The Economics of Poverty

Introduction to Economics Series

Kenyon A. Knopf, *Editor*

ECONOMIC DEVELOPMENT AND GROWTH
Robert E. Baldwin

THE ECONOMICS OF POVERTY
Alan B. Batchelder

NATIONAL INCOME AND EMPLOYMENT ANALYSIS
Arnold Collery

THE MARKET SYSTEM
Robert H. Haveman and Kenyon A. Knopf

INTERNATIONAL ECONOMIC PROBLEMS
James C. Ingram

WELFARE AND PLANNING: AN ANALYSIS OF
CAPITALISM VERSUS SOCIALISM
Heinz Köhler

TOWARD ECONOMIC STABILITY
Maurice W. Lee

CASE STUDIES IN AMERICAN INDUSTRY
Leonard W. Weiss

The Economics of Poverty

SECOND EDITION

ALAN B. BATCHELDER

Kenyon College

John Wiley & Sons, Inc.   New York · London · Sydney · Toronto

To Mary Hutchins Batchelder
and William G. Batchelder, Sr.,
who have taught
"Seek truth, then act with justice."

Introduction to Economics Series

Teachers of introductory economics seem to agree on the impracticality of presenting a comprehensive survey of economics to freshmen or sophomores. Many of them believe there is a need for some alternative which provides a solid core of principles while permitting an instructor to introduce a select set of problems and applied ideas. This series attempts to fill that need and also to give the interested layman a set of self-contained books that he can absorb with interest and profit, without assistance.

By offering greater flexibility in the choice of topics for study, these books represent a more realistic and reasonable approach to teaching economics than most of the large, catchall textbooks. With separate volumes and different authors for each topic, the instructor is not as tied to a single track as in the omnibus introductory economics text.

Underlying the series is the pedagogical premise that students should be introduced to economics by learning how economists think about economic problems. Thus the concepts and relationships of elementary economics are presented to the student in conjunction with a few economic problems. An approach of this kind offers a good beginning to the student who intends to move on to advanced work and furnishes a clearer understanding for those whose study of economics is limited to an introductory exposure. Teachers and students alike should find the books helpful and stimulating.

Kenyon A. Knopf, Editor

Preface

Of every 1000 babies born to white Americans, 19 die before reaching their first birthday. Of every 1000 babies born to American migrant laborers (many of whom are white), 43 die before they are a year old. The additional infant deaths occur among migrant laborers because migrant laborers are among the poorest Americans. Poverty has many facets. The most cruel one is the relatively high incidence of dead babies.

There are large differences between poor Americans and non-poor Americans. There are larger differences between Americans as a group and most of the other people in the world. Poverty is not as severe in Chile as in most Asian, African, or Latin American countries but, of every 1000 babies born to Chileans, 80 die before they are a year old because so many Chileans are very poor.

A larger material output per person does not always mean fewer poor people or fewer infant deaths. Infant mortality rates often have been reduced without any increases in per capita production. Some babies born to the rich die. Sweden and Denmark, with a smaller output per person, have lower infant mortality rates and a lower incidence of poverty than the United States.

But in most times and places, the general rule holds true: the larger the per capita output of a region, the lower its poverty and its infant mortality rates. In most times and places, an increase in output per person leads to reductions in a region's incidence of poverty and in its infant mortality rate.

One half of the people in the world live in countries with a per capita output (in American prices) of less than $300 a year. In the United States, the real output per person *rises* by about $150 a year. In the poorer countries, government officials celebrate when per capita output rises as much as $8 a year, since such a "large" increase rarely occurs. Most babies born in 1970 will be born in these countries and will be born poor. Most of them also will die poor. They will die poor because the output per person is now rising very slowly in most African, Asian, and Latin American countries.

The output per person is exceptionally low for so many people because they and their countries have so little physical capital (machinery and power plants, for instance) and so little human capital (education and production training) per person. The output per person rises very slowly for them because, despite high infant mortality rates, they have added rapidly to their population but have been unable to add very rapidly to their stock of physical and human capital. At present, there is little evidence that the poverty of the less-developed countries will be considerably reduced during the next generation.

World poverty could be reduced by a revolutionary change in world attitudes toward international migration. If millions of untrained people moved from the less-developed countries to countries that are rich in physical capital, and if millions of people of average developed-nation education moved from the developed to the less-developed countries, the extent and severity of world poverty would decline. Today, few people advocate massive international migration or any other change that is likely to have great impact soon on the pervasive poverty of the people of Africa, Asia, and Latin America.

I repeat: world poverty could be reduced. Areas of American poverty have been much reduced and are now being further reduced. Some of the reductions are so large that they could not possibly have been foretold at the time they began.

The most spectacular change has been the rise of black Americans. In 1910, 89% of black Americans lived in the South, most of them on farms. In 1940, 77% of black Americans lived in the South; of these, 45% lived and worked on farms, nearly all in grinding poverty. Most other black Americans earned their living from the lowest-paid laboring and service occupations. Southern whites limited black "schools" to little more than child-sitting care. Black Americans, who left those schools, were able to do the work that the Southern way of life asigned to them: in cotton culture, as laborers, or in menial occupations. But this education and this work left nearly all black Americans poor. They could escape poverty only if they could acquire productive education and mobility within the capital-intensive, technologically advanced, national economy.

No one in 1940 could have foreseen that by 1970 only 4% of black Americans would remain on farms and that the majority of blacks, despite their heritage of Southern educational ignorance, would be well on their way toward productive equality with white Americans. The economic gap between black and white Americans remained large in 1970. The changes that reduced the gap were brutally painful to millions. Changes yet to come also will be brutally painful. But the great movement of black Americans out of rural servile poverty and into the economic mainstream is far advanced. Black culture and life styles may remain distinctly different from white culture and life styles, but black education, mobility and productivity will continue to move closer to white education, mobility and productivity; and the incidence of poverty among black Americans will continue to decrease.

This book is concerned principally with the fall in the incidence of poverty among Americans—black, white, red, yellow, and brown. Economic analysis is applied here to the character and the extent of poverty in America and to the character and causes of the decline in the incidence of poverty in America, but this analysis can be applied largely to the poverty that characterizes much of the rest of the world. It explains the stubborn persistence of poverty throughout Africa, Asia, and Latin America. Those who care to persevere may be able to use this analysis to participate in an effective war against poverty in Africa, Asia, and Latin America, but *that* war must yet be declared.

I have restricted this book to poverty in America and have limited its coverage to an objective description and economic analysis. I have not defended any program nor argued on behalf of any program or group of programs. Many controversial programs are described and many controversial issues are raised, but the reader must make his own judgments.

The first two chapters describe the character and extent of poverty in America. The next four chapters analyze the causes of American poverty. Chapter 7 describes charity, social security, and other programs that transfer money from the nonpoor to the poor. Chapter 8 analyzes programs designed to help the poor to work and earn their way out of poverty. The final chapter describes many of the choices affecting poverty that must be made by Americans. My objective here is to help Americans make choices that will lead to the results that the decision makers desire.

Kenyon A. Knopf and John P. Young (formerly of Wiley) originally conceived the idea of this book as a useful tool of analysis for college students and laymen. Deborah Herbert of Wiley edited the manuscript and made the prose more fluent than it otherwise would have been. Mrs. Hope Weir, a most excellent typist, translated the manuscript into text copy.

Professor R. W. Pfouts of the University of North Carolina read the manuscript and made numerous suggestions, nearly all of which I was delighted to incorporate in textual revisions. I bear full responsibility for any remaining faults or errors.

ALAN B. BATCHELDER

Kenyon College

Contents

Chapter 1
Where To Draw the Line?   1

    I. The War on Poverty: Understand, Criticize,
        Look Ahead   2
   II. The Importance of Numbers   4
  III. The Social Security Administration Statistics   4
  IV. Are There Objective Natural Criteria
        Defining Poverty?   5
    V. An Aside about Census Bureau Definitions   7
  VI. Resources Available: Income and Assets   8
 VII. Resources Available: Money Income and
        Income in Kind   10
VIII. Resources Needed: Size of Household, Location;
        Age and Health of Members   11
  IX. A Materialistic Criterion   12
   X. Diversity of Opinion and Use of the Statistics   13
  XI. Summary   14

Chapter 2
How Many Poor?   16

    I. Bureau of the Census Income Statistics   16
   II. Social Security Administration Poverty
        Income Criteria   19
  III. Total Poor in 1968 and in 1969   21
      A. Age and Poverty in 1968   22

B. Sex and Poverty in 1968   22
C. Race and Poverty in 1968   23
D. Farming and Poverty in 1968   24
E. Statistics Needed but Not Available   24
IV. Few Americans become Poor   25
V. Decline in the Incidence of Poverty: 1961 to 1968   25
   A. Change in the Poverty Cross Section:
     1961 to 1968   27
   B. The Working Poor   28
VI. Dollar Width of the Poverty Gap   30
VII. Summary   31

Chapter 3
Per Capita Production   33

I. Measures of Total Output   33
II. Per Capita Output, Per Capita Income   37
III. International Comparisons of 1966 Per Capita GNP   37
IV. When the Ratio is Small, Most Must Be Poor   41
V. When the Ratio Is Large, the Division May Leave
   Some Poor   43
VI. Population   44
VII. What Determines the Size of Output in the
   Short Run?   44
   A. Extent and Character of the National Domain   44
   B. The Quantity of Physical Capital   45
   C. The Quantity of Human Capital   46
   D. Technological Quality   48
   E. Economies of Scale   48
   F. Hours Worked   49
   G. Attitude   49
   H. Aggregate Demand   50
VIII. What Determines the Rate at which the National
   Product Grows?   53
   A. Growth of Physical Capital   54

B. Growth of Human Capital 55
C. Improvements in Technology 56
IX. Labor's Average Product Curve 57
X. Summary 61

Chapter 4
Dividing the National Product 62
I. Government's Share, Private Investment,
Private Consumption 62
II. Dividing the Household Share among Households 64
A. Equality 65
B. Dividing Output in Proportion to Needs 66
C. Authority 68
III. Output Divided in Proportion to Contributions to
Production 69
A. Genetic Potential for Contributing to
Production 72
B. Actual Contributions Differ from Genetic Po-
tential for Many Reasons 72
C. Potential and Actual Productive Intelligence:
A, B, C 73
D. Allocating Physical and Human Capital among
Workers 75
E. Interest Income and the Marginal Physical
Product of Capital 76
F. Economic Rent: the Bounty of Nature 78
G. Perfectly Competitive Markets, VMP,
and Poverty 79
IV. Luck 79
V. Summary 80

Chapter 5
Why One Is Poor When One's Equal Is Not 83
I. From Intelligence A to Intelligence B 84
II. From Intelligence B to Intelligence C 85

	A.	From B to C: Nutrition		86
	B.	From B to C: Education		88
		1.	Ignorance of Opportunities	89
		2.	Achievement Motivation	90
		3.	Inadequate Education	92
		4.	From Conception Through School: Summary	93
III.	Family Obligations			94
IV.	The Social Minimum Wage			95
V.	Inadequate Aggregate Demand			96
VI.	The Near Poor			99
VII.	Rising Productivity: Not a Cause			99
	A.	For Example		99
	B.	Four Options		101
	C.	1929 to 1969, American Agricultural Productivity Doubled		102
VIII.	Summary			104

Chapter 6

White Power Discrimination 106

I.	Slavery		107
II.	Freedom?		109
III.	The Twentieth Century		110
	A.	Agriculture	111
	B.	The Federal Government	114
IV.	Why Are So Many Blacks Poor?		116
	A.	Americans Do Not Become Poor	116
	B.	Banker, Realtor, John Doe Conspiracy	116
	C.	Low Intelligence A?	117
	D.	Little Inherited Physical Capital	119
	E.	From A to B: Inadequate Prenatal and Obstetrical Care	120
	F.	From B to C: Malnutrition	121
	G.	From B to C: Inadequate Knowledge of Opportunities	123

H. From B to C: Inadequate Education and
Training   124
I. Maternal Responsibility   126
J. Insufficient Aggregate Demand   127
K. Racial Discrimination Distinguishing Black Poor   128
L. Self-Image   130
V. Labor Supply and Demand   131
VI. Indians   133
VII. Summary   135

Chapter 7
Transfer Programs Now Operating   137
I. Private Transfers: Within Families   138
  A. Other Private Transfers   139
  B. Hiding the Poor in Cities   141
II. Government Transfers   145
  A. Transfers Alleviating Poverty Associated with
    Old Age   146
    1. OASDHI   146
    2. OAA   148
  B. Transfers Alleviating Poverty Associated
    with Youth   149
    1. AFDC   149
    2. OASDHI   151
    3. Veterans' Administration Payments 151
  C. Transfers Alleviating Poverty Associated
    with Injury, Disease or Congenital Handicap 151
    1. Workmen's Compensation   151
    2. TDI   152
    3. APTD   153
    4. AB   153
    5. Veterans' Disability   153
    6. Medicaid   153

D. Transfers Alleviating Poverty Associated with
Unemployment 154
E. Food 155
1. The Surplus Commodity Distribution
Program 157
2. The Food Stamp Program 157
3. The School Lunch Program 158
4. The Extended School Lunch Program 158
5. Child Nutrition Act of 1966 158
6. Milk Program 159
7. Elementary and Secondary Education Act 159
F. Housing 159
1. Public Housing 159
2. Leased Housing 159
3. Rent Supplements 159
4. Urban Renewal 160
G. Social Service 160
H. General Assistance 160
I. The Philosophy behind Government Transfers 161
J. Portion Helped, Portion Left Poor 163
III. Taxes on Poor and Nonpoor 165
IV. Summary 169

Chapter 8
*Reducing Poverty Through Increases in the Per Capita
Productive Contribution of the Poor* 170

I. Increasing Per Capita Product Using
Existing Resources 171
A. Increased Aggregate Demand 172
B. Improved Knowledge about Job Opportunities 173
C. Increased Resource Mobility 175
D. Reduced Obstacles to Labor Force Participation 177
E. Reduced Racial Discrimination 177
II. Raising the Average Product Curve 178
A. More Physical Capital per Worker 180

B. Increase in Human Capital: The Home   181
C. Increase in Human Capital: Public Schools   182
D. Increase in Human Capital: Adult Training and
    Education   186
    1. OJT   186
    2. Apprenticeship   187
    3. Defense Department Training   187
    4. MDTA   188
    5. JOBS   190
    6. WEP-WIN   192
    7. Other   193
III. The Ratio of Population to other Resources   193
IV. Summary   196

Chapter 9
Policy Issues   198
I. The "Changeless Race of the Poor"   198
II. Policy Issues   200
III. Lower Unemployment or Less Inflation?   201
    A. The Dilemma   202
    B. Who Gains, Who Loses, and Why   203
    C. The Statistics   206
    D. Why the Dilemma?   206
    E. Easing the Dilemma   207
    F. Where Should We Be?   208
IV. Government Spending to Raise the Productivity of
    the Poor   209
    A. Moving Workers to Jobs and Jobs to Workers   209
    B. Permitting Mothers to Enter the Labor Force   211
    C. Government as Employer of Last Resort   211
    D. More Human Capital for Children   212
    E. More Human Capital for Adults   215
V. Zero Population Growth?   216
VI. Minimum Wage Laws   217
VII. Tax Revisions to Benefit the Working Poor   219

VIII.   Racial Discrimination   221
  IX.   Reducing Poverty among People Who Cannot Work   224
        A.   Tax Forgiveness for the Elderly   225
        B.   Federalizing Welfare Programs   226
        C.   The Family Assistance Program   226
   X.   Summary   227
  XI.   Conclusion   228

Index   231

1

Where to Draw the Line?

If poverty is a great evil then Americans are, in at least one respect, significantly better off today than in the past. Poverty, once
the general rule, is now the exception. What is more, the number
of poor Americans seems likely to continue to decrease from
year to year.

That improved condition and that favorable prospect are new
in this world.

Throughout most of recorded history, the majority of people
have been poor and have had every reason to expect that the poverty in which they would die would be very much like the poverty
into which they were born. Poverty remained ubiquitous for thousands of years because of the inability of men to raise average
output per person. Under those conditions, the chief business of
kings and nations was often the formulation and execution of policies designed to increase their income and wealth by acquisitions
taken at the expense of other kings and nations. More for one
meant less for another as long as output per person changed
little from decade to decade.

That was the past, improvement for some only at the expense
of others; almost universal poverty taken for granted. Over the
centuries per capita output rose gradually, but as recently as the
middle of the nineteenth century, Lincoln could think it reasonable to observe fatalistically, "God must have loved the poor; he
made so many of them."

Today in America, a principal concern of the federal government is the formulation and execution of policies designed to accommodate the national economy as it pushes up output per person. Once, more for one meant less for another; today, the rule is that rising output raises the incomes of most Americans every year. Because annual output per American has risen greatly over the past century, the incidence of poverty (that is, the poor as a percent of total population) is at an unprecedented low. Nevertheless, poverty persists in America, not just for tens of thousands but for several tens of millions.

I. THE WAR ON POVERTY: UNDERSTAND, CRITICIZE, LOOK AHEAD

The incidence of poverty is much less than in the past and is falling, but the rate of fall during the 1950s and early 1960s was too slow to satisfy the nation. In 1964, Congress passed the Economic Opportunity Act and made official, in the words of that act,

. . . the policy of the United States to eliminate the paradox of poverty in the midst of plenty in this Nation by opening to everyone the opportunity for education and training, the opportunity to work, and the opportunity to live in decency and dignity.

Thus the official policy of Congress became "to eliminate the paradox of poverty in the midst of plenty." Most Americans agree that this is a desirable goal, but differences of opinion arise among them in connection with all the programs that affect the incidence of poverty.

Since President Johnson's original declaration of war on poverty in his January 1964 State of the Union message, many decisions have been made, in and out of government, that are calculated to further the aims of that war. Many other decisions made before and since that time and directed primarily to other ends have had significant effects on the character and the extent of poverty in America.

Differences—sometimes angry—differences of opinion have arisen among Americans regarding both the general strategy and the specific tactics adopted by governments and by private agencies engaged in the War on Poverty. These differences of opinion arise partly because individuals have different value systems and partly because individuals differ in their knowledge of the facts of poverty and of how those facts fit together. Value systems will continue to differ from person to person, but the facts and their interrelationships are the same for everyone.

When factual knowledge is inadequate, differences of opinion may arise that have no factual basis. Worse yet, personal and public policy decisions then may lead to totally unforseen and unwanted results. How disappointing for conservatives to take power, set policies, implement programs, and then discover that their policies and programs bring results quite different from the ones intended. Equally chagrined are the liberals who take power, shift policies, adjust old programs, implement new programs, and discover that their policies and programs bring net results both unforeseen and undesired. These mistakes are made when decisions are based on inadequate or inaccurate information.

The nature of the world is such that most decisions must be based on incomplete information, but obviously, the results achieved come closest to the results intended when policies are based on all accessible information and on an accurate understanding of that information. The purpose of this book is to provide readers—whether their values be liberal, conservative, middle-of-the-road, reactionary, or radical—with the available facts and with an economic analysis of the causes of poverty and of the operation of the forces that serve to reduce poverty.

Economic analysis involves the arrangement of economic facts in a tight and logical sequence of cause and effect. Subsequent chapters develop this kind of analysis to answer two questions:

1. In Chapters 3 through 6: Why are some Americans poor when most are not?

2. In Chapters 7 through 9: What are the observed or probable effects of various actual and proposed programs that might help the poor or that might permit the poor to help themselves?

Out of that analysis can come both a better understanding of the character and causes of poverty in America and a more confident basis for constructive criticism of past, present, and projected programs that affect Americans who are poor—and that also affect Americans who are not poor.

II.   THE IMPORTANCE OF NUMBERS

In general, the economic analysis of this book will be as valid for ten hundred thousand as for twenty-five million poor. Nevertheless, numbers are important, and applications of the analysis to formulate, to administer, and to adjust policies require information about the number of poor at present, about the relative numbers of different categories of poor, and about trends in the number of poor.

When programs are formulated to combat poverty, the number of poor and also the degree of their poverty must be known if a rational decision is to be made about the size of the overall antipoverty program—whether it is designed to eliminate or only to alleviate poverty. Because different people are poor for different reasons, programs designed to attack particular causes of poverty can be scaled to appropriate sizes only if fairly accurate counts have been made of the subcategories of poor. Over time, recounts are needed to show the effects of past events and to permit the revisions appropriate to plans for further actions.

III.   THE SOCIAL SECURITY
ADMINISTRATION STATISTICS

The particular count of the poor used in this book shows:

1. Between 1961 and 1968, the total number of poor declined from 39.6 to 25.4 million, or from 21.9% to 12.8% of the American population.

2. In 1959, 8,015,000 (50.5% of all) American farm residents were poor; in 1968, only 2,300,000 (23% of all) American farm residents were poor (yes, the number of farm residents fell sharply between 1959 and 1968).

3. In 1961, 67%, in 1968, 43% of all black American children were members of poor families.

4. In 1961, 15.6%, in 1968, 63% of families headed by men under 35 were poor .

These numbers, as well as others presented in the next chapter, are derived from counts made by the United States Bureau of the Census on behalf of the United States Social Security Administration (hereafter, the SSA).

Are these numbers to be believed?

They assert that the incidence of poverty is spectacularly high among particular groups. They assert that changes in the incidence of poverty were very rapid during the 1960s.

Are the SSA poverty statistics to be believed as accurate measures of the character—and of changes in the character—of poverty in America? The SSA figures rest on the particular set of criteria used by the SSA to distinguish poor from nonpoor. The final count is only as meaningful as the criteria and the criteria's rationale on which that count is based.

What are the criteria of the SSA? What is the rationale behind the selection of those criteria? What other criteria might be used? This last question is the subject of the rest of this chapter. The two preceding questions are answered in Chapter 2.

IV. ARE THERE OBJECTIVE NATURAL CRITERIA DEFINING POVERTY?

To be able to count the poor, criteria must be established whereby the poor man can be distinguished from the nonpoor man. But what criteria are the "right" criteria to obtain a count that:

includes everyone who is poor and

excludes everyone who is not poor?

Any one man's precise criteria for counting the poor are likely to differ from everyone else's, since men differ in their views of how much is needed to be nonpoor. As a result, the right criteria are a matter of subjective choice, and honest men will disagree about that choice.

But why are there no objective criteria? Poverty exists when the quantity of resources available to a person is less than some particular quantity of resources "needed" by that person. That is an imposing definition, but it is not easy to use it in a poverty count. The hitch here is that nothing in the nature of man or in the nature of the world suggests the minimal resource "needs" that must be satisfied if a person is to be nonpoor.

But is that true? Is not "enough to keep from starving or freezing to death" a criterion all could agree on as a biologically objective rock bottom dividing line between nonpoor and poor? No. Only a moment's thought is needed to recognize, although many men have starved to death quickly, that men may—and millions do—starve to death slowly. Most of the citizens of the less developed nations have life expectancies only 70% down to 50% of those of Swedes, Swiss, and Japanese. Those short life expectancies are due in large part to diets too poor to support good health.

No food brings death within two months or so (much sooner if no water is available); inadequate diet also shortens life though not so spectacularly. There is no objectively precise food consumption line to distinguish between poor and nonpoor (although, as the next chapter will show, the SSA poverty-nonpoverty criteria make use of what the SSA calls "minimal nutritional needs").

If one were to persist in attempting to use a measure based on objectively definable biological needs, then, at the other health extreme, "enough food, shelter, and medical care to maintain the best possible state of health" would avoid much of the ambiguity of the nonstarving criterion but would establish a very, very high poverty-nonpoverty dividing line. Each year many Americans die who could have been saved by artificial kidneys or by heart transplants, but the best possible medical care in these and in most other specialties is available only in very limited quantities; only a few can receive it. Many people who consider themselves far from poor nevertheless must settle for less than the best in medical care. Thus the "best-health" criterion is not a satisfactory definition for nonpoverty.

The point of these observations is to show that criteria distinguishing the poor from the nonpoor cannot be plucked full-blown from nature. Yet an understanding of the extent and character of American poverty and of poverty programs requires a count of the poor; and this requires criteria, reasonable although necessarily subjective criteria, by which the poor can be distinguished from the nonpoor.

The particular criteria chosen are surely critical. Different sets of criteria would yield different numbers of poor and different groups of poor. Thus different criteria would delineate different sized and different shaped poverty problems. What, then, are the factors that subjective judgment must face and evaluate when the Social Security Administration or any other group or person is establishing criteria that are to be used when counting the poor?

As was said above, and as common sense affirms, poverty exists when the quantity of resources available to a person is less than some particular quantity of resources needed—"needed" in some pressing sense—by that person. Thus the factors to be considered when establishing poverty-nonpoverty criteria involve the following.

(a) Resources available, involving issues of
    (i) income as distinct from assets and of
    (ii) money income as distinct from income in kind.

(b) Resources needed, involving considerations such as
    (i) family—or household—size,
    (ii) location, and
    (iii) the age and health of individuals.

Respecting each factor, an important consideration to bear in mind is that the criteria sought are not platonic definitions suitable to the conceptual perfection of the cave but instead, are, practical standards that can be used in the present world to count the poor in a way that will be of use to policy makers, and to their critics.

V. AN ASIDE ABOUT CENSUS BUREAU DEFINITIONS

Earlier, references were made to the resources available to and the resources needed by an individual. Many people do live alone, but most people live in groups; some of these groups are families (related persons), other are unrelated and share a housing unit as a matter of convenience. The United States Bureau of the Census uses the term "household" to include all of these kinds of living units. According to the Bureau of the Census:

The term "family" refers to a group of two or more persons related by blood, marriage, or adoption and residing together; all such persons are considered as members of the same family. Thus if the son of the head of the household and the son's wife are in the household, they are treated as part of the head's family. On the other hand, a lodger and his wife not related to the head of the household or an unrelated servant and his wife are considered as additional families, and not a part of the household head's family.

"Unrelated individuals" refers to persons 14 years old and over (other than inmates of institutions) who are not living with any relatives.

A "household" comprises all persons who occupy a "housing unit," that is, a house, an apartment or other group of rooms, or a room that constitutes "separate living quarters." A household includes the head of the household, others in the housing unit related to the head, and also the unrelated persons, if any, such as lodgers, foster children, wards, or employees who regularly live in the house. A person living alone or a group of unrelated persons sharing the same housing unit as partners is also counted as a household.[1]

Three students sharing an apartment are, if unrelated, both one "household" and three "unrelated individuals." If they are siblings they are both one "household" and one "family." Thus the sum of families and unrelated individuals is not the sum of households in the country. For convenience, subsequent references to people's needs and resources will use households to represent both families and unrelated individuals.

VI.   RESOURCES AVAILABLE: INCOME AND ASSETS

The resources available to a household consist of income (a flow), what a household receives as earnings or from gifts during some period of—between two points in—time, and assets (a stock), what the household owns (gross and net, since this includes loans and borrowings) at a single point in time. Most income flows to a household as money; some comes as "income in kind," goods and services. A household's stock of assets comprises physical property such as a house, food, and clothing, and paper claims such as bonds, stocks, bank accounts, IOUs, and dollar bills.

A household with no assets on January 1 can live quite comfortably during the subsequent year if its income is ample. A household with no income during that year but with large assets can live quite comfortably by drawing down its assets.

When income criteria alone are used to count the poor, some

---

[1] Bureau of the Census, *Statistical Abstract of the United States: 1969*, G.P.O., Washington, D.C., 1969, p. 3.

households with low incomes are counted as poor even though they possess large assets. For example, a household owning 100,000 shares of stock paying no cash dividends during a year might enjoy an affluent existence during that year by selling several thousand shares of that stock.

The difficulty, thus far, concerning the establishment of poor-nonpoor criteria is that at the present time the Census Bureau collects fairly reliable household income statistics, but no agency, either public or private, collects very extensive data regarding the assets of individual households. Thus, as a practical matter, most poverty criteria must be based solely on incomes.

How much error will unconsidered assets introduce into a poverty count based exclusively on income criteria? Fortunately, not much because most people with large assets receive large incomes in the form of profits, rent, and interest. For one particular group, the error has appeared to be large, and in 1964 the Social Security Administration undertook a special survey of the assets of elderly people; since, as a major group, they include the largest portion of households with money incomes that are low relative to the size of their assets. The SSA calculated the extra spendable income elderly people could have if each year they would draw on their assets (other than equity in their homes) at a rate calculated actuarially to exhaust these assets over the average years of life remaining. Under SSA poverty criteria, these calculations showed that allowance for these assets would reduce the number of elderly poor by a little less than 10%. If younger people with low incomes have smaller assets relative to income than do elderly people with low incomes, similar calculations for people under age 65 would reduce the number of poor among them by less than 10%. Allowing for equity in homes of course, would reduce the number further.

A roundabout method of approximating the availability of assets to a household would be to consider household income over a period of years rather than over a single year, which is the general practice; since, apart from inheritances, most household assets are accumulated out of past income. If, to imagine a simple case, an annual money income of under $3500 were to be judged "a poverty income," and if household incomes over ten-year periods were to be considered, then the household with an income under $3000 in each of the 10 years considered could be distinguished from the household with an income above $10,000 during each of the first six and last three of the ten years, but with a $1200 income during the seventh year. Since the latter household's average annual income would be above $3499, that household would be labeled "nonpoor" during the seventh as well as during the other years. It, in nearly all cases, would have access to more of its own assets during that seventh year than would the other household just described. In most cases, this nonpoor household would also, during the seventh year, have access to far more credit than would the household with a persistently low income.

The Department of Commerce once experimented with a poverty criterion of a $6000 family income for two years and concluded that "a poverty criterion based on a two-year income average of $3000 yields nearly as many low-income families as is indicated by the one-year" family-income criterion.[1]
The difference in this case may have been small, but the poverty count based on the two-year income criterion was more accurate than the count based on one year, and counts based on five-year or on ten-year income averages would be more accurate still. If information regarding two-year (or three- or five- or ten-year) household income becomes available on a national basis, the count of the American poor will be improved, and the need to know about household assets will become less pressing. As yet this information is not available.

VII.   RESOURCES AVAILABLE: MONEY INCOME AND INCOME IN KIND

A second factor complicating the use of money income criteria to count the poor is the circumstance that some American households receive all of their income in cash while others receive some income in cash and some in kind. "Income in kind" refers to goods and services individuals receive either from land and water or homes they own or from an employer in lieu of or in addition to

---

cash wages. For example, servants or farm laborers may receive room and board as part of their pay. This room and board is income in kind. Like Dr. Pangloss and Candide, many households cultivate their own vegetable gardens; their produce from these gardens is income in kind. The same is true of poultry, livestock, game, and fish raised or caught by its consumers. Some people own clear title to their homes, the use of such houses is income in kind (this, we notice is another aspect of the ownership of assets).

Money income and total income are the same for households receiving all of their income in cash. In contrast, the total income of most people with income in kind is money income *plus* the goods and services received as income in kind. When using money income criteria to count the poor, the problem of income in kind can, in the abstract, be resolved in either of the following two ways,

1. The money value of income in kind can be calculated and added to the cash income of each household.
2. Lower money income poverty criteria can be used for households with income in kind than for households with no income in kind.

In practice, in most cases the first of these alternatives is not feasible.

The Social Security Administration, after some trial and error, has used the second of the two methods just described to calculate, for farm families, money income poverty criteria that are different—by being lower—than the criteria used for nonfarm families. That difference is based on the general rule that farm families receive significantly more income in kind than do nonfarm families. The SSA farm-nonfarm poverty criteria differences are shown in the next chapter.

VIII. RESOURCES NEEDED: SIZE OF HOUSEHOLD, LOCATION; AGE AND HEALTH OF MEMBERS

A household consisting of one healthy elderly man clearly has fewer needs than the household of a young couple with two children; and the young couple with two children has fewer needs than the older couple with three teenagers and three younger children. When efforts were made during the early 1960s to count the number of poor in America, a cash income line was drawn between $2999 and $3000. All households of two or more people with incomes below $3000 were counted poor. Households of two or more people with incomes above $2999 were counted nonpoor. This procedure was unsatisfactory. Why? Because it counted as poor many two-person households with incomes of $2500 to $2999 but counted as not poor many households of three, four, five, or more people with incomes of between $3000 and $3500. Thanks to improved statistics, this single criterion for all two-or-more person households now has been abandoned.

Other variables also affect resource needs. A household in central Florida has lower insulation and heating and clothing costs than a household in North Dakota. Health can make a big difference. A diabetic must pay more than the average cost for food, and he must buy insulin; an invalid must have special care; a blind person must pay more for books and newspapers.

If American households are classified as poor or as nonpoor on the basis of an income criterion that makes no allowance for the size or the location of the household or for the age or health of household members, the final count must be inaccurate—or, perhaps, more usefully described, must carry many reservations. When using any particular collection of poverty statistics, an individual will find that he understands their strengths and weaknesses far better if, after reading about the resource "availability" and "need" characteristics that *were* considered, he identifies the availability and need characteristics that were *not* considered when the count was being made.

IX. A MATERIALISTIC CRITERION

Men speak sometimes of "poverty of spirit," but that concept is not included within the meaning of "poverty" as it is used in this book. The term, poverty, as used here is narrowly materialistic.

To be happy, most individuals require:

1. Enough income or assets to be confident of their ability to satisfy minimal materialistic needs for food and shelter.
2. Reasonable health.
3. Intimate friends and loved ones.

4. Successes doing challenging work.
5. The respect of their peers.
6. Parenthood, for some.

Few people can be happy when deprived of any of these things, and men can experience a kind of poverty with respect to any one of them.

Happiness encompasses a wide sweep of factors, but the subject of this book is relatively narrow, since it treats only the availability of or lack of goods and services bought and sold in the market—the material things underpinning physical life. Many whom the SSA criteria identify as nonpoor nevertheless will suffer from a poverty of spirit.

X. DIVERSITY OF OPINION AND USE OF THE STATISTICS

To evaluate existing programs affecting the poor, to modify those programs, to formulate new programs, and to administer programs, the critic, the policy maker, and the administrator must have counts of the total number of poor, of the subcategories of poor, and of the changes over time in the number of poor in total and in the subcategories. Given the present state of statistics, the number of poor must be counted by setting an annual money income criterion for particular types of household and by identifying as poor every household with annual money income below the relevant line.

For each type of household, the poverty income criterion is, in practise, drawn at the level of minimum "need." But what is minimum "need"? It is a matter of opinion regarding which honest men disagree. This means that when one man or one agency, for example, the Social Security Administration, sets poverty income criteria, the criteria established and the resulting counts will be different from the ones that another individual or agency would produce.

But these differences of opinion concerning need do not prevent the use of the SSA poverty statistics by people of widely dissimilar views with respect to poverty. If an individual considers the SSA's idea of minimum needs to be unreasonably low, he can make what he believes to be an appropriate upward adjustment in the number of poor counted by the SSA in total and in each subcategory. Conversely, if an individual considers the SSA's idea of minimum needs to be unreasonably high, he can make what he believes to be an appropriate downward adjustment in the total and subcategories of poor counted by the SSA. By making modifications of this kind, persons of very different opinions can use the same basic set of poverty figures.

XI. SUMMARY

In the past, output per person was very low throughout the world, and most people died in the same poverty into which they had been born. In these circumstances, one man could have more only at the expense of someone else. Today, because output per person is high and rising, only a minority of Americans are poor, and the number of poor is expected to continue to decline.

Nevertheless, the rate of that decline has been too slow to satisfy many Americans; and, following President Johnson's leadership, Congress in 1964 committed the nation to a policy aspiring to eliminate poverty. This book is intended to help proponents, policy makers, administrators, and critics of the War on Poverty by providing an economic analysis of the causes of poverty and of the forces that reduce the incidence of poverty. Since policy makers and critics also need statistics, this book reports on the statistics of poverty and on the problems involved in counting the poor.

Most of the poverty statistics cited in this book were compiled by the United States Social Security Administration. They show a spectacularly high incidence of poverty among particular groups and a very rapid overall decline during the 1960s. Can these figures be believed?

The SSA poverty criteria are necessarily subjective for nature provides no objective criteria. When measuring the resources available to the poor, both assets, money income, and income in kind, should be considered, but statistics are lacking regarding assets and the money value of income in kind. When determining the needs of the poor, size of household, its location, and the age and health of its members should be considered. In practice, the

SSA has allowed for household size and for the age of household members.

The poverty criteria used in this book ignore many spiritual values and stand narrowly materialistic. Thus any particular set of poverty statistics are likely to prove unsatisfactory for one reason or another to nearly everyone, but nearly everyone still can utilize them by making some rough upward or downward adjustments in the reported numbers.

2

How Many Poor?

Ideally, a count of the poor would consider "needs," assets, money income, and income in kind. Of necessity, contemporary counts must do without statistics of assets and of income in kind, but the estimates of need have been rationalized and standardized, and the income statistics seem to be reliable.

I. BUREAU OF THE CENSUS INCOME STATISTICS

The United States Constitution requires a census of population every 10 years so that seats in the House of Representatives can be allocated among states in proportion to their populations. A new census has been taken every tenth year since the first one in 1790, and the most recent one was in April 1970. Each census has attempted to reach every American. In the censuses of 1950, 1960, and 1970, each person was asked to report his income during the preceding year.

Governments (state, local, and federal) and businesses often need population census information as current as the problems that legislators and businesses face. But decennial censuses come but once in 10 years, and each complete census is expensive (the 1960 census cost $128 million). To meet the current information needs of governments and businesses, the Bureau of the Census began a monthly population survey in the late 1940s. This "Current Population Survey" sends interviewers to approximately 35 thousand households every month of every year. One third of the households are changed each month, but all are selected so that, as a group, they will typify the entire nation. From each month's sample, generalizations are extended to the entire population. The techniques of mathematical statistics provide the users of these data with precise measures of the reliability of these generalizations. Most are highly reliable.

The Census Bureau interviewers could ask each household: "Are you poor?" The affirmative answers would give a national poverty count of people poor by their own testimony. This question is not asked.

Neither do census interviewers ask questions regarding assets, income in kind, or all the aspects of need relevant to the identification of poverty (for example, no questions are asked about medical expenses). Both the decennial censuses and the March Current Population Surveys do ask about the number in each household and about the age, sex, and employment status of each member of the household. They also ask how much, if anything, each member of each household received in *cash* income during the preceding year. The income questions are phrased in the following manner:

40. Earnings in 1969—Fill parts a, b, and c for everyone who worked any time in 1969 even if he had no income. (If exact amount is not known, give best estimate.)

a. How much did this person earn in 1969 in wages, salary, commissions, bonuses, or tips from all jobs? (Before deductions for taxes, bonds, dues, or other items.)

$ _____ .00
(Dollars only)
OR _____ None

b. How much did he earn in 1969 from his own nonfarm business, professional practice, or partnership? (Net after business expenses. If business lost money, write "Loss" above amount.)

$ _____ .00
(Dollars only)

c. How much did he earn in 1969 from his own farm? (Net after operating expenses. Include earnings as a tenant farmer or sharecropper. If farm lost money, write "Loss" above amount.)

$ _____ .00
(Dollars only)

41. Income other than earnings in 1969—Fill parts a, b, and c. (If exact amount is not known, give best estimate.)

a. How much did this person receive in 1969 from Social Security or Railroad Retirement?	$ _____ .00 (Dollars only) OR None
b. How much did he receive in 1969 from public assistance or welfare payments? Include aid for dependent children, old age assistance, general assistance, aid to the blind or totally disabled. Exclude separate payments for hospital or other medical care.	$ _____ .00 (Dollars only) OR None
c. How much did he receive in 1969 from all other sources? Include interest, dividends, veterans' payments, pensions, and other regular payments. (See instruction sheet.)	$ _____ .00 (Dollars only) OR None

Information is requested of all persons 14 years of age and older in households reached by the census interviewers. In this book, the term, "annual income," refers to the total amounts given in answer to the two census income questions. For families, annual income is the sum of the incomes for all family members 14 years old or over.

How good are the census income figures? Intensive spot checks against factory pay records and income tax returns and Census Bureau re-interviews have uncovered many errors. Interest and dividend payments are under-reported by about 10%, but reports of wages and salaries are generally accurate on average. Individual reports are often wrong, but particularly among low income households overstatements virtually balance understatements. In short, the annual cash income data are reliable for low income families.

One might expect the decennial census of all the people to give results that are more reliable than the ones obtained by the Current Population Survey 35,000 household sample. Rechecks have repeatedly shown that the Current Population Survey generalizations are more accurate than the complete count so far as concerns income statistics. The difference is mostly explained by the contrast between the inexperience and brief training of the tens of thousands of decennial census interviewers and the experience and lengthy training of the hundreds of Current Population Survey interviewers.

II. SOCIAL SECURITY ADMINISTRATION POVERTY INCOME CRITERIA

Reliable income statistics are available. In 1965, the Social Security Administration formulated poverty income criteria that allow for farm-nonfarm residence, the age and sex of the household head, the total number in the household, and the number of children under 18. These criteria do not allow for household assets (stocks, bonds, houses) or for variations in household needs other than the ones implied by the variables just listed. Thus most, but not all, of the considerations discussed in Chapter 1 are taken into account by SSA calculations.

The Social Security Administration (SSA) identified more than 100 categories of household, each distinguished by its peculiar farm-nonfarm, age-and-sex-of-head, number-of-members, number-of-children combination. The SSA then calculated a dollar-income poverty line appropriate to each household type. These lines have been revised each year to allow for the effects of year-to-year price changes.

To calculate a dollar-income poverty line appropriate to a particular household category, the SSA begins with the assumption that low income families spend one third of their total income on food; this was the average food-cost-to-family-income ratio observed by the Department of Agriculture in a 1955 survey.[1] Then, using appropriate prices, for example, 1968, the SSA computed the minimum cost of minimally nutritious meals for each of the household categories; these minimally nutritious meals are what the Agriculture Department calls an "economy food plan" for "emergency or temporary use when funds are low." This food cost times three gives the poverty line.

---

[1] See U.S. Department of Agriculture, *Food Consumption and Dietary Levels of Households in the United States,* Agricultural Research Service Series 62-6, G.P.O., Washington, D.C., August 1957.

For example, a four-person family of father and mother, under age 65, and two children, under 18, was found to need 27.05¢ per person per meal in 1968. It follows that this family would need 27.05¢ × 3 × 4 = $3.246 a day for food and 2 × $3.246 = $6.492 a day for all other items: housing, including utilities and furnishings, clothing, transportation, medical care, soap and other personal care, and everything else. The total figure came to $9.738 a day. The poverty line for this particular family of four was, therefore, between $3554 ($9.738 × 365 = $3554.37) and $3555. With a 1968 income of $3554, such a family was classified "poor"; with a $3555 1968 income, it would be classified "nonpoor." The calculations are a bit elaborate, but the key figure is the 27.05¢ per meal.

Table 2-1 gives poverty thresholds for a dozen different nonfarm family categories. The figures are called "weighted averages" because the age of family members is not considered; thus, each figure in Table 2-1 is an average of the poverty thresholds of several family categories;

Table 2-1.   Weighted Average Nonfarm Poverty Thresholds
for 1968 by Size of Family and Sex of Head

Number of Family Members	Male Head	Female Head
1	$1827	$1700
2	2272	2202
3	2788	2678
4	3555	3536
5	4191	4142
6	4709	4670
7 or more	5804	5638

Source: U.S. Bureau of the Census, "Poverty in the United States 1959 to 1968," *Current Population Reports*, series P-60, No. 68, 31 Dec. 69, G.P.O., Washington, D.C., p. 11.

the "weight" allows for the relative importance of each category. Each threshold figure is built up from the cost of an economy food plan meal. The threshold figures are changed from year to year to allow for the effects of inflation. For 1969, the threshold figure for a four-person family with a male head was $3740.

In 1965, the SSA allowed for farm households' real income by making poverty thresholds for farm households just 60% of those of equivalent nonfarm households. For 1966, the adjustment was raised to 70%; for 1968, it was raised to 85%, and all earlier poverty counts were readjusted to reflect the 85% threshold adjustment.

Having established a poverty threshold income criterion for each household category, the SSA used them to distinguish between poor and nonpoor in the March Current Population Surveys. Generalizations then were made from the samples to the entire nation.

III. TOTAL POOR IN 1968 AND IN 1969

According to SSA criteria, 25,389,000 Americans, 13.8% of the population, were poor in 1968. Of the total number poor, 20,695,000 lived in families, 4,694,000 lived alone as what the Census Bureau misleadingly calls "unrelated individuals," a term defined in Chapter 1. In 1969, the number of poor fell to 24.3 million, 16.7 million whites (10% of all whites) and 7.6 million nonwhites (31% of all nonwhites).

Subsequent chapters emphasize the distinction between two groups of poor: first, those whose poverty can be eliminated by increases in their productive contribution and in their earned income; second, those whose poverty can be eliminated only by increases in transfers, directly or via government, from other people's earned income. This chapter divides the 1968 poor into categories that are relevant to this distinction between poor people who might earn their way out of poverty and poor people who are unlikely to earn their way into nonpoverty.

Two kinds of percentage calculations will be mentioned often in this chapter. One kind looks only at the poor and calculates the percent of the poor who belong in a particular category. For example, of the 1968 poor, 18% were unrelated individuals; 82% lived in families.

The other kind of calculation looks at a population category, for example, all unrelated individuals, and shows "poverty incidence," the number poor in that category as a percent of all the people in that category. For example, of America's unrelated individuals, 34% were poor in 1968.

Poverty incidence calculations show the extent of poverty

within a particular population category. The other percentage calculation breaks down total poor into subcategories. The statistics that follow below will feature a distinction between the subcategories of poor most likely to earn their way out of poverty and the subcategories least likely to do so.

Unless one is a glutton for mind-boggling statistics, the best way to proceed through the following lettered subsections may be to skim through very quickly (the same advice applies to the statistical section opening Chapter 3). These statistical sections may be most useful if readers refer to them with care only when their curiosity is aroused by the analytical discussion of subsequent chapters.

A. Age and Poverty in 1968

Of the 20,695,000 1968 poor in families,

        10,739,000 were children under age 18,

        2,091,000 were past age 64;

thus   52% of the family poor were children,

        10% of the family poor were past 64,

while   10% of all American children were poor.

    Of the 4,694,000 1968 poor unrelated individuals,

        2,584,000 were past age 64;

thus   55% of these poor were past 64,

while   49% of all unrelated individuals past 64

        were poor.

Few among the 10,379,000 poor children 17 and younger were in a position to earn their way out of poverty until they acquired more years and more education. The years were sure to come. The additional education might or might not come, and enormous differences in educational quality were certain to appear, as among those children in poor families.

Few of the poor people past 64 had any prospect of earning their way out of poverty. These people could cross from poverty to nonpoverty only if they were to be given larger transfers.

B. Sex and Poverty in 1968

Of the 3,846,000 families poor in 1968 with heads aged over 17 and under 65,

        1,501,000 were headed by women;

thus	39% of these poor families were headed by women,
while	35% of families headed by women 18 to 64 were poor.

Of the 2,110,000 unrelated individuals aged 18 to 64 and poor in 1968,

	1,365,000 were female;
thus	65% of these poor unrelated individuals were women,
while	29% of all female unrelated individuals, aged 18 to 64 were poor in 1968.

Only 11% of American families are headed by women, but women, especially women with children to care for, are as a rule less well equipped than men to earn above-poverty incomes. Many poor women aged 18 to 64 are potentially able to earn their way out of poverty; whether or not those with children should leave home to work is another question.

C. *Race and Poverty in 1968*

Only 11% of Americans are black, but blacks made up more than 30% of all American poor in 1968. For more than 300 years, white Americans have restricted the education and training of black and red Americans, and the effects show up in the poverty statistics.

Of the 25,389,000 Americans poor in 1968,

	7,616,000 were black;
thus	30% of the poor were black,
while	35% of all blacks were poor.

Of the 5,047,000 families poor in 1968,

	1,366,000 were black;
thus more than	27% of poor families were black,
and	29% of black families were poor,
while only	8% of white families were poor.

Of the 10,739,000 children in poor families in 1968,

	4,188,000 were black,
thus almost	40% of poor children were black,
while	43% of all black children were poor.

Of the 1,501,000 1968 poor families with a female head aged 18 to 64,

	649,000 were black,

thus   43% of these families were black,
while   58% of families with black female heads
                        aged 18 to 64 were poor.

D. *Farming and Poverty in 1968*

Americans have been moving off the farms throughout this century. Only 5% of Americans lived on farms in 1968.
  But of the 10,454,000 living on farms in 1968,
                    2,318,000 were poor,
                      599,000 were black and poor,
so almost   10% of all poor Americans lived on farms,
and although   10% of white nonfarm residents were poor,
                    18% of white farm residents were poor,
                    33% of black nonfarm residents were poor,
and   67% of black farm residents were poor.

Most of the poor who remain on farms can become productive enough to earn their way out of poverty—but only if they move to nonfarm employment.

E. *Statistics Needed but Not Available*

Data on poverty among Indians, continental American residents of Puerto Rican origin, and white persons of Spanish surname in the Southwest would be useful, but no SSA statistics are available. The 1960 census did count the number of families—of all sizes, 2, 3, 10 or more persons—with 1959 income below $3000. In this category were

                    18% of white majority families,
                    54% of Indian families,
                    49% of black families,
                    32% of families of Puerto Rican origin,
and   35% of white persons of Spanish
                    surname in the 5 southwestern states.

  Poverty figures for people of different educational attainment also would be useful. Again, no SSA data exist, but the 1960 census statistics showed that of 9,700,000 families with 1959 income below $3000 only 665,000 were headed by white men aged 25 to 65 with 12 or more years of education.

IV. FEW AMERICANS BECOME POOR

The making of the American poor could be a process in which the children of the last generation's poor and the children of the last generation's nonpoor alike are winnowed so that the weakest in each group become the poor of the new generation. This is not the way it works.

Few Americans become poor—except in old age. Most children born to the American nonpoor remain nonpoor all their lives. Of children born to the poor some remain poor until they die, others find the means to attain above-poverty productivity though many who rise above poverty during their working lives fall back into poverty after they retire.

The preceding survey of the 1968 poverty statistics provided a brief introduction to the characteristics of people who remain poor. The next section surveys the changes in numbers and portions poor that occurred between 1961 and 1968 and provides an introduction to the kinds of forces that reduce poverty.

V. DECLINE IN THE INCIDENCE
OF POVERTY: 1961 TO 1968

Figure 2-1 shows the drop in the incidence of poverty that occurred over the years 1961 to 1968 (note that throughout this text, "1961 to 1968" means inclusive of 1961 and 1968). This drop was not an illusion of price inflation, since the SSA criteria did allow for price increases.

If the size of the drop between 1961 and 1968 (from 39,600,000 to 25,400,000) is repeated between 1968 and 1975, only 11,200,000 will be poor in 1975. A similar drop during subsequent years would eliminate poverty after 1981.

The sex trend lines in Figure 2-1 show that trends alone will not eliminate American poverty by 1981. The lines for white males and for nonwhite males trend down (though even they are unlikely to reach zero by 1982), but the white female line has fallen only slightly and the nonwhite female line has gone up since 1959. A further look within the statistics will distinguish more precisely those groups whose poverty incidence seems likely to continue in most rapid decline.

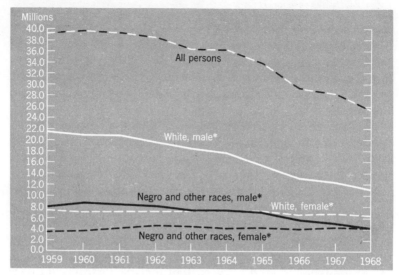

Figure 2-1. Number of persons below the SSA poverty thresholds, by sex and race of head, 1959 to 1968.

Source. Bureau of the Census, "Poverty in the United States, 1959 to 1968," Current Population Reports, Series P-60, No. 68, 31 Dec. 69, G.P.O., Washington, D.C., p. 1.

Table 2-2 shows the increase or decrease in the number of poor Americans as between successive years. A sharp contrast is shown between the years 1959 to 1961, when the number of poor rose, and the years 1961 to 1968, when the number of poor fell. During the last years of the Eisenhower Administration, fiscal-monetary policy stressed control on inflation; and high unemployment and a high incidence of poverty were accepted in order to have stable prices.

After 1961, rising prices were accepted in order to have lower unemployment rates and a lower incidence of poverty. After 1964, the Vietnam War gave a super boost to the economy and cut unemployment rates and the incidence of poverty while it accelerated the rate of increase of prices. Clearly, a booming economy is associated with a falling poverty incidence for households headed by men.

The 1966[R] figure is a note of caution. SSA revisions in methods

Table 2-2. Increase or Decrease in Number of Poor Americans since the Preceding Year: 1960 to 1968

Year	Change in Number Poor
1960	+361,000
1961	−223,000
1962	−1,003,000
1963	−2,189,000
1964	−381,000
1965	−2,870,000
1966	−2,761,000
1966R	−1,914,000
1967	−741,000
1968	−2,380,000

Source: Bureau of the Census, "Poverty in the United States, 1959 to 1968," *Current Population Reports, Series* P-60, No 68, 31 Dec. 69, G.P.O., Washington, D.C., p. 21.

of calculation produced this drop in number of poor between 1965 and 1966. The new methods are presumably more precise than the old ones; but the jump warns everyone that every poverty statistic is to be taken as an educated approximation.

A. *Change in the Poverty Cross Section: 1961 to 1968*

Table 2-3 makes a comparison between 1961 and 1968 in the percent of poor who were, (a) children, (b) elderly, (c) unrelated individuals, (d) farm residents, and (e) black. In 1968 as in 1961, 42% of the poor were children, but the portion of aged among the poor rose from 15% in 1961 to 18% in 1968. Because so many unrelated individuals are elderly, their representation among the poor rose from 12% in 1961 to 18% in 1968.

Table 2-3. Percent of Poor Persons Who Were Children, Aged, Farm Residents, or Black: 1961 and 1968

	1961	1968
Children under 18	42%	42%
Aged over 64	15%	18%
Unrelated individuals	12%	18%
Farm residents	16%	9%
Black	26%	30%

Source: Same as for Table 2-2, pp. 21-23.

The increasing importance of the elderly among the poor occurred because the full employment years of the 1960s drew many of the younger poor into jobs but left older people in poverty that could be reduced only by larger transfer payments.

The continued migration from farms cut the farm resident portion of the poor from 16% in 1961 to 9% in 1968. Some of those poor farm migrants left both the farms and poverty when they moved. Others simply moved from farm poverty to nonfarm poverty.

The portion of the poor who were black rose from 26% in 1961 to 30% in 1968 and to 31% in 1969. Partly because of poor education, partly because of white racial prejudice, blacks continued to be the last hired and the first fired.

The effects of full employment also appear in figures for the heads of poor families (not shown in Table 2-3). Males under age 65 headed 58% of the poor families in 1961, but only 46% in 1968.

Within these 1961 to 1968 statistics, the important distinction is between people most able to leave poverty via higher earnings —their own or their relatives—and people least able to leave poverty via higher earnings. Between 1961 and 1968, federal monetary-fiscal policy permitted private business to expand and to press down unemployment, in the process making jobs available to the unemployed poor. Between 1961 and 1968, the nation's stock of machinery increased, the state of technology was improved by invention and innovation, and the education and training of the poor were improved; all these changes tended to raise the productivity of an hour of labor and, thereby, to raise the 1968 income of persons who were poor in 1961 and who were working during 1968. In contrast, the 1961 poor who could not work because of age, illness, or other causes, and who could not share in the income of other people (as most children can), remained poor through 1968—except in cases where transfer payments were increased more rapidly than prices rose.

B. *The Working Poor*

Many of the poor work and remain poor. Table 2-4 shows the portion of family heads aged 25 to 64 who worked but remained poor in 1961 and 1968. The Table distinguishes between male and female, white and black.

In both 1961 and 1968, half of the 25 to 64-year-old males heading poor families worked full time year-round. These cases are easily pictured: 52 weeks times 40 hours times $1.65 an hour is $3432 a year, well below the poverty threshold of a four-person family (see Table 2-1). Most of the other poor male household heads aged 25 to 64 worked part of the year.

Table 2-4. Of Poor Family Heads Aged 25 to 64, Number and Portion Who Worked during 1961 and 1968

	1961		1968	
	Number	Percent	Number	Percent
Total white male	3,274	100	1,587	100
Worked 50 to 52 weeks				
Full time	1,596	49	803	51
Part time	123	4	54	3
Worked 1 to 49 weeks	1,174	36	420	26
Total working	2,893	89	1,277	80
Total black male[a]	1,078	100	465	100
Worked 50 to 52 weeks				
Full time	456	42	220	47
Part time	42	4	12	3
Worked 1 to 49 weeks	478	44	156	34
Total working	976	90	388	84
Total white female	878	100	727	100
Worked 50 to 52 weeks				
Full time	84	10	91	13
Part time	39	4	27	4
Worked 1 to 49 weeks	298	34	198	27
Total working	421	48	316	44
Total black female[a]	573	100	579	100
Worked 50 to 52 weeks				
Full time	114	20	101	17
Part time	59	10	45	8
Worked 1 to 49 weeks	185	32	185	32
Total working	358	62	331	55

[a] The figures for 1961 are for all nonwhites.
Source: Same as for Table 2-2, pp. 51, 53, and 112.

As between black and white men aged 25 to 64, the differences are small. A slightly larger portion of the poor whites worked full time; a larger portion of the poor blacks worked part time. As between 1961 and 1968, the portion working fell. Men in part-time work switched to full-time work and left poverty. Rising productivity raised wages and carried full-time workers out of poverty. The ones who remained behind were increasingly those who potentially were least able to earn their way out; these least-able people are another reason the downward trend lines of Figure 2-1 will flatten out before reaching zero in 1982.

The figures for female family heads aged 25 to 64 show a much smaller portion working full time and a slightly smaller portion working part time than was the case for men. The changes between 1961 and 1968 in percentages working were similar for men and women aged 25 to 64. Black women aged 25 to 64 heading poor families were special in that their numbers rose between 1961 and 1968. A decade of "full employment" had minimal effect on them.

VI. DOLLAR WIDTH OF THE POVERTY GAP

For selected years, the SSA has measured the gap between actual money income received and the poverty threshold of each poor unrelated individual and of each poor family. The sum of these figures measure the "poverty gap," the additional income the poor would have had to have received during a particular year to have been not poor—just barely not poor.

In 1959, the poverty gap was $13,668,000,000.
In 1968, the poverty gap was $ 9,849,000,000.

For the average poor family, the gap was $1179 in 1959 and $1278 in 1968. For the average poor unrelated individual, the poverty gap was $783 in 1959 and $724 in 1968. The size of the gap did not change much for individuals or for families because the relative position of the individual poor did not change much during the decade.

The size of the total poverty gap fell between 1959 and 1968 despite inflation because of the drop in number poor. Between 1959 and 1968, the number of poor fell 36% and the poverty gap fell 28%; the discrepancy was largely accounted for by inflation.

VII. SUMMARY

Both the decennial census and the Current Population Survey collect information regarding earned and transfer money income of individuals during the calendar year preceding the census. The income statistics include many errors, but the errors seem to average out for low income families.

The Social Security Administration (SSA) has calculated poverty income thresholds for unrelated individuals and for families of various characteristics. Individuals or families with cash incomes equal to or above those thresholds are counted nonpoor; those with incomes below those thresholds are counted poor by the SSA. The basis of the SSA threshold calculations is the assumption that poor families spend one third of their income on food, and the Department of Agriculture "economy food plan" calculations of the cost of minimally nutritious meals, for example, 27.05¢ a meal in 1968 for a four-person family.

According to the SSA poverty thresholds, 25.4 million Americans, 13.8% of the population, were poor in 1968; 10.7 million were children, and 4.7 million were past age 64. Of the 5.05 million poor families, 39% were headed by women and 1.4 million were black.

Since most poor Americans were born poor, statistics showing changes over time show the extent to which people born poor are able to move out of poverty.

The drop in the incidence of poverty was so great between 1961 and 1968 that if the 1961 to 1968 trend were to continue through 1981, America would have no poverty. But the trend cannot continue; much of the 1961 to 1968 decline in poverty was the result of the expansion of aggregate demand and of the rise in labor productivity during the 1960s. The able-bodied poor of 1961 were helped most by those changes. From 1961 to 1968, the portion of the poor made up of the aged and of mothers with small children rose persistently. By 1968, a larger portion of the poor were those who could be lifted out of poverty only by increased transfer payments. Many of the 1961 poor who could work their way above poverty had done so by 1968. But even in 1968, more than a million family heads worked full time year-round and were nevertheless poor. These people can leave poverty only by becoming more productive—or by transfers from the nonpoor.

The "poverty gap" is the difference between the earned and transfer money income of the poor and the poverty threshold of each family and unrelated individual. The dollar width of the poverty gap was $13.7 billion in 1959 and $9.8 billion in 1968. It averaged $1179 per family in 1959 and—after inflation—$1278 in 1968.

3

Per Capita Production

The Social Security Administration has counted a minority—a large minority—of Americans as poor. Outside the United States, no carefully organized count is required; the most casual observer sees that a majority of the people in the world are poor. Yet in Denmark, Norway, Holland, and Sweden, a smaller percent of the population is poor than in the United States.

Why should anyone anywhere be poor?

Why should most be poor when so many are not?

A start can be made on finding answers to those questions by looking at the value:

$$\frac{\text{total annual production by one nation}}{\text{total population of that nation,}}$$

which shows a nation's annual production per person (or, if one prefers, "output per capita"). Obviously, if the value of that ratio is very small, all or nearly all of the people in the nation must be poor. Conversely, if the value is large, it is at least arithmetically possible that everyone in the nation will be nonpoor.

I. MEASURES OF TOTAL OUTPUT

To measure the value of the ratio, one must have a measure of total annual production, and that means adding apples and oranges, and cars, and airplane rides, and restaurant meals. Fifty years ago no one could do it; forty years ago, some were learning. Now there are three widely used conceptually distinct measures of total annual production:

1. Gross National Product, GNP: the sum of the market prices of all goods and services produced during a year.

2. Net National Product, NNP: GNP minus the value of all depreciation and other capital consumption during a year (that is, NNP = GNP — c.c. allowances).

3. National Income, NY: the sum of the market value of all factor inputs during a year net of capital consumption allowances (that is, NNP — indirect taxes — surplus of government enterprises + subsidies).

GNP is the most widely used measure of the value of annual production, but it overstates the value of annual output available for disposition by the poor and the nonpoor of a nation. GNP overstates the value of what becomes newly available for the following reasons:

1. It makes no deduction allowance for replacing capital consumed during the production year (NNP corrects this overstatement).

2. It includes the value of indirect taxes loaded on top of the production value of output (NY corrects both overstatements).

The production process is a little like running up a muddy hill in 60-inch strides with a 5-inch backward slip accompanying each stride. During a year's production of a GNP worth, say, $60 billion, the buildings and equipment (the physical capital) with which the nation begins the year will suffer extensive depreciation and some damage from flood, earthquake, fire, and other causes. Such "capital consumption" might total $5 billion, in which case GNP would be $60 billion, but NNP would be only $55 billion. The general rule, if a nation's stock of physical capital is not to fall, is that a portion of output must be used to replace capital consumed. England and other combatants demonstrated during World War II that the replacement does not have to be made, but Europe's output was smaller in 1946 than it would have been if worn out machinery had been replaced during the war.

NNP is the sum of the market prices of all production after a deduction for the replacement of capital consumed.

NNP still overstates the productive value of what becomes

newly available because it includes the value of indirect taxes and the surplus of government enterprises. This overstatement can make year-to-year comparisons misleading. For example, if in Year 1 and in Year 2, physical production is exactly the same car for car, haircut for haircut, apple for apple, and Senator for Senator, and if wage, interest, rent, and profit rates remain unchanged while sales taxes of the second year are double the ones of the first (similarly if the surplus of government enterprises, for example, state liquor stores, is increased), then NNP (and GNP) will rise between the two years by the amount of the added tax (or surplus of government enterprises) even though physical output is unchanged. In contrast, one should notice that if physical output and factor receipts remain unchanged while personal and corporate income taxes double between Year 1 and Year 2, both GNP and NNP remain the same in the second as in the first year. The indirect-tax overvaluation of GNP and of NNP and the surplus-of-government-enterprises overvaluation of GNP and of NNP are excluded from National Income since NY = NNP — (indirect taxes) — (surplus of government enterprises) + (subsidies).

GNP and NNP tend to overstate the production value of what becomes newly available during a year because they include indirect taxes and the surplus of government enterprises. They tend to understate the production value of output because, when summing market prices, they omit the production value bought by government subsidies. For example, when the 83rd Congress met in 1953, their first fiscal action was a law providing for federal cash payments to wool growers. Because of that law, wool farmers receive part payment for their work from the market prices (less sales taxes) of their wool and part payment in the form of treasury checks from the federal government as a heritage from President Eisenhower's era. To obtain the total value of all the inputs going into a year's production, subsidies must be added in. National Income calculations do this though GNP, and NNP do not.

In summary, National Income, NY, sums the factor cost of a year's production. NY measures the total factor (input) value of production made newly available to the poor and nonpoor of a nation during a year. If factor prices would hold constant from year to year, then NY would be the best measure of year-to-year changes in the real output of a nation and, hence, of year-to-year changes in the value of the

$$\frac{\text{annual output}}{\text{population}} \quad \text{ratio.}$$

But, of course, factor prices do not remain constant from year to year; wage, interest, and profit rates change from year to year and so do product prices. The United States Department of Commerce constructs index numbers by which GNP figures can be adjusted for price changes to yield a series that portrays year-to-year changes in real output (and in indirect taxes). The department, however, does not "correct" either NNP or NY for price changes. Thus, although NY is the preferred numerator for output per capita calculations, GNP is the only total output measure permitting year-to-year comparisons free of the effects of price changes.

There is one other income (not ouput) series that the Department of Commerce adjusts for price changes and that, for some purposes, serves best as the numerator of an income-to-population ratio measuring the absolute level of and changes in the purchasing power of the average citizen of a nation. This is Personal Disposable Income.

National Income measures the value of a nation's total output, but households receive command over only a portion of that output after distributions to governments and corporations. The households' claim on output is measured by Personal Disposable Income, PDY. It is calculated (using 1969 figures for illustrative purposes) as follows:

National Income		$772 billion
Less: Retained earnings of corporations,	64	
Social insurance taxes,	54	
Personal taxes (mostly income)	118	236
		536
Plus: Government transfers to persons	62	
Government interest payments	29	
Business transfers to persons	4	95
Personal Disposable Income		$631 billion

II. PER CAPITA OUTPUT, PER CAPITA INCOME

In 1969, the value of the output-to-population ratio with each of the several numerators just discussed was:

> Per capita GNP: $4590
> Per capita NNP: $4200
> Per capita NY: $3800
> Per capita PDY: $3100

Over recent decades, the value of per capita GNP (stated as though the prices of every year had been those of 1958) and of per capita PDY (stated as though the prices of every year had been those of 1958) were as follows.

	Per Capita GNP	Per Capita PDY
1929	$1670	$1236
1933	1120	893
1939	1600	1190
1947	2150	1513
1958	2560	1831
1969	3580	2507

Per capita output and per capita income have risen persistently in the United States.

The growth of American GNP is the sum of the growth of the output of goods and of services. The figures would be smaller if the Department of Commerce summed the growth of output of goods and services and bads. Pollution, beginning with Alice's garbage in Stockbridge, Massachusetts, and congestion could be added into GNP as negative items. Then the greater the pollution, the smaller would be GNP net of "bads." Estimates of GNP net of bads are not yet available but should become available sometime during the 1970s.

III. INTERNATIONAL COMPARISONS
OF 1966 PER CAPITA GNP

Even for a recent year, GNP statistics are rough estimates for the less developed nations, but they are good enough to indicate the order of magnitude of per capita GNP in these nations. By way of contrast with the United States, the per capita GNP figures for 91 of the 94 countries with more than three million people each (no estimates are available for China, North Korea, or North Vietnam) and for Kuwait, Israel, and Brunei (the only three Asian nations with per capita GNP above $1000) were as follows in 1966, according to the World Bank. For the less developed nations, the figures include the output of both their market and their nonmarket economies:

$3500	The UNITED STATES
3400	Kuwait
2300	Sweden
2200	Switzerland, Canada
1800	Australia, Denmark
1700	France, West Germany, *Norway*
1600	Belgium, The United Kingdom, Finland
1400	The Netherlands
1300	Brunei
1200	East Germany, Israel, Austria
1000	Italy, *Czechoslovakia*
900	RUSSIA, Japan
800	Venezuela, Hungary, Argentina
700	Poland, Greece
600	South Africa, Romania, *Spain*, Bulgaria, Hong Kong
500	Chile, Jugoslavia, Mexico
400	Portugal
300	Cuba, Guatamala, Peru, *Colombia*, Iraq, Malaysia, Turkey
250	El Salvador, Dominican Republic, Iran, Brazil, Saudi Arabia
225	Ghana, *Taiwan-China*, Algeria, Ivory Coast
200	Senegal, S. Rhodesia, Tunisia, Ecuador
175	Syria, Zambia, Angola, *Morocco*
150	Bolivia, Philippines, United Arab Republic, Ceylon, S. Korea
125	Thailand, Cambodia, S. Vietnam

100   Cameroon, INDONESIA, Mozambique, Sudan,
      Uganda
 90   INDIA, Kenya, Malagasy R., PAKISTAN, Yemen
 80   Guinea, *Niger*, Nigeria, Tanzania
 70   Afghanistan, Chad, Haiti, Nepal
 60   Burma, Congo (Kinshasa), Ethiopia, *Mali*
 50   Burundi, Malawi, Upper Volta
 40   Rwanda

The numbers are rounded, but the countries with per capita GNP above $100 are in order according to the unrounded figures. Every tenth country is underlined to facilitate rank calculations.

Comparisons between the $40, $50, and $60 per capita GNPs of Rwanda, Upper Volta, and Ethiopia and the $3500 per capita GNP of the United States are somewhat misleading. Pretty clearly, a family of 6 with a total annual income of $300 could not survive a year in New York City. Climate and crowding account for substantial differences in needs between Manhattan and the rural tropics, but the statistics are themselves in need of qualification.

These dollar estimates were obtained in most cases by the use of official exchange rates to convert each country's per capita GNP figure from its national currency to dollar terms.[1] This procedure understates the dollar value of the GNP of many countries, especially of the poorest countries. The understatement results because official exchange rates derive from goods and services traded internationally, but in the less developed countries, the prices of food, transportation, clothing, and housing that comprise most of the cost of living of most people are lower relative to international trade produce prices than is the case in the United States. Thus exchange rates may appropriately value internationally traded products while undervaluing much that is not traded internationally but that is of great importance in the consumption of the ordinary Nigerian, Indonesian, and Brazilian.

---

[1] For a more detailed (but still incomplete) explanation of the derivation of these dollar estimates, see the "Technical Note," on page 42, at the end of the section, "World Bank Atlas: Population and Per Capita Product of the World," pp. 30-42, *Finance and Development* magazine, No. 1, 1969.

As a rule of thumb, the figures at the bottom of the above list should be multiplied by as much as 2 before being compared with the per capita GNP of the United States. Then, as against the American per capita GNP of $3500, the comparable figures are near $400 for Senegal, Tunisia, and Ecuador; near $200 for Indonesia, Sudan, and Uganda; and near $100 for Burundi, Malawi, and Upper Volta.

All these figures are per capita. To convert them to per household, each must be multipled by about 4. Such adjustments make the figures grow.

But neither per capita GNP nor per household GNP make any allowance for the portion of output taken by government for administration, defense (or aggression or repression), and other uses that are of little direct benefit to households. Neither does either of these GNP-per figures allow for the portion of output used for gross investment. Because of these government and investment expenditures, the GNP figure exceeds—to a degree that varies from country to country—the value of the portion of production available for consumption.

Since no country practices income equality, the per capita and per household GNP figures also overstate the position of about half of each country's population because that population half is the lower end of the income distribution.

After due allowance for each of these considerations, the per capita GNP figures of these 94 countries illustrate the point made earlier: most of the people in the world are poor.

More than half of the people in the world live in China, India, Russia, the United States, Indonesia, or Pakistan, the six nations with populations of more than 100 million. Five of these appear in capital letters in the above list. China is not listed because no estimate of per capita GNP is available more precise than "something under $100." Of these six, four had per capita GNP of $100 or less in 1966.

Two thirds of all people live in countries with 1966 per capita GNP of $300 or less. Half live in countries where the 1966 figure was $100 or less.

The list shows "the AALA gap" between Africa, Asia, and Latin America on the one hand, and Europe, Canada, America, New Zealand, and Australia on the other. All countries with 1966 per capita GNP below $400 are in the AALA group. Of countries with 1966 per capita GNP above $800, only Japan, Israel, Brunei, and Kuwait are in the AALA group. Expressing this in another way, it can be pointed out that the difference is closely associated with color; the Japanese and the mainly white countries are not poor; most colored people are poor.

IV. WHEN THE RATIO IS SMALL, MOST MUST BE POOR

Most of the people in the world are poor. Why? They are poor because they live in countries in which output is low relative to population, or where—which is saying the same thing—population is large relative to output. Obviously, India would not be a poor nation if output were 20 times as large from the present population or if output were at the present level and the population was only one twentieth the present figure.

The output-to-population ratio is fundamental. If that ratio has a very small value, say $50 to $100 as in Indonesia, India, Nigeria, and the Congo, then the nation has only two possibilities (assuming no foreign gifts of unprecedented size): either everyone in the nation must be poor, or a minority can be nonpoor while the great majority are a little poorer than if everyone had the same income.

Let us suppose that a nation of 30 million with a $3 billion GNP initially displays great income inequality with

10,000 people averaging $10,000 income, man, woman, and child, and the other 29,990,000 people averaging about $97 per capita.

A revolution might then abolish income inequality in favor of an equal division of the national product in which case, if population and output remained unchanged, everyone would receive $100 a year. Everyone would be poor.

The 3+% improvement in the income of most people would be modest. If, however, that nation of 30,000,000 with $3 billion GNP had begun with

100,000 people averaging $10,000 and the other 29,900,000 averaging about $67 per capita,

An income-equalizing revolution would lift most incomes by nearly 50% by raising them from about $67 to $100. Still, all would be poor.

In circumstances of this kind the only way poverty can be eliminated is by an increase—by an enormous increase—in the ratio of output to population. The elimination of income inequality can make the poor less poor but cannot eliminate poverty. Time may do so, but England required 500 years (from the fifteenth to the middle of the twentieth century) to raise output from $100 to $1000 per head.

Through all but the past dozen decades of the history of man, the choice has everywhere been between universal poverty and an arrangement whereby a few can be rich because the many are each a little poorer than under a system of income equality. In Periclean Athens, income inequality left most residents in poverty while it provided a few with comfortable incomes and the time for the conceptual work that contributed so much to the ideas and ideals of Western civilization. The splendors of the Roman Empire required great income inequalities. So did that "fleeting wisp of glory . . . that was known as Camelot." Each modern American is enormously indebted to past systems of income inequality that left most somewhat poorer while they allowed a minority opportunities to make disproportionately large contributions to culture and technology. Those income inequalities also permitted (the next chapter will emphasize this point) the accumulation of the great stock of machinery and of education that permits production of a $4590 per capita GNP.

In the nineteenth century, Karl Marx protested what he called the "exploitation of the working class." But even as recently as Marx's time, the hard fact was that national products were still so small that an equal division of the German, or of the English, or of the Swedish national product would have left everyone in the nation poor. The poor were poorer because of income inequality, but income equality could not have eliminated poverty.

In classical Greece, in Arthur's, and even in Victoria's England, there could be no end to poverty. There was not enough output. Today, in Nigeria, in China, in India, and in Brazil, there can be no end to poverty, at least, not in the short run. Using the SSA definition of poverty and looking at the world as a whole instead of at individual nations, there can be no end to poverty for many decades, since the ratio of world output to world population is less than $300 and rises but slowly. Mankind as a whole remains in the category it has been in since the species first appeared; that is to say, *poverty cannot be eliminated for all men either this year or any time in the foreseeable future.* Poverty cannot be eliminated until enough men work enough harder and until enough capital and technology accumulate to double or triple the world output-to-population ratio.

V. WHEN THE RATIO IS LARGE, THE DIVISION MAY LEAVE SOME POOR

When the output-to-population ratio does have a very large value, say $4590 as for the United States in 1969, then a wide range of possibilities opens up: most people can be poor while a majority receive enormous incomes; or all can be nonpoor; or some can be very poor, and some very far from poverty, with others scattered in between. Given a high output-to-population ratio, a nation can eliminate poverty through income transfers from its well-to-do to its poor and still can retain wide income differences among its citizens. For example, the United States (as Chapter 9 will point out) would have had no poverty in 1968 if about $25 billion had been transferred (notice how this figure exceeds the $9.8 billion poverty gap) from the well-to-do to the people labeled poor by SSA criteria. After such a transfer, the income differences between the newly nonpoor and the well-to-do would have remained large. The elimination of poverty can occur only when a nation's output-to-population ratio is large.

These statistics and this discussion have distinguished two fundamental causes of poverty:

1. A small output-to-population value.
2. Unequal distribution of output as among households.

This chapter considers the factors that determine the size of the output-to-population ratio. The next three chapters discuss the processes whereby the household share of the total is divided among individual households.

VI.　POPULATION

It is an immutable truism that no matter how large the size of a nation's output, a big enough population denominator will cut the output-to-population ratio to a level that condemns most of the citizens to a life of poverty.

Over time, growth in output may yield each citizen a larger portion. But if population grows faster than output, a drop in output per person must follow. So far as concerns the objective of escape from poverty, growth in output is not important, growth in output per person is important.

The not-so-mythical Republic of Fecundia provides an illuminating negative example. The size of its national product increased 10% between 1959 and 1969. During the same period, its population increased 20%. Consequently, output per person fell more than 8% during the decade. Such a combination of changes has characterized many nations in the past. It will characterize some nations this year.

VII.　WHAT DETERMINES THE SIZE
OF OUTPUT IN THE SHORT RUN?

A.　*Extent and Character of the National Domain*

Quite obviously the size of a nation's land and water resources is a fundamental determinant of national output. Just as obviously size is not everything.

Hong Kong, with just 398 square miles, manages a total output eight times and a per capita output ten times that of 106,000 square-mile Upper Volta; and as one jolts over the Voltaic corrugated roads during the dry season, one wonders where these 4,000,000 people and their more numerous sheep, goats, and cattle find enough water, much less enough food, to keep alive. Indeed, they would have much less food if they did not receive almost as much in pensions to veterans of the "Senegalese" units of the French Army as they receive from merchandise exports and if, in each recent year, they did not export many men to labor in the Ivory Coast.

Kuwait, with 491,000 people and 5300 square miles, enjoys a GNP half again as large and a per capita GNP 50 times as large as that of Afghanistan with 16,000,000 people and 251,000 square miles. The fertility of the soil, the amount of rainfall and of river water available, the amount of oil and of other minerals under the surface—each of these factors can make a big difference in national output.

To produce a large output, people, raw materials, semifinished parts, and final products must be moved around. If transportation is especially difficult, residents must devote extra effort to *moving* things, and, consequently, they will have less time and energy left to *make* things. When producers decide as among locations, they shun areas where transportation is difficult and, instead, settle where transportation is easy. Thus Holland, Hong Kong, and New Jersey with flat plains and/or with easily accessible navigable waterways are favored, but landlocked mountainous nations such as Afghanistan, Bolivia, Zambia, and Nepal are at a big transportation disadvantage.

The size, the rainfall, temperature, topsoil, and subsoil conditions and the lay of the land and water of a country are important determinants of total output. But disadvantages in these respects can be compensated for and can be overcome by accumulations of physical capital (machinery, bridges, railroads, power plants) and of human capital (education and training) as the citizens of Japan and of Hong Kong have demonstrated on their rocky mineral-short lands.

B. *The Quantity of Physical Capital*

There are about 99 million Japanese living on the Japanese islands. Japan's per capita GNP is about one fourth that of America's. If a playful Olympic deity were to grasp all 99 million Japanese, pick them up, and put them down in the United States in place of 99 million Americans transplanted to Japan, what would happen to the total production in each country? Would the GNP of the Japanese islands quadruple under American hands so that per capita GNP would be the same from 99 million Americans in Japan as for those same 99 million Americans when in the United States? Would output in America sharply contract under half-Japanese operation? The answers would be, "Yes," if the chief reason for the differences between America and Japan in per capita GNP were because of variations between Americans and Japanese in their willingness and ability to work. But how big in fact are those variations, if any?

The answers to all three of these questions become clearer after one other question is answered: How does the quantity of physical capital used by the typical Japanese worker compare with the quantity of physical capital used by the typical American worker? The answer is easy. The typical American worker uses two to three times the quantity of tools, buildings, and infrastructure used by his Japanese counterpart (these are averages; the contrast, for example, would not apply to the steel industry). More of these things, meaning more physical capital, permits more output per worker. Much of the Japanese-American difference in GNP per capita is the result of the Japanese-American difference in physical capital per worker.

The population exchange between Japan and the United States would strand Americans in Japan with a small amount of physical capital per worker and would give the Japanese in America some two to three times as much physical capital per worker as they had had in Japan. After the exchange, time would be required to permit workers to adjust to unfamiliar equipment (presumably, the Olympic deity would obviate any potential language problem). Following the transition period, the GNP of Japan would be about the same as before the switch. American GNP would be about the same under fifty-fifty Japanese-American hands as under 100% American hands. Thus Americans in Japan would produce about one fourth as much per worker as they had produced at home; the Japanese in America would produce about four times as much per worker as they had produced in Japan. This assumes that the Japanese willingness to work longer hours and harder than Americans would almost offset the greater education and training of the American labor force.

India, Nigeria, and Brazil are poor countries largely because they possess much less physical capital per worker than Sweden, Switzerland, and Canada. Puerto Rico, Arkansas, Mississippi, and nearly all black American farmers are poor, in part, because they possess much less physical capital per worker than Connecticut, Illinois, Michigan and nearly all white farmers in the Midwest.

C. *The Quantity of Human Capital*

As a variation on the previous population switch, suppose that this god on Mt. Olympus traded the entire American population for an equal number of Indians. What would the Indians be able to do in the United States with their sudden wealth of physical capital?

Among the Japanese population, 98% are literate. Among the United States population, 97% are literate. Among the Indian population, 20% are literate. Because of these differences in literacy and because of differences between India and Japan in experience with machinery, the question, "What could the Indians do with America's physical capital?" is answered differently from the question: "What could the Japanese do with America's physical capital?" For the Indians, the question can be reworded to ask: "What use could be made of America's physical capital by a largely illiterate population with little experience in the use of nuts, bolts, and lubricants, much less of pistons, transistors, and IBM cards?" Clearly, the answer is, "Relatively little."

It is not enough to *possess* a tractor, a lathe, or a computer, that is to say, it is not enough to *have* physical capital. Workers also must know *how* to use the machinery to produce efficiently. To be able to produce efficiently with a particular piece of equipment, one must know more than how to run the equipment under ideal conditions. The effective operator must be able to coordinate with other machines, other operators, and with managers. The effective operator must be able to deal with predictable contingencies by following established procedures. He also must know enough about mechanical relationships, about cause and effect, to be able to deal with the unpredictable in order to prevent damage to his machine and to minimize impediments to production.

Reading, writing, arithmetic, casual analysis, on-the-job training, and all other *productive* skills are *human* capital. Physical capital and human capital together derive from the portion of output that is produced during one time period but is held over instead of being consumed during that time period. Held back from consumption, this portion of output is added to the stock of physical and human capital, and this increased stock becomes available to increase the level of production in future time periods.

Human capital derives from parental instruction, formal education, and the years of experience on and off the job. The size of a nation's National Income is as directly dependent on its accumulation of human capital as on its accumulation of physical capital. America's per capita NY exceeds Japan's because America has nearly triple the per capita physical capital of Japan and because America has accumulated more human capital per person than has Japan.

D. *Technological Quality*

Some lathes are better than other lathes; some engineering students are taught techniques superior to the ones taught other engineering students; some farmers learn better farming methods than the ones other farmers learn. A nation's output derives from accumulated physical and human capital whose potential is a function of quantity *and* quality. The higher the quality of a nation's physical and human capital (in other words, the better its technology), the larger its potential national product.

E. *Economies of Scale*

If sheet metal costing 10¢ a square foot is used to make a storage tin in the shape of a cube 1 ft. × 1 ft. × 1 ft., the cost of metal for the six sides will be 60¢. If the same metal is used to make a storage tin 2 ft. × 2 ft. × 2 ft., the cost of metal for the six sides will be $2.40. But in the latter case, the cost per cubic foot of material stored will be $2.40 ÷ 8 or 30¢; in the first case, the cost per cubic foot of storage space was 60¢. A container 3 ft. × 3 ft. × 3 ft., would involve a cost of $5.40 for the metal in the six sides; but this would be only $5.40 ÷ 27 = 20¢ per cubic foot of storage space.

This example illustrates the geometric basis of the economies of scale that characterize most manufacturing processes in the United States and that permit low-cost production because of the enormous scale of operations. Economies of scale cannot go on indefinitely. In the example cited, for example, the weight of the contents would beyond some particular size of cube, be too great to be contained by metal of this gauge. Then the walls would have to be made thicker, and unit costs would be pushed up.

In almost every manufacturing or transportation process (think of the jumbo jets) known to engineers, unit costs are lower with large-scale than with small-scale production. Some of these economies of scale are directly due to the circumstance that square measures (area) grow less rapidly than cubic measures; part is because of the secondary effects of the growth difference between square and cube; for example, heat loss would be relatively far larger from a Bessemer converter one foot in diameter than from one 50 feet in diameter. Part of these economies are due to the limited divisibility of a man; the manager capable of supervising 1000 employees will produce at lower unit costs in a plant employing 1000 than will his peer in a plant employing 100.

The American Constitution created the first great common market of modern times and gave the United States unsurpassed opportunities to enjoy the benefits of economies of scale. In contrast, parts of Europe and of Asia, much of Latin America, and almost all of Africa is splintered into nationettes with markets too small to afford opportunities for production for domestic consumption on a scale that permits significant economics of scale. The ranks of the nationettes were swelled in 1960 when General de Gaulle, with thoughtful malice, divided into 13 parts the French-speaking portion of Africa awarded nominal independence in that year. Only by joining nationettes as nations or as free trade areas can economies of scale be put within the reach of producers in the multiple small nations in the world.

F. *Hours Worked*

In 1900, most Americans worked 60, 70, or more hours a week; vacations were infrequent and brief. Since then, the length of the average work week has fallen to 55 to 48 to 44 to 40 hours; the frequency and length of vacations have grown. In many other countries, most people work far more hours per year than Americans. Given the quantity and quality of capital per worker, it is clear that, up to some physical maximum, the more hours worked by a nation's labor force, the greater will be the total and the per capita national income.

G. *Attitude*

Above all, there is attitude toward production processes. At one extreme is the view—as in traditional societies—that production, rice growing or steel making, should continue to be carried on in every detail as it was carried on by one's father and grandfathers. At the other extreme is the view that every possible improvement in productive efficiency should be sought out and put into effect. The former view predominates throughout the less developed countries and nationettes. The latter view more nearly predominates in America and in Japan than anywhere else in the world, and it accounts for a substantial portion of the difference in output per capita as between Europe and America.

Professor Edward Denison is now regarded as America's most accomplished measure of productivity. He has concluded that Western Europe's workers are about 60% as productive as American workers. He has further concluded that much of the difference is due to America's advantages in physical capital per worker and in economies of scale but that *more* than one half of the difference is because of the greater air of innovative enthusiasm that permeates American society.[2] This characteristic has not yet yielded to arithmetic measurement, but its presence in America—where the young have recently applied it with unprecedented vigor to social customs—is apparent, and its absence from the less developed countries is equally apparent.

H. *Aggregate Demand*

The considerations just cited determine how large national income *can* be. Aggregate demand determines how large it *will* be.

In 1932, the idle ships and freight cars, the silent, padlocked mines, the oiled but inactive cranes, and the motionless assembly lines were American physical capital in disuse. The unemployed patternmakers, the former personnel managers selling apples, and the skilled brick masons employed as common laborers were unused American human capital.

Mark Twain once observed that those who could read but did not were no better off than those who could not read. Similarly, a nation that has resources but does not use them may be no better off than the nation without them. Land, buildings, equipment, education, and training are productive only if they are used, and they are used only if there is an effective demand for their use.

---

[2] Edward E. Denison, *Why Growth Rates Differ, Postwar Experience in Nine Western Countries*, The Brookings Institution, 1967, pp. 334-335.

The relevant phrase is "aggregate demand"—the demand from all businesses, all governments, and all households. If aggregate demand is "sufficient," then most available resources will be used, and the national product will, assuming no special distortions, be maximized. If aggregate demand is insufficient, then some resources will stand idle. If aggregate demand is excessive, most resources will be used *and* prices will rise.

The most used measure of the degree of resource utilization, more precisely, of nonutilization, is the unemployment rate of the civilian labor force. On behalf of the Bureau of Labor Statistics, the Census Bureau collects statistics monthly to measure employment and unemployment rates. In America, few job hunters are able to find jobs—much less start working—the day or even the first week after they begin looking for work. Delays in finding work are common partly because some people want work but not very badly (often the case with teenagers of working parents and with wives whose husbands are employed), partly because many inexperienced and uneducated people in the labor force are qualified for only the least demanding jobs, and partly because America is so big and communication is so imperfect that the most eager and able job seekers often require weeks or even months to locate suitable jobs. Because these factors prolong the job search and because of delays between finding a job and actually starting work, "full" employment of "all who want to work" leaves 3½ to 4% of America's civilian labor force unemployed in the statistical count. Thus demand is "sufficient" when unemployment stands at about 3½ to 4% of the civilian labor force. Demand is "deficient"—in the sense used here—when unemployment moves up beyond 4%. Demand is "excessive" when aggregate demand presses unemployment below 3½% and pushes prices up rapidly. (Chapter 9 points out how rapidly prices rise in the United States at unemployment rates below 3½%.)

To survey the forces affecting the strength of aggregate demand, it is helpful to separate GNP into its three components by distinguishing among goods and services used (1) for consumption, (2) for gross investment (including net foreign investment), and (3) for public (government) use. This breakdown may be written as:

$$\text{aggregate demand} = \text{actual } GNP = C + I + G.$$

A great many factors act together to determine the amounts households, businesses, foreigners, and governments are able and willing to buy. Household, business, and foreign demands are influenced by current levels of employment, income, prices, and profits and by expectations regarding the future levels of employment, income, prices, and profits. Inventions, politics, wars, rumors of wars, fashions, and fads all play a part as do actual and expected tax rates. Government demand fluctuates with the decisions of Congress, state legislatures, city councils, school boards, and public tax referenda.

Two factors affecting aggregate demand require special attention. They are the federal government's fiscal and monetary programs. Government has discretion to vary these programs and can use them to prod aggregate demand toward sufficiency without excess.[3]

Monetary policy is important because, in the United States, the money supply and money market conditions are subject to the discretionary initiatives of the Board of Governors and the Open Market Committee of the Federal Reserve System. Month by month, the American labor force and labor productivity rise. Every increase in labor-force size and in labor productivity raises America's production potential. If the Federal Reserve implements a sufficiently expansive monetary policy, America's growing production potential is realized. If the Federal Reserve applies a restrictive monetary policy, production rises less rapidly, or may even decline, unemployment rises, and the war on poverty becomes less effective. If the Federal Reserve undertakes a sufficiently expansive monetary policy, unemployment will fall and price increases will become large.

The "correct" monetary policy is a matter of opinion, in large part because of the trade-off America experiences between unemployment and inflation (more of either is associated with less of the other). The question of the "right" unemployment level

---

[3] For a more extensive analysis of the relationships among monetary and fiscal policy, other variables, and aggregate demand, see Arnold Collery, *National Income and Employment Analysis,* in this John Wiley series. For a study of fiscal policy in all its ramifications, see Robert Haveman, *Public Finance,* also in this series.

for which monetary policy should aim is discussed in Chapter 9 below.

Monetary policy is not the only means by which the government affects unemployment rates and price levels. Fiscal policy also plays a large role. Fiscal policy refers to changes in the levels of government spending and of tax collections. When the federal government spends more, aggregate demand rises. When the federal government cuts taxes (here, emphasis is on the federal instead of on state and local governments because the federal government has much more discretion to vary spending independently of taxes, and vice versa), households and businesses will have larger disposable incomes and will be able to raise the consumption and investment components of aggregate demand.

In the other direction, when the federal government cuts spending or raises taxes, the government component or the consumption and investment components of aggregate demand are reduced (or their rate of increase is reduced) and production, and sometimes even prices, fall (or cease to rise as rapidly as otherwise).

Fiscal policy can be very effective in pushing actual output close to potential output. It was spectacularly effective in 1942 and, again, in 1951, 1964, and 1965. But in each case, monetary policy pointed the same way. In 1948 and during 1952 to 1953, fiscal policy, supported by monetary policy, slowed the pace of inflation.

Monetary and fiscal policy affect the level of aggregate demand. Chapter 5, below, will show how variation in the level of aggregate demand influences the incidence of poverty.

VIII. WHAT DETERMINES THE RATE AT WHICH THE NATIONAL PRODUCT GROWS?

The preceding discussion applies to the very short run in which technology and its applications are unchanged and in which the quantities of natural resources and of human and physical capital are fixed. These fixed factors determine the size of potential product; aggregate demand determines the size of actual product in this very short-run period.

In the real world, of course, most of the factors discussed above change with the passing of minutes. These changes determine whether potential and actual national product will rise or fall over time. Along with changes in the size of population, these changes determine whether the ratio of output to population can and will rise or fall over time.

A. Growth of Physical Capital

In 1969, the United States contained about $1.5 trillion worth of business merchandise inventories, of residential, government, institutional, and business structures, and of producers' durable equipment (for example, assembly lines, bottling machinery, and oil refining equipment). This was the physical capital used to produce the national product of 1969.

As the year's output took shape, this $1.5 trillion stock of physical capital suffered extensive depreciation as the wear and tear of use wore it down. Some portions dropped in value as innovations rendered old equipment obsolete. Some portions were destroyed by fire or other accident. During 1969 approximately $78 billion of private capital was "consumed." As was mentioned above, this $78 billion in private capital consumption allowances was the difference between 1969 GNP and NNP. Additional portions of government-owned capital also were consumed.

While this destruction was going on, new houses, new machines, new factory buildings, and new roads were being built. During 1969, about $132 billion worth of new private structures and equipment were produced and about $8 billion worth of merchandise was added to business inventories. Thus, during 1969, private physical capital (household inventories are overlooked) was worn back by $78 billion while receiving $140 billion in new increments (Gross Private Domestic Investment) for a net gain of about $62 billion (Net Private Domestic Investment). In addition, billions of dollars worth of new plant and equipment were built for governments.

Put differently, about 15% of America's GNP goes into GPDI; about 6% goes to NPDI. In Japan in contrast in recent years, about 37% of GNP has gone into GPDI, and approximately 28% has been NPDI. This means 28% of each year's production is not used up but is added, *net*, to Japan's stock of private physical capital.

By way of contrast, medieval Europe had, and much of the contemporary underdeveloped world has, an NPDI of zero. NPDI is zero when total output is divided in only two parts: the greater part for consumption, mostly food; the lesser part to offset the year's depreciation of tools and buildings. Nothing is then left over for the net investment in physical capital. If physical capital is not increased, output per capita is unlikely to rise, since increases in human capital and improvements in technology are unlikely to appear in circumstances in which physical capital changes but little.

Contemporary Japan's willingness and ability to hold consumption (plus depreciation offset) well below total output results in substantial annual increases in Japanese physical capital. The growth of physical capital has been accompanied by rapid growth in human capital and by changes in technology. Because of these annual increases, the potential size of Japan's national product has grown substantially year after year. Because aggregate demand has grown proportionately and because the Japanese population has remained roughly constant for a decade, the actual size of Japan's per capita product has grown by 13% a year, a rate of increase well above that of any other large nation.

The larger the portion of a nation's output going to NPDI the more rapid the growth of that nation's potential total output. The smaller the portion to NPDI, the slower the growth of that potential.

B. *Growth of Human Capital*

Estimates have been made of this nation's stock of physical capital. Annual calculations are made of the size of additions to that stock.

Human capital is as important as physical capital in the production process, but no one has yet devised a practical means of estimating the value of America's total stock of human capital or the value of net annual additions to that stock. Nevertheless, the output-to-population ratio is as much affected by changes in the stock of human capital as it is by changes in the stock of physical capital.

Whenever people acquire more education and training of a kind they can utilize in their work, potential output rises. Obviously, more and better education and training add to a nation's stock of human capital. Less obviously, an increase in the length of the working life of a nation's population will add to the nation's potential output even though population size remains unchanged. Increased length of working life has approximately doubled America's stock of human capital during the past century.

If all the members of the labor force are trained by age 20 and die at age 40, the entire stock of human capital must be renewed every 20 years. If people trained at 20 can work on average until age 60, the stock of human capital need be renewed but once in 40 years. Put differently, when human capital is created in a labor force, the returns to that investment when people average 40 years of work are double (more if experience adds to productivity) the returns when people average only 20 years of work. The significance of this consideration may be inferred from the following life expectancy figures:

United States of America:	70
Mexico	57
India	46
Tanzania	38
Morocco	47
Ethiopia	35
Chad	32

Thus a nation's stock of human capital is larger the larger the portion of annual output devoted to training, education, and health. Furthermore a nation's stock of human capital is larger the longer the working life of its people.

C. *Improvements in Technology*

When one lathe is replaced by two lathes exactly like the original one, the change that takes place is neither invention nor innovation. But when a lathe that is superior to the original one is conceived and built for tests, invention occurs. When the superior lathe replaces or supplements the original lathe, the change is properly called innovation.

Invention is the conception, construction, and use of new machines and techniques in a laboratory or testing facility. Innovation is the application of the new machine or technique in production. The discovery and application of ever-superior technology is a major source of year-to-year increases in the American national product. These changes in technology that raise the value of the output-to-population ratio occur so rapidly in America in large part because the American business community is—for better or for worse—very receptive to change. American business schools concentrate on teaching how to innovate. Businesses promote successful innovators. The entire institutional system is geared to change.

As pointed out above, the institutions of most of the people in the world are not geared to change. As a result, people in these societies do not originate changes that raise the output-to-population ratio. What seems stranger to most Americans, people in poor countries are extremely slow and awkward at transplanting American technology into their institutional systems, and most have proved to be extremely reluctant to modify their institutions to facilitate the transplantation of American technology.

The thousands of Appalachian and Ozark residents of isolated mountain coves and millions of blacks cut off from education by Southern white school systems are products of a similar mold. They have been educated to perpetuate the conditions into which they were born. That education and those practices endured for many generations. They can no longer continue, but they have crippled millions of Americans by severely limiting their ability to learn new skills and to adapt to urban institutions.

IX. LABOR'S AVERAGE PRODUCT CURVE

The more machinery, the greater is output per worker; the more education and training, the greater is output per worker; the better technology, the greater output per worker. Easy enough. But the potential output per worker depends on both:

> quantity of other resources (land, capital, technology),
> *and* on the size of the labor force.

The character of this relationship can be illustrated by a homely example and by some geometry.

Given 1000 cleared arable acres, some farm buildings, and some farm machinery, there are a number of mutually exclusive ways in which these resources can be combined with labor:

If one worker uses these resources to grow strawberries, he can produce 5000 pecks during one year.

If two workers use these resources to grow strawberries, they can produce 9500 pecks during that year.

If three workers use these resources to grow strawberries, they can produce 13500 pecks during that year.

If four workers use these resources to grow strawberries, they can produce 17000 pecks during that year.

And so on through many other mutually exclusive possible inputs on this farm during a particular year.

The numbers used here are arbitrary, but the general principle is not. The principle of "diminishing average returns to a variable factor combined with fixed factors" observes as a general rule in this world that given some fixed quantity of resources (for example, land, buildings, machinery), the larger the quantity of some other resource (in this case, labor) used with the fixed resources, the smaller the $\dfrac{\text{output}}{\text{variable input}}$ ratio (which in this case is the average product of labor).

The arithmetic of the strawberry example is:

Labor Quantity	Total Product	Average Product
0	0	0
1	5,000	5,000
2	9,500	4,750
3	13,500	4,500
4	17,000	4,250

Figure 3-1 presents a geometric elaboration respecting the average product of labor on this strawberry farm. The dots in Figure 3-1 represent the information given in the columns above. The dashed lines through those four dots show the average product of labor if fractional amounts between 1 and 2 and 3 and 4 laborers are used. The dashed line extended to the right of the dots shows the average product of labor on this farm if more than four laborers are used.[4]

---

[4] In *Case Studies in American Industry*, in this Wiley economic series, Leonard W. Weiss uses some actual statistics on feed input and milk output per cow to illustrate the principle of diminishing average returns to a variable factor.

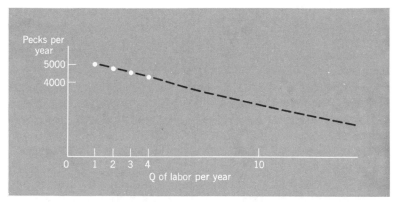

Figure 3-1. Average product of labor on a 1000-acre strawberry farm.

The above example used a strawberry farm, but any farm would do to make the point. Moreover, the principle of diminishing average returns to a variable factor applies to the entire nation.

Given the entire area of the United States, and given the national stock of capital, and the state of technology, the average product of American labor slopes down to the right as in Figure 3-2. If the labor force is *ox*, then if resources are fully employed with maximum efficiency, realized average product would be *oq*. If the labor force is *ox'*, then if resources are fully employed with maximum efficiency, realized average product would be *oq'*. If

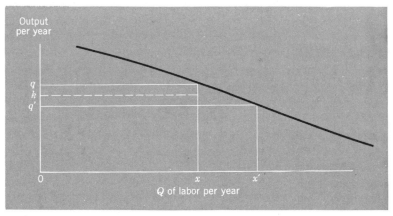

Figure 3-2. Average product of American labor.

the labor force is *ox*, and if some resources are unused or are used inefficiently, realized average product would be some amount, for instance, *ok*, below *oq*.

Figure 3-3 shows what happens to the average product of American labor following increases in the quantity of resources other than labor. Given an initial quantity of all other resources, the average product curve of American labor would be *AP-1*. With a labor force of *ox*, realized average product could be *oq*.

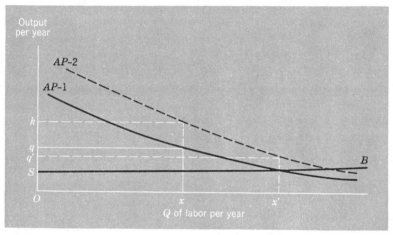

Figure 3-3. Average product of American labor as affected by changes in quantity of other resources.

An increase in the quantity of physical or human capital or an improvement in technology would raise labor's average product curve to *AP-2*. If there were no change in labor force size, labor's realized average product could be *ok*. But despite the rise in the AP curve, if population increases to raise the labor force to *ox'*, realized average product can be only *oq'*. Three general principles are illustrated here:

1. Labor's average product curve slopes down to the right.

2. An increase in the quantity of other resources raises labor's average product curve.

3. The larger the labor force, the lower is possible average product.

The height of the line *SB* represents an average product that would mean poverty for everyone in the nation. No matter how high other resources raise labor's AP curve, the nation as a whole will be poor if the population becomes so large that realized average product is cut to *OS*.

The annual rate of population growth now ranges from 1% in Europe to 1.5% in the United States to more than 3% in Latin America. Latin America seems determined to remain near *OS*. The United States is far from *OS*. But even the United States could reach *OS* if population growth were to exceed the rise of labor's average product curve for a long enough period of time.

X. SUMMARY

Most people in the world are poor. Most Americans are not poor. Most of the people in the world are poor because they live in countries in which per capita national income is so low that even an equal distribution of output would leave everyone poor. This condition characterizes the world as a whole, since the world's total output is so small relative to the world's 3.5 billion people (there were 2 billion in 1930) that an equal distribution would leave everyone poor.

Most people in America are not poor, and most people in several other countries are not poor because they live where per capita national income is high. Nevertheless, even in these countries many people are poor, not because their country's per capita national income is low, but because of their country's system of dividing output among its residents.

Subsequent chapters consider the American system of distributing output. This chapter has considered the elements determining the size of a country's output-to-population ratio. Total output and growth in total output depend upon the stock and upon growth in the stock and physical and human capital, upon technology and technological improvements, upon economies of scale, upon working hours, upon attitudes and institutions, and upon aggregate demand. Output per person depends upon those factors and upon the size of population.

4

Dividing the National Product

Through most of the years of man's history, widespread poverty has been inevitable because of the small size of the output-to-population ratio. In the less developed countries today, widespread poverty is still inevitable because the value of the output-to-population ratio remains small. In all such times and places, that low ratio is the primary cause of poverty.

But even in such low output societies, the degree of poverty of a particular individual depends on the way in which output is distributed as among individuals. In societies in which the output-to-population ratio is large, the extent and character of poverty are entirely the consequence of the way in which output is distributed.

In the United States, the output-to-population ratio is now so large that, at least so far as concerns simple arithmetic, total output could be distributed in ways that would leave everyone not poor. Almost every year there is a drop in the number of Americans left poor by the distribution of output. But every year millions are left poor.

This and the next two chapters are principally concerned with the system by which American output is distributed. In addition, this chapter considers some other ways in which output could be distributed.

I. GOVERNMENTS SHARE, PRIVATE INVESTMENT, PRIVATE CONSUMPTION

Of a country's total output, most is taken directly by the private sector for consumption and investment; the remainder is used by government. Part of government's share is used up, immediately in government consumption, as with dogcatchers', Senators', and policemen's time; and part is transformed by government investment into capital as with the construction of highways and with the construction of schools and the operation of schools. Most government activities do benefit households; so the distinction between the private share and the government share of output is not a distinction between private benefits and private nonbenefits. It is a distinction between private choices and public choices of the use of output.

Table 4-1 shows how American output has been divided between the government and private sectors during 1929, during 1969, and during each election year 1932 to 1968. When interpreting these figures, one must bear in mind that social security payments, veterans' pensions, aid to the blind, and other *transfers* from governments do *not* show up in the government columns of Table 4-1.

Table 4-1. Division of the Gross National Product in 1929, 1969, and in the Election Years 1932 to 1968, by Percentage Shares

	Percent of Gross National Product going to:				
	The Public Sector			The Private Sector	
	Federal		State		
	National		and	Invest-	Consump-
Year	Defense	Other	local	ment	tion
1929	1.3[a]		7.1	16.7	74.9
1932	2.5[a]		11.3	2.4	83.8
1936	6.0[a]		8.5	10.5	75.0
1940	2.2	3.8	8.1	14.9	71.0
1944	41.5	0.8	3.6	2.5	51.5
1948	4.2	2.3	5.8	20.3	67.4
1952	13.3	1.7	6.6	15.7	62.7
1956	9.6	1.3	7.9	17.7	63.5
1960	8.9	1.7	9.2	15.7	64.4
1964	7.9	2.5	10.0	16.2	63.4
1968	9.0	2.4	11.6	14.9	62.0
1969	8.5	2.3	12.1	15.2	61.8

[a] These figures are for national defense and other federal uses combined.

Source: Calculated from the *Economic Report of the President: 1970*, G.P.O., Washington, D.C., 1970, p. 177.

This table shows neither total tax collections nor the total of government checks written. This table is about output, not about money or money payments. It shows the division of output between government and private uses.

The federal government's portion has varied with the nation's military activities. The state and local government portion has risen persistently from its 1944 low, and is now more than 60% above its 1929 level. The private share has remained about the same since 1956.

Not all of the private share goes into consumption. Part goes to investment. The choice between "more or less investment this year" is also a choice between "more or less poverty this year, less or more poverty in the future." The larger this year's consumption, the less there will be left over for investment and the less poverty there will be this year, but the lower the production and the greater the poverty in the future. Conversely, the smaller this year's consumption, the more there will be left over for investment and the greater will be the poverty this year, but the greater the production and the smaller the poverty in the future. The poverty of nineteenth-century England and America was greater than otherwise because a large share of nineteenth-century output went into net investment. The low incidence of poverty in the United States in the 1960s is the consequence of the high levels of net investment in the past.

The last two columns of Table 4-1 disclose the share of GNP going to private gross investment and the share going to private consumption. In the past, these shares have fluctuated when depression or war disrupted the economy. Since the Korean War of 1950 to 1953, the consumption share has remained almost constant and the investment share has varied only enough to cause mild economic fluctuations.

II. DIVIDING THE HOUSEHOLD SHARE AMONG HOUSEHOLDS

As a country's output is being divided between government and households, and as the household's share is being divided between investment and consumption, the household share is being divided among households.

Who should receive what share of output? Should everyone in the world receive an equal portion of world output? (That would be about $250 each; about $1250 a year for a five-person household.) Should everyone in the United States receive an equal portion of the nation's output?

Should those whose parents received a relatively large share of output also receive a relatively large share? (As between America and India, this is the case. It is also the case as between white Americans and black Americans.)

Everyone has his own opinion as to how output "should" be distributed, but no law of nature exists to determine how output is to be divided. As among societies many different systems of distribution have been and are being used. The loaves and fishes were distributed on a different basis than was the output of imperial Rome. The output of South Africa is now being distributed on a different basis than is the output of the United States. Nature has not identified any one system as The Right System.

The system used in the United States today "works" well in the sense that its results are so generally accepted that only a small portion of Americans favor fundamental changes in the basic system. Advocates of fundamental change may eventually win out; but unless they become much more successful in persuading others to change their views, the present system can be changed radically during the near future only if a large portion of the population is put in jail while many of the rest are subjected to close police control.

Other distribution systems could be used in the United States. Three of these other possibilities are considered here: (1) equality, (2) to each according to his needs, and (3) authority. After a brief examination of each of these three possible systems, the remainder of this chapter concentrates on distribution in proportion to contribution to production; this latter system is used extensively in America.

A. *Equality*

Equal output per person is a simple concept. But equal division of output merits only passing attention as an arithmetic curiosity. No society has ever divided output equally; no one advocates that output should be divided equally as among men, women, the elderly, youths, infants, the sick, and the well. When pressed, those who use the term, "income equality," usually explain that what they mean is division of output in proportion to needs. Division in proportion to needs was once the general rule throughout North America and all of the world.

B. *Dividing Output in Proportion to Needs*

Division in proportion to needs still governs the distribution of most output in the AALA world. This is not a matter of choice, but of necessity in many places.

By definition, a "subsistence society" is one in which the output-to-population ratio is so small the population barely manages to reproduce its numbers even though it makes no effort to restrict population growth. In circumstances of this kind, output must be distributed nearly equally; but more must go where needs are greater, less where needs are less; more for pregnant and nursing women, even more for the most active men, less for the elderly, even less for the unproductive senile, and amounts appropriate to the various other ages and conditions of infancy, youth, and age.

The principle, "from each according to his faculties; to each according to his needs," was enunciated as a revolutionary rallying cry by the anarchist, Bakunin, in 1870, and by Marx in 1875. In late nineteenth-century Europe, the proposal was revolutionary; but through much of man's history, the principle has stood at the center of man's traditions.

When *Australopithecus africanus* gave way to *Homo erectus*, the succeeding species remained locked into a subsistence society. In all of his hunting-fishing societies, in most of his agricultural societies, *Homo sapiens* has lived in close to subsistence output-to-population ratios. When all Americans were Indians, most lived near subsistence levels most of the time. Today, in the interior of Africa, Asia, and Latin America, one still can find subsistence societies forced, as were all the subsistence societies before them, to distribute output in proportion to needs. This division was so often necessary because subsistence was for millenia the natural state of man.

This distributive system has been tried in societies with output-to-population ratios well above the subsistence level, but none of these attempts have been successful for long. Many nineteenth-century collectivist and cooperative societies in Europe and America attempted to implement Bakunin's principle, "from each according to his ability; to each according to his needs." The distribution of subsistence food, clothing, and shelter, was handled easily according to the Bakunin principle. Trouble arose because this principle offers no obvious measures to guide a society in dividing above-subsistence output. Ideally, these goods and services should be distributed so that the last item going to each person satisfies exactly the same intensity of personal need as the last item going to every other person. But who can make interpersonal comparisons of need? Who can measure the intensity of each person's above-subsistence needs?

As a practical matter, most nineteenth-century communal societies eventually chose one person or group to decide whose needs were greatest. At that point, the society became authoritarian, and volunteer members who disagreed with the deciders began to drop out.

Twentieth-century Communists frequently pay lip-service to Marx's restatement of the ancient principle, but European Communist nations have not applied the principle much more extensively than have other Western nations. Cuban and Chinese Communists have applied the principle to a much greater degree, but this may be only because their economies are still so near the subsistence level.

Communes begun in America in recent years are dedicated to the Bakunin principle; so are Israel's kibbutzim. Only time can tell if their members can make the system work for more than a few years.

Could America be converted to a system of distribution in proportion to needs? Perhaps it could if someone could measure comparative needs. If such a system could be made to work, involuntary poverty would disappear—although total output might be less than under the present system where there is a connection between the contribution to output and the share of output received.

At present, the most extensive American applications of the Bakunin principle are within families, where parents divide family income with children on the basis of needs as determined by the parents, and in the welfare-charity system, which for several decades has assured most northern and western Americans of a large enough share of output to meet just-above-starvation needs for food, clothing, and shelter (although not much for medical care). Because public and private welfare-charity have provided a bit more than minimal subsistence, infant mortality rates, the incidence of disease, and the life spans of poor Americans are somewhat above those of the poor in AALA countries.

C. *Authority*

When a society is near subsistence levels, output is distributed in proportion to needs. When the output-to-population ratio rises a bit above the subsistence level—at it has in most AALA countries, the above-subsistence portion of output can be divided among individuals in equal shares or in proportion to subsistence needs. As a rule, neither of these kinds of divisions occur. Instead, a new system of distribution appears: authoritarianism; and the extra output goes in disproportionate part to the chief and priest and to their retinues. Generals then appear to share in the surplus and to undertake to obtain a share of the product of neighboring societies. This system, of course, was inchoate in the to-each-according-to-need societies, for tribal leaders had to participate in decisions dividing output among the needs of competing individuals.

Slavery is the most extreme form of this system of output distribution. The sharecropping system evolved by Southern white property owners after the Civil War was a form only a little less extreme. The "authority" in these cases rests with individuals able, with government backing, to control the input, output, and income of other individuals. This authority may be in decline in most countries. Not in decline is the use of a government's authority to tax the public and to pay selected individuals in proportion to their influence instead of in proportion to either their contribution to production or their needs. Federal agricultural-assistance legislation authorized the payment during 1968 by the federal government of $116,978 to Mississippi Senator Eastland, a farmer and the chairman of the Senate Agricultural Committee that drafts the laws providing federal aid to farmers. The birth of many new nations since 1945 has brought as many complete—

and, often, superfluous—government bureaucracies into being. Those bureaucracies are staffed in large part on the basis of "pull," not ability or need. Pay is often based much more on authority than on contribution or need. Perhaps with Senator Eastland in mind, a deputy to an African French-speaking parliament pays himself, for one one-half month's work, as much as an African farmer earns in 36 years—in a lifetime of hard work. Thus is authority still used to cream off part of the above-subsistence portion of a country's output.

III. OUTPUT DIVIDED IN PROPORTION TO CONTRIBUTIONS TO PRODUCTION

Some of America's output is distributed on the basis of need; that is what the welfare and charity systems are supposed to be all about. Some is distributed on the basis of authority. Monopoly and monopsony influence most American incomes. But the central principle guiding the division of American income is "to each in proportion to his contribution to the total value of output." In fact, almost no one ever receives a year's income exactly equal to his contribution to the total value of output. Nevertheless, most American incomes *tend* to equal the value of that contribution.

The general principle is shown in microcosm in a simple arithmetic (or geometric) example of a market where products are sold perfectly competitively and inputs are bought perfectly competitively. These assumptions mean no outside agent imposes controls on prices or wages, and buyers and sellers in both the product (output) market and the factor (input) market are individually so small that, although output and input prices are free to fluctuate, neither the entrance into the market of one more seller or of one more buyer nor the departure from the market of one buyer or of one seller will have any effect on price.

Table 4-2 assumes such a case with a strawberry grower buying labor for $6000 a year in a perfectly competitive market and selling strawberries for $2.00 a peck in a perfectly competitive market. Table 4-2 shows his mutually exclusive output possibilities:

If he hires 1 man, total product is 5000 pecks, marginal product is 5000 pecks, value of marginal product is $10,000.

If he hires 2 men, total product is 9500 pecks, marginal product is 4500 pecks, value of marginal product is $9000.

If he hires 3 men, total product is 13,500 pecks, marginal product is 4000 pecks, value of marginal product is $8000.

Table 4-2. Mutually Exclusive Numerical Possibilities for Total Product, Marginal Product, Dollar Value of Marginal Product, and Marginal Resource Cost of Labor for a Strawberry Grower in Perfectly Competitive Markets (Product Measured in Pecks)

Number of Laborers	Total Product	Marginal Product	At $2 a Peck, Value of Marginal Product	Marginal Resource Cost
0	0			
		5,000	$10,000	$6,000
1	5,000	4,500	9,000	6,000
2	9,500	4,000	8,000	6,000
3	13,500	3,500	7,000	6,000
4	17,000	3,000	6,000	6,000
5	20,000	2,500	5,000	6,000
6	22,500	2,000	4,000	6,000
7	24,500	1,500	3,000	6,000
8	26,000	1,000	2,000	6,000
9	27,000	500	1,000	6,000
10	27,500			

And so on, through the infinitude of mutually exclusive possibilities including 2.5 men and 3.05 men. The principle of diminishing marginal product is illustrated here. It does not always apply, but it is the usual case. The similarity between this principle and the principle of diminishing average returns to a variable factor is not accidental. Both principles derive from the same basic physical relationships.

Because the going wage in this case is $6000 a year, the marginal resource cost (MRC) of each man is $6000. Since the first man brings a value of marginal product (VMP) = $10,000 and his MRC = $6000, he will be hired by a profit maximizing employer. Since the second man brings VMP = $9000 and MRC = $6000, he will be hired—and so on. Even the fifth man will be hired assuming that the employer prefers the largest employment short of marginal losses. But because a sixth man would bring VMP = $5000 and MRC = $6000, he will not be hired.

With perfect competition in both the product market and the factor market, the general rule is that an employer hires the largest number for which VMP exceeds or equals the wage rate (MRC). Then, given equilibrium, which would be reached in this particular case with five workers employed, a reduction in employment of any one person (all workers are assumed to be equal) would cut output by the number of units (3000 in this case) whose value (at $2 each in this case) equals the wage paid that worker. In this sense, every worker (and every unit of capital) is paid the value of his (its) marginal product.

This strawberry example can be sketched, as in Figure 4-1, with number of homogeneous workers measured along the x axis and with both physical output, for MPP, and dollars, for VMP, and MRC, measured on the y axis. A horizontal line, drawn at the

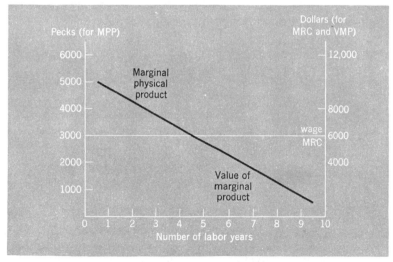

Figure 4-1. Mutually exclusive numerical possibilities for marginal product, dollar value of marginal product, and marginal resource cost of labor for a strawberry grower in perfectly competitive markets.

$6000 height, represents labor supply, since this employer can hire any number of laborers at the rate of $6000 a year. The points of the VMP represent demand for labor by this firm.

Where MRC exceeds VMP, the employer would net more by hiring fewer rather than more laborers. Where VMP exceeds MRC, the employer would net more by hiring more rather than fewer laborers. Where VMP equals MRP, the firm is in equilibrium, and each laborer is being paid the value of his contribution to the total value of output.

A. *Genetic Potential for Contribution to Production*

What determines the value of the contribution an individual can make to output? At the moment of conception, the new human being receives the genetic inheritance of his ancestry. This heritage does not determine what the individual will do or be. It does place outer limits on what the individual can do or be. One is conceived with a capacity to learn to do certain things. Many of these potential acts would be contributions to production (although the most productive skills in a tribe of fishermen may not be productive in New York in 1970) if the individual were to be given the opportunity to perform those particular acts.

The economic system might be arranged so that the following obtains:

1. Output is distributed among individuals in proportion to individuals' contributions to production.

2. Individual workers' contributions to production are proportional to individual workers' inherited capacity for learning productive skills.

But contributions to production are not proportional to workers' inherited capacity for learning productive skills.

B. *Actual Contributions Differ from Genetic Potential for Many Reasons*

There are many reasons why individual workers' contributions to production are not proportional to their inherited capacity for learning productive skills. Some of these reasons can be understood by imagining the case of two boys conceived at the same instant with identical capacities for learning productive skills. Despite this identical genetic inheritance, the two will not make identical contributions to production if:

1. The two, through training, education, and experience, acquire equal ability, but one is employed while the other is unemployed.

2. The two, acquire equal and superior ability, but one is employed where he can be most productive while the other, for some reason such as racial discrimination, is employed as a common laborer.

3. The two are born with identical capacity for learning, but one attends a good school while the other goes to school in rural South Carolina or Georgia or in the Chicago black ghetto.

4. The two are conceived with identical potential, but one's mother receives excellent nutritional and medical care during the prenatal period and during the delivery, while the other mother is ill fed, under extreme emotional strain, and poorly cared for during her pregnancy and delivery.

C. *Potential and Actual Productive Intelligence: A, B, C*

What a man can contribute to production depends on his intelligence—his productive intelligence. This is not the relatively narrow concept measured by IQ tests.

What is productive intelligence? It is the whole range of human physical and mental abilities valued in the marketplace. The determinants of an individual's productive intelligence may be studied more conveniently if the phrase "productive intelligence" is (1) restricted to behavior valued in the marketplace, and (2) subdivided to be applied to three different time periods in each person's life. By doing this, one can distinguish among Intelligence A, the individual's marketable potential at the moment of conception, Intelligence B, the individual's marketable potential at the moment of birth, and Intelligence C, the individual's marketable ability at any point in life after birth.

Intelligence A is a limiting concept. The genes joined by sperm and egg may carry the potential for a mathematical genius or may limit the individual so narrowly that he will be unable to write, count, or even speak. Barring as yet unknown processes in surgery and biology, the person with defective genes cannot be lifted out of idiocy. He is doomed to zero production.

Babies with low Intelligence A cannot rise. Babies with high Intelligence A may not rise. Kept after birth in a room with blank walls, kept from contact with other people, an individual with an Intelligence A potential for mathematical genius will, nevertheless, remain an idiot unable to talk or count, much less create new concepts. Given an appropriate education, he would become a creative master of mathematical concepts; uneducated, he has no productive ability.

Intelligence A refers to all kinds of marketable productive potential: ability to count, to persuade, to organize production, to teach, to use a shovel, to take initiatives, to write novels, to assemble transistor radios. The list is long. One may think of Intelligence A as a single measure that is comprised of thousands of different kinds of potential ability, or one may conceive of there being many Intelligence A's, one for each kind of ability potential.

For each kind of marketable ability, Intelligence A is the genetic potential at the time of conception. This genetic potential may or may not be realized—that will depend on events after conception. But the genetic potential, given the present state of biological-medical knowledge, can never be surpassed.

Between conception and birth, a great deal can happen to lower an individual's potential. The devastating effects on the baby of German measles in the mother during the second month of pregnancy are well known.

Millenia have favored the reproduction of genes of women who bore children over the genes of women who did not. Through the years, women have become endowed with a body chemistry that will sacrifice its own welfare to protect and to preserve the baby. During the months between conception and birth, the mother's body will do all it can but, sometimes, the mother's body cannot do all that is needed. Malnutrition, incompatible Rh factor combination, mental stress, and physical mistreatment can cripple the ability of the mother's body to serve the needs of the fetus. Then the baby may die or its Intelligence B may suffer. Intelligence B may be cut below the potential granted in Intelligence A at the time of conception.

The child's intellectual potential can be eroded by maternal malfunctioning or by the malfunctioning of those attending the delivery. In extreme cases, infants die; in less severe instances, babies suffer cerebral palsy, mental retardation, epilepsy, or other neurologic disorders.[1] In these cases, Intelligence B and, later, Intelligence C suffer.

The erosion of infants' Intelligence A, caused by incompetence or by inadequate care during the obstetrical period, can be avoided by mothers who have access to proper food, shelter, security, and medical care before and during delivery. This evasion is more difficult for poor women. The lower the socio-economic group of the mother, the further is the Intelligence B of her baby likely to be cut below that baby's Intelligence A and the more likely is the poverty of parents to be passed to the children.

After birth, environment operates directly, rather than through the mother, on each person. Intelligence C is the summary combination of environment and heredity. Much of Intelligence C derives from formal schooling: grade school, high school, and college. Much of Intelligence C comes from home, relatives, and friends. These people can teach the child to be ambitious, complacent, or despairing, to be polite or impolite, to want to learn or to be indifferent, to want to contribute to existing society or to want to revolutionize society.

While accumulating Intelligence C, individuals enter the market. There, in perfect competition, their share of output is as large as their contribution to its making. That contribution depends on the job the individual has, on the quantity and quality of the physical capital with which he works, and on the fitness of that job and physical capital for his Intelligence C.

D. *Allocating Physical and Human Capital Among Workers*

Individuals in a perfectly competitive market are presumed to be able to use the most efficient available production methods in order to obtain the maximum output consistent with individuals' willingness to work. To obtain this maximum output, each individual must be in the job where he can be as productive or more productive than any other person could be in that job. To

---

[1] Benjamin Pasamanick and Hilda Knoblock, "Some Thoughts on the Inheritance of Intelligence," *The American Journal of Orthopsychiatry*, July 1961, pp. 454-473.

achieve this ideal arrangement, every person would have to have perfect knowledge of the existing alternatives and perfect mobility to get to the most attractive positions. Another way of describing this most productive matching of workers and physical capital is to say that perfect competition would allocate physical capital among workers so that the added product from the marginal unit of physical capital assigned any one worker would be exactly equal to the added product from the last unit of physical capital assigned to his neighbor and to every other worker. Additions to the inherited stock of physical capital would be made until the value of the added product from the last unit of net addition to physical capital would just equal the value of the added cost of that added unit.

What a worker can produce with his tools, machinery, and natural resources depends on the human capital he has acquired. In perfect competition, training and education would be allocated with the object of maximizing output, and every individual would receive an amount of training such that the value of added product from his last unit of education would just equal the cost of that last unit of education. Medical care would be allocated in a similar manner. This system would make Intelligence A the guide for the allocation of human capital formation, and output would be larger than from any other possible combination of the particular society's Intelligence A, its technology, and its inherited stock of physical capital and natural resources.

E.   *Interest Income and the Marginal Physical Product of Capital*

Output derives from inputs of labor, of physical capital, and of natural resources. In an economic system where physical capital and natural resources are privately owned, individuals receive income from the contributions to production made by their labor, by their physical capital, and by their land.

Table 4-2 illustrates the concept of the marginal physical product of labor by showing a number of mutually exclusive strawberry production possibilities differing only in the quantity of labor used in each option. Figure 4-1 drew on Table 4-2 for values for the MPP, VMP, and MRC of labor to show that in a perfectly competitive market every laborer will be paid the value of his marginal physical product.

Another table could be made up for the strawberry farm, showing mutually exclusive production possibilities differing one from another only by the number of units of physical capital used in the production of strawberries. MPP and VMP figures could be calculated for capital. Again, the usual case would show diminishing marginal physical product associated with larger quantities of any one input, in this case, of physical capital.

The MPP and VMP of physical capital figures could be taken from the table and combined with MRC of physical capital figures in a sketch, for instance, Figure 4-2. If strawberries cost $2 a

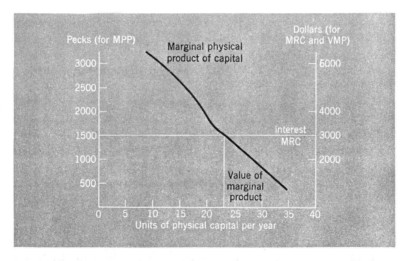

Figure 4-2. Mutually exclusive numerical possibilities for marginal product, dollar value of marginal product, and marginal resource cost of physical capital for a strawberry grower in perfectly competitive markets.

peck and if the price of a unit of physical capital were $3000 a year, then the strawberry grower would employ 23 units of physical capital and would pay $3000 to the owner of each unit. Each owner would be paid interest equaling the value of his physical capital's marginal physical product.

F.   *Economic Rent: The Bounty of Nature*

When individuals pay "rent" on a house, most of what they pay is interest on the physical capital they are living in, only a small portion of house rent is "economic rent." A numerical example will illustrate the concept of economic rent better than words. Given in Table 4-3 are 50-acre parcels of each of four grades of land. If $1000 is put into production costs on each parcel, output will differ from parcel to parcel because of differences among the parcels in natural fertility. If the crop sells for $2 a bushel,

Table 4-3.   Total Cost, Total Product, Total Revenue, and Economic Rent from 50-Acre Parcels Each of Four Grades of Land

	A	B	C	D
Total cost	$1000	$1000	$1000	$1000
Total Product	750 bushel	600 bushel	500 bushel	400 bushel
At $2, total revenue	$1500	$1200	$1000	800
Economic rent	$ 500	$ 200	0	—

total revenue on parcel A would be $1500, costs would be $1000 (inclusive of wages, interest, and profit), and the lucky owner would have $500 left over as economic rent accruing to him because of the relatively high fertility of his land. At $2 a bushel, the owner of B land would clear $200 in economic rent; the owner of C land would just cover all costs of production; and the owner of D land could not afford to farm it.

If demand for the product lifted the price to $2.50 a bushel, then the D landlord could spend $1000, grow 400 bushels, sell it for $1000 and break even; the C landlord would receive $1250 for his 500 bushels and would collect an economic rent of $250; Landlord B's economic rent would be $500; Landlord A's $875. Wages must be paid to elicit labor effort; interest paid to elicit waiting (during the interval between production of capital and the time when it is used up in consumption), profit must be paid to induce risk taking. Reduce profit, there will be less risk taking; reduce interest, there will be less waiting and less physical capital; reduce wages, there will be less labor effort. But economic rent need not be paid to bring high-fertility land into being, for land fertility is the free gift of nature. If economic rent were all taxed away by governments (as Henry George advocated), the quantity of available land would remain the same.

The amount of economic rent received on a parcel of land is determined by the size of the difference between the productivity of that parcel and the productivity of the least fertile parcel in cultivation. The less fertile the marginal parcel in use, the greater the economic rent accruing to the owner of every other parcel in use.

G. *Perfectly Competitive Markets, VMP, and Poverty*

If the American economy consisted exclusively of perfectly competitive markets; if there were full employment; if human capital were allocated among Intelligence A's and if physical capital were allocated among Intelligence C's so as to maximize production; and if everyone were paid the value of the marginal products of his labor and physical product, then poverty would be widespread. Individuals conceived with low Intelligence A—manifested in either mental or bodily defects and limitations—would be incapable of attaining high Intelligence C. Accidents, disease, mental breakdown, and age would limit or reduce the Intelligence C and the marginal physical product of labor of individuals. People with low labor MPP and with little or no physical capital or land would be poor.

IV. LUCK

Americans are inclined to be critical of a person who receives a large income because he is lucky enough to have obtained a position of power that commands a high income, even though he does no work. In the real world, many income differences exist because luck puts people in positions of this kind. Luck operates in several other ways that would cause income differences as among individuals living and working in a perfectly competitive economic system.

First, luck determines whether one is born of parents who will bequeath land and an income flow of economic rent to their child or children. Second, luck determines whether one is born of parents who will bequeath physical capital and an income flow of interest to their child or children.

Critics of these consequences of luck have argued for inheritance taxes that would wipe out or would reduce the role of property inheritance as a cause of income differences. These critics have had little to say about the third way luck contributes to income differences in a perfectly competitive economy.

This third effect follows when luck determines whether one is born of parents who will bequeath, in the instant of conception, a high Intelligence A that will lead to a high Intelligence C that will permit a high value of marginal physical product of labor and a large income flow to that Intelligence A's contribution to the value of production. One might ask why, for example, Joan Baez should have the income she receives as a result of her luck in the Intelligence A draw.

Finally, luck determines whether a person is born into an economy with a large stock of natural resources and physical and human capital (for example, the United States, Sweden, or Japan), or into an economy with a small stock of these factors. If the former, the value of one's marginal product will be larger than if the latter.

The man who loafs on the job but who, nevertheless, receives a high income in an imperfectly competitive economy is not productive; luck has given him his high income. The man in the perfectly competitive economy who inherited land, physical capital, and a high Intelligence A (that may permit him to acquire more land and physical capital) is productive, but luck has given him his high productivity with high income just as luck has given the other man high income without high productivity.

V. SUMMARY

The extent and character of poverty in a nation depends on the size of its GNP and the way in which GNP is distributed. The larger the portion of GNP taken by the public sector, the smaller the portion available to the private sector. The federal share is largest during the war. During recent peacetime years, the private share remained about 80% of GNP although the state and local share grew a bit more rapidly than the federal share fell.

The private share is divided between investment and consumption. The greater the consumption share, the lower the incidence of poverty can be in the current year. The greater the investment share, the lower the incidence of poverty can be in the future years. Since 1945, about one sixth of America's total product has gone to investment while more than five eighths of it has gone to consumption. Per capita gross investment has fluctuated over time, but it has remained high enough to permit the doubling of per capita consumption between 1938 and 1968.

As the American national product is being divided between public and private sectors, and as the private sector's share is being divided between consumption and investment, consumption and title to the investment portions are being distributed among members of the total population. Output can be distributed by any of a number of methods. Several methods have been described briefly here: (1) perfect equality, with every person receiving exactly the same amount as every other person, (2) distribution according to need so that the last unit of output going to each person satisfies exactly the same intensity of personal need as the last unit going to every other person, and (3) authoritarianism with the politically powerful using that power to take part of other peoples' output away and to transfer it to themselves or to others. If the United States were peacefully converted to either the first or second alternative, poverty would disappear in America—and total output might be reduced.

The present American system of distribution works in the sense that only a few Americans favor fundamental change in the basic system. This American system is a mixture of many elements, but its central principle is, "To each according to the value of his productive contribution." This is the general rule, but monopoly, charity, and tax-transfers provide numerous exceptions to the rule by providing many people with more than their productive contribution while leaving others with less.

Given the general rule, productive intelligence is of primary importance in determining the distribution of output. In this chapter, "intelligence" has been restricted to abilities valued in the marketplace and has been subdivided to be applied at three points in each person's life. In this scheme, Intelligence A refers to genetic potential at the moment of conception, Intelligence B to a baby's potential when delivered, and Intelligence C to productive ability at any time after birth.

If output is to be maximized then, given the Intelligence A's of the population, medical care, education, and training, and physical capital must be allocated among members of the labor force so that the last unit going to each person brings forth the same addition to output; and new capital is created as long as the additional units add more to output than to costs. If all markets are perfectly competitive, then each person is paid the value of the marginal product of his labor, plus the value of the marginal product of his capital (if he owns any), plus the rent on his natural resources (if he owns any). Even though a nation's output-to-population ratio is very large, this system of production and distribution leaves many people poor: a portion because of low Intelligence A; others because accident, disease, mental breakdown or age limit or reduce their Intelligence C, the determinant of the distribution of output to labor. Above all, luck operates to determine whether one is born into an economy with a large or a small stock of physical capital and to determine whether one inherits much or little physical capital and land and a high or a low Intelligence A.

5

Why One Is Poor When Ones Equal Is Not

In a perfectly competitive world, most people will be poor if they are so unlucky as to be born into an economy that has accumulated little physical and human capital. Even when a production-maximizing perfectly competitive society has accumulated a large stock of physical and human capital, some people will be poor if they are so unlucky as to inherit a low Intelligence A and small amounts of land and of other physical capital. The previous chapter considered these causes of poverty. This and the next chapter discuss factors that cause adults to be poor despite an inheritance of high Intelligence A in an economy with large quantities of physical capital.

One such factor that causes poverty is racial discrimination. Some people with high Intelligence A and B are kept from developing Intelligence C because of discrimination. Others are kept by discrimination from applying the Intelligence C they have developed. Undeveloped Intelligence A and unused Intelligence C inhibit American productivity and leave many Americans with incomes below the poverty line. These effects of racial discrimination are quantitatively so large that the entire next chapter is devoted to an analysis of discrimination as a cause of poverty.

The rest of this chapter deals with other causes that bring poverty to persons conceived with Intelligence A equal to that of fellow citizens who grow up to enjoy above-poverty income. These causes are grouped under five headings here: the first of these is misallocation and underallocation of resources to the care of prospective mothers during pregnancy and delivery.

I. FROM INTELLIGENCE A TO INTELLIGENCE B

Nutritional needs rise dramatically during pregnancy; but nutrient availability does not rise for poor families just because a family member is pregnant. The Citizens' Board of Inquiry into Hunger and Malnutrition in the United States found both in hearings and studies that pregnant women in poverty suffered from nutritional deficiencies and were constantly anemic.[1] The effects on the fetus of maternal nutritional deprivation were mentioned above in Chapter 4. The Citizens' Board of Inquiry (brought together by Dr. Jean Mayer of the Harvard Medical School) quoted Dr. Frederick Solomon respecting the connection between poor nutrition during pregnancy and repressed development of Intelligence B:

It is well known that low income women have greatly increased chances of producing premature infants and/or having "complicated" pregnancies and deliveries. It is also known that off-spring will then have greatly increased risk of brain damage or (in the case of prematures) slow development and special needs. As far as I can tell from the medical literature, the causes of prematurity and other complications of pregnancy . . . include: (1) small bone size in the expectant mother (probably due to poor nutrition and illness in her childhood); (2) poor nutrition and infectious disease during the pregnancy.[2]

Because of differences between pregnant women in nutrition and medical care, individuals conceived with identical Intelligence A emerge to face the world with unequal Intelligence B. Some of the differences in obstetrical care are because of chance and women's choices of doctors, hospitals, and treatment; many of the differences are the result of differences in family income. Consequently, persons conceived by the poor are more likely to suffer restricted development of Intelligence B than are persons

---

[1] Citizens' Board of Inquiry, *Hunger, U.S.A.*, Beacon Press, Boston, 1968, p. 19.
[2] Quoted in *ibid.*, p. 29.

conceived by the nonpoor. Thus does lack of money combine with biology to pass poverty from generation to generation.

The inhibition of Intelligence B would be less if more resources were devoted to obstetrics. The inhibition of Intelligence B might be less—net—if a larger proportion of resources currently devoted to obstetrics were devoted to women with low incomes.

II. FROM INTELLIGENCE B TO INTELLIGENCE C

In *Let Us Now Praise Famous Men*, James Agee wrote:

All that each person is, and experiences, and shall never experience, in body and mind, all these things are differing expressions of himself and of one root, and are identical: and not one of these things nor one of these persons is ever quite to be duplicated, nor replaced, nor has it ever quite had precedent: but each is a new and incommunicably tender life, wounded in every breath and almost as hardly killed as easily wounded; sustaining, for a while, without defense, the enormous assaults of the universe.[3]

Hardly killed and easily wounded, each person moves through life experiencing the diversity and the unity of man. Growing and experiencing, a man touches more of life than is reached through Intelligence C as here defined. But Intelligence C is the chief means to income; and in America, people born with equal Intelligence B grow up to face the labor market with unlike Intelligence C, while some people born with low Intelligence B have the good fortune to enter the labor market with Intelligence C higher than that of their Intelligence B betters.

No matter how great the mechanical, literary, managerial, artistic or leadership potential of the newborn, inadequate or inappropriate education will prevent that potential being realized and applied in the marketplace by one person, although it is realized and applied by another. Thomas Gray cried out:

Full many a flower is born to blush unseen,
And waste its sweetness on the desert air.
And in the country churchyard, there is laid

---

[3] James Agee and Walker Evans, *Let Us Now Praise Famous Men*, Boston, Houghton Mifflin, 1941 and 1960, p. 56.

Some heart once pregnant with celestial fire;
Hands, that the rod of empire might have sway'd,
Or wak'd to extasy the living lyre.
But knowledge to their eyes her ample page
Rich with the spoils of time did ne'er unroll;
Chill Penury repress'd their noble rage,
And froze the genial current of the soul.[4]

A. *From B to C: Nutrition*

After as well as before birth, nutrition is important. Before a child is four, his brain reaches about 90 percent of its adult weight. If there is not enough protein during those critical four years, the brain may not develop fully, and later compensatory nutrition may be unable to recover the earlier losses.

There is accumulating evidence to show that an inadequate and un-balanced diet, occurring at a highly crucial and prolonged period in the development of an infant or young child, may affect its mental capacities to a degree where its ability to learn is seriously impaired. The visible effects of malnutrition may be corrected and may disappear, and the child may seem to be restored to full health and vigor. But the effects on mental development may not be readily apparent and often may be perceived only when the child manifests difficulty in competing with normal children.[5]

If malnutrition erodes part of the potential of an infant's Intelligence B, his ability to learn particular skills will be reduced.

But Intelligence C involves technical ability, imagination, *and* attitude toward learning and toward using what has been learned. Dr. Robert Coles, author of *Children of Crisis: a Study of Courage and Fear*, found that children who are more or less hungry most of the time:

. . . become tired, petulant, suspicious and finally apathetic.

One will talk with them and play with them and observe their behavior and ask them to draw or paint pictures. From all that one can learn the aches and sores of the body become for a child of four or

---

[4] *Elegy Written in a Country Churchyard*, Heritage Press, New York, 1951, pp. 12-14.
[5] George Harrar, *Quarterly Report*, Rockefeller Foundation, 1967.

five more than a concrete physical fact of life, being in the child's mind a reflection of his worth, and judgment upon him and his family of the outside world by which he not only feels but judges himself.

They ask themselves and others what they have done to be kept from the food they want or what they have done to deserve the pain they seem to feel.

In my experience with families in the Delta, their kind of life can produce a chronic state of mind, a form of withdrawn, sullen behavior. I have seen some of the families I know in the South go North and carry with them that state of mind and I am now working with them in Boston. They have more food, more welfare money, and in the public hospitals of the northern city certain medical services.

But as one tape records their expressed feelings and attitudes month after month, one sees how persistently sickness and hunger in children live on into adults who doubt any offer, mistrust any goodness or favorable turn of events as temporary and ultimately unreliable.

I fear that we have among us now in this country hundreds of thousands of people who have literally grown up to be and learned to be tired, fearful, anxious, and suspicious and in some basic and tragic sense simply unbelieving.

All one has to do is ask some of these children in Appalachia who have gone north to Chicago and Detroit to draw pictures and see the way they will sometimes put food in the pictures or draw pictures of trees which they then explain are ailing with branches in some way falling. All one has to do is ask them what they want, to confirm the desires for food and for some kind of medical care for the illnesses that plague them.[6]

Both the poor and the nonpoor are forbidden to sleep under bridges. Both the poor and the nonpoor may be malnourished. But the poor are more likely to need to sleep under bridges, and the poor are more likely to have children who are malnourished and whose accumulation of Intelligence C is inhibited by the scars left on brain and psyche by malnourishment. Whether the cause is poverty or something else, when two children are born with equal Intelligence B and one is undernourished and the other is not, the former is likely to reach a lower Intelligence C than is the latter.

---

[6] Senate Subcommittee on Hunger, *op. cit.*, p. 25 *et seq.*

B. *From B to C: Education*

At any point in time, a man's Intelligence C is the result of his Intelligence B, his health, and of all the life experiences that contribute to Intelligence C as here defined in terms of ability to make productive contributions valued in the marketplace. Those life experiences contributing to Intelligence C will be referred to here—for want of a better word—as "education." This definition gives "education" in some respects a wider meaning and in some respects a more narrow meaning than is usually given to it. Wider in that it includes learning in the bassinet, at the dinner table, in the streets, and at the machine. Narrower in that it excludes learning that does not in any way contribute to ability to make productive contributions valued in the marketplace.

To repeat a point made in Chapter 4, if output is to be maximized, then additional resources should be devoted to the education of each individual so long as they bring an increase in Intelligence C that induces an increase in the value of output (marginal revenue, MR) greater than the associated increase in cost of resource inputs (marginal cost, MC). (These MR and MC comparisons must be made not in terms of a month or a year but in terms of the individual's lifetime; therefore, each MR or MC figure implies a summation of discounted values of future as well as of present revenues and costs.)

When resources are being allocated to education, decisions based on the following questions must be made.

1. Of all the ways in which a given quantity of resources can be used in the education of one individual, which particular way gives maximum returns (that is, which way is most efficient)?
2. What portion of the economy's total stock of resources shall be devoted to education?
3. Given the portion of resources going to education, how much shall go to each individual?

Similarly, three kinds of mistakes can be and are made during the process of allocating resources to education:

1. The inefficient use of resources devoted to a particular individual (for example, teaching him a subject he cannot learn or using a person to teach who cannot teach).
2. The under- or over-allocation of resources to education.

3. The misallocation of educational resources by directing more to one than to another of equal Intelligence B or by directing more to an individual of less, than to one of more potential.

An economy can err in all or in any one or any combination of these ways. America errs in education in several ways that result in poverty for households and individuals. Each of these several ways involves two or more of the above three kinds of allocation mistakes. Separating out the relative importance of each of the three would be very difficult.

1. *Ignorance of Opportunities.* For example, ignorance of opportunities results because of all three kinds of errors. Many do not learn what they could best learn and apply, and many who have learned do not apply in the best way what they have learned because they do not know about the occupation, industry, and geographic opportunities that are open or that would become open to them if they would move or if they would learn more.

Many youths feel obligated to follow their parents' calling. Sometimes this is the best occupational choice for the child (he has, after all, been learning the trade—for example, plumbing, farming, or medicine—at the dinner table since infancy); sometimes it is not; it may simply be the trade appearing closest at hand. When the father or mother is not followed, the odds are that relatives, neighbors, or other family friends will be. Many important occupational decisions, therefore, are based on restricted and biased information.

Each year, hundreds of thousands of Americans move long distances to reach better jobs; but other hundreds of thousands are ignorant of opportunities far from their homes. In 1965, the federal government's Aid to Appalachia program was under attack for spending too much of its limited money on roadbuilding. A West Virginia professor of economics replied, "Don't criticize. That's the best way to use that money. Spend half the money to build roads into Appalachia, and spend the other half to teach people who live there to use those roads to get the hell out."

When choosing occupations, when choosing locations, when choosing jobs, most Americans operate from a vast amount of ignorance. Most Americans, knowing little of existing opportunities, choose jobs through the "buddy system." Newspaper advertisements and employment service agencies are secondary.

The typical American chooses a job because a buddy (friend or relative) tells him of its availability. This means that the typical American's knowledge of job opportunities is limited to what his friends and relatives know. This is far short of the ideal.

Ignorance of choice is more than a matter of not knowing what options exist today. The slogan "You can't get tomorrow's jobs with today's skills" emphasizes the importance of also knowing how the labor market of the future will differ from the labor market of the present. To the extent that a future job requires lengthy training, the prospective jobholder must know what the future market will be like so that he can begin the prerequisite training in time to be qualified when the new job opens. Again the buddy system is, in the 1970s, the chief determinant of most individuals' expectations regarding the future. And, again, knowledge falls short of the ideal.

People ignorant of the choices today work in jobs where their productivity is so restricted as to leave them below the poverty line. If they were aware of other opportunities, many could move to jobs where their productivity and income would rise above the poverty line. People ignorant of impending change in their present jobs are not currently training in the skills that would maximize their productivity in the future. Unprepared for the change, some of these people will drop below the poverty line when change comes. If they knew of prospective changes, they could begin to train now for the future.

Many Americans who are poor now would not be poor if they had known more about opportunities open to them when they were choosing occupations and locations. Others would not be poor now if they knew of opportunities open to them now.

2. *Achievement Motivation.* Some people who do know of opportunities choose not to learn; some who have learned and who know of opportunities choose not to move to them because of a lack of ambition. Ambition, like the ability to read, is learned. In the context of this chapter, ambition means motivation to develop Intelligence C and to apply acquired Intelligence C to attain maximum income (given social customs respecting working hours). For several decades, American psychologists have been examining the childhood origins of this kind of "achievement motivation." They have studied the character of high achievers and the en-

vironments that engendered high achievement motivation in the past, and they have begun to search for ways to teach achievement motivation within formal academic programs.[7]

Most Americans do learn achievement motivation and work to develop and to apply their Intelligence C's in the ways most valued in the market of their times. Many, however, fail to develop suitable Intelligence C's because their environments never teach them—or sometimes teach them *not*—to work to develop and to apply the kinds of skills and imagination the market values. Some are not taught because their families and friends cannot visualize participation in the high-productivity sectors of the economy (one thinks at once of Thomas Lincoln, "Why must that boy spend so much time with those books when I need him for the farm work?" and of the ghetto father, "Why aintcha out playin' with the boys insteada lookin' at them books and workin' your back off for the Man?"). Others clearly are opposed to efforts to cooperate with the system as it now works. One would be hard put to sort out for an individual the extent to which his lack of achievement motivation was the result of failure to learn of opportunities and to what extent his lack of motivation was due to correct information that turned him off given his learned value system.

Many people from well-to-do homes have had the opportunity to observe some of the good and some of the bad features of the high-productivity sectors of the economy and have concluded that on the basis of what they have seen, they do not want to work in those sectors. Their lack of ambition to participate and "succeed" in the marketplace is learned in a different way but to the same effect as the lack of "ambition" in poor families.

Achievement motivation may be lacking in one other respect: geographic mobility. Many Americans have learned values that make them unwilling to move from a position of low productivity (on a small farm) or chronic unemployment (in Appalachian coal mining) to an area with a job of higher productivity. Contemplating geographic change, some men are eager to move, for some express the classic wish, "I sure would like to move any-

---

[7] See, for example, David C. McClelland, *Motivating Economic Achievement,* Free Press, New York, 1969.

where far away from my mother-in-law." Others say, "I'm too old to move" or "All my friends and relatives are here; I can't leave them" or "I just can't see taking my kids away from the country and making them live in the city."

People who lack the ambition to strive to acquire Intelligence C, or to be eager to apply their Intelligence C, or to be willing to move to the locations where their Intelligence C can be used most productively are headed for low productivity and for low incomes.

But not even knowledge of opportunities and ambition together are enough to develop high Intelligence C if an individual does not have access to appropriate teaching. Quite obviously, when teachers are ill-prepared or disinterested, or when texts, equipment, and facilities are inadequate, students will not learn as much as they would learn in more favorable circumstances.

3. *Inadequate Education.* Equally obviously, individuals do not benefit when given training they cannot apply. High school vocational agricultural courses are a case in point. Many "Future Farmers of America" members are not future farmers. In 1950, the United States had 5.4 million farms and 765 thousand high school vocational agriculture students; in 1967 there were fewer than 3 million farms and 783 thousand vo-ag students. Many of those 783 thousand were spending months learning skills they could never use.

Previous education often proves inadequate when technology and consumption patterns change and end the jobs of men who have been trained in particular specialties. The carriage makers and glassblowers are famous examples; bituminous coal miners are a more recent example. Agriculture continues to be a case as the relative efficiency of large heavily capitalized farms rises and the ability of a small farm to support a family falls. When job opportunities change, the only education that counts is Intelligence C appropriate to the new production techniques. Education involving an obsolete technique is scarcely better than no education at all and may leave its owners as unproductive and poor as would no education.

"Many" Americans have not known of available opportunities; "many" have not learned ambition; "many" have not had access to appropriate education. But how many is "many"? No one knows; yet several fairly reliable statistics are available to suggest the large number of Americans with little education and the close connection between little formal education and poverty income.

In 1968, about 6.3 million Americans past the age of 20 (5.4% of all Americans past 20) were "functional illiterates" in that they had failed to complete the fifth grade. They had little to offer in the marketplace. Some of them had not been born with the Intelligence B that would have justified keeping them in school beyond the fourth grade. Most of them had been born with that Intelligence B but were victims of the underallocation of resources to education, of the misallocation of educational resources, or of the inefficient use of educational resources. The same considerations apply to the 46.6 million Americans past age 20 (40% of Americans past 20) who had completed fifth grade but had not completed high school in 1968.

During 1959, 9.65 million American families received incomes of less than $3000. Men aged 25 to 64 headed 4.48 million of these families. Among the 4.48 million male family heads, 709 thousand were high school dropouts and approximately 3.0 million left school with an eighth-grade education or less. Much of this poverty is due to low Intelligence A and B in individuals; but fewer people would have been poor in 1959 and in 1970 if in earlier years more resources had gone into education and if the resources that did go into education had been better used.

4. *From Conception through School: Summary.* Thus far this chapter has considered factors that affect the development of Intelligence C from conception through adolescence. These factors have been considered one by one and rather abstractly. Herbert G. Birch, Ph.D. in psychology and doctor of medicine, has been working directly with disadvantaged people. In a 1970 book, *Disadvantaged Children: Health, Nutrition, and School Failure,* he assesses the effect of poverty on the intellectual potential of children. He sums up:

The data we have presented in this book have made it abundantly clear that the environments in which disadvantaged children develop from conception on are far less supportive to growth and health than are those of children who are not disadvantaged, and that this relative environmental impoverishment is exaggerated when the disadvantaged child is non-white. The differences are profound and prolonged.

Mothers of such children tend to be less well fed, less well grown, and less well cared for before they reach childbearing age. When they reach it, they begin to bear children younger, more rapidly, and more often, and they continue to bear them to an older age. When such a mother is pregnant both her nutrition and her health will tend to be poorer than that of a woman who is better off, but she will be far less likely to get prenatal care and far more likely to be delivered under substandard conditions.

Children of such mothers are smaller at birth, die more readily, and are generally in poorer condition in infancy than are children born to the more affluent. If they survive the first month of life, their mortality thereafter is excessively high and their illnesses more frequent, more persistent, and more severe. Their early nutrition is negatively influenced by their mother's health, her age, her income level, her education, her habits and attitudes, so that among such children in the preschool years frank malnutrition, as well as sub-clinical manifestations of depressed nutritional status (reflected in anemia and poor growth), are markedly more prevalent. During the school years they eat irregularly, their health care continues to be almost totally inadequate, and family disorganization commonplace.[8]

In addition to these factors that inhibit the development of Intelligence C in some people, there are other considerations that keep some Americans poor while others of equal Intelligence A are not. These other considerations are discussed below.

III. FAMILY OBLIGATIONS

Family obligations keep some individuals from attaining above-poverty productivity, even though these individuals have an above-poverty productive potential and have access to jobs befitting their potential. Some of these individuals are men who must stay home to care for their wives. Most of these individuals are women with small children but without men at home. Many of these women would work outside the home if they could; but the small children force most of them to remain at home. In 1966, 3.0 million American families with children (10.4% of all families with children) were headed by a woman. About 1.5 million of these families were poor in 1966; many of them would

---

[8] Herbert C. Birch and Joan Dye Gussow, Harcourt, Brace & World, Inc., New York, 1970, pp. 266-267.

not have been poor if the mothers had been free to work outside their homes. Whether those mothers and their children would have been better off in terms of psychic income with the mothers at work is, of course, another question.

The SSA counts the poor on the basis of gross family income and, hence, fails to count as poor a family whose head takes a job and hires someone to care for the dependents and whose income net of the cost of the dependent care is below the poverty line. No estimate has yet been made of the undercount that results from these situations.

IV. THE SOCIAL MINIMUM WAGE

Governments, unions, and businessmen's pride combine to introduce a social minimum wage that sometimes makes poverty more severe than it would be in perfectly competitive markets. Governments set minimum wages by establishing laws that forbid employers to pay employees less than a minimum hourly amount. Unions obtain contracts that specify minimum wage levels for each occupation in a plant. Businessmen set minimum rates they feel they can, in self-respect, pay employees.

Together, these considerations determine what economist Clarence D. Long (who, since 1962, has been a Maryland congressman) calls the "social minimum wage"; this is the minimum a businessman feels that law, contracts, and self-respect permit him to pay.[9] If this wage is $1.60 an hour, individuals whose productivity is less than $1.60 an hour do not get hired. Instead of a low-earned income in the absence of the social minimum, these least-able people then have a zero earned income—or find work with employers who ignore the social minimum.

If the social minimum wage is $1.60 an hour, which is $3328 for 52 weeks of 40 hours each, people employed at the minimum, in most cases, will have incomes below the poverty line for their household type. Consequently, when a social minimum wage causes unemployment, it does not ordinarily cause poverty. The

[9] C.D. Long, "An Overview of Postwar Labor Market Developments," in *Proceedings of the 4th Annual Social Security Conference*, W.E. Upjohn Institute, Kalamazoo, 1962.

social minimum wage aggravates poverty by moving some families from a high-poverty earned income to the deeper-poverty income of unemployment.

V. INADEQUATE AGGREGATE DEMAND

This last cause of poverty has effects more pervasive than any of the others considered in this chapter. When aggregate demand falls, the effects of that fall touch nearly everyone in America.

When aggregate demand is deficient, three of its consequences cause poverty. First, people unemployed for long periods drop into poverty (unemployment lasting only a few months of a year may permit individuals to earn above-poverty incomes during the remaining months of the year). Second, people who are forced to settle for part-time work (only a few days each week, or a few hours each day) drop into poverty. Third, people who in a full-employment economy would have high-productivity jobs but who can obtain only low-productivity jobs because of deficient demand may also drop into poverty.

One way of showing the impact of demand fluctuations on the number of American poor is the following (this assumes "poverty" means a family income of under $3000 a year):

. . . to divide the fifteen years 1948-1963 into categories of strong economic expansion (1950, 1951, 1953, 1955, 1959, and 1962), slow expansion (1952, 1956, 1960, and 1963), and no expansion (1949, 1954, 1957, 1958, and 1961), and then to note what happened to the amount of poverty during each group of years. If the $3000 family-income measure is used, the results show that in years of strong expansion, the number of poor families declined by an average of 667,000 per year; in the slow-expansion years the decline was a third less: 425,000 families per year; and in the no-expansion years of downturn or recession, the number of poor families *rose* by 400,000 per year. Thus, the difference between strong expansion and recession has been more than a million families (from a decrease of 667,000 to an increase of 400,000) among the poor."[10]

Using the SSA poverty criteria, the *1969 Report of the Council of Economic Advisers* goes further in describing the role of de-

---

[10] Burton A. Weisbrod (ed.), *The Economics of Poverty*, Prentice-Hall, Englewood Cliffs, N.J., 1965, pp. 15-16.

ficient aggregate demand and of its opposite in causing increases or decreases in the total number of poor:

Virtually all the progress in reducing poverty over the past 20 years has occurred during periods of general prosperity. In three periods of sustained economic expansion—1949-1953, 1954-1956, and 1961 to the present—the annual decline in the number of individuals in poverty averaged two million or more a year. In contrast, during recessions the number of poor people has increased. The brief recession of 1954 wiped out half of the gains of the preceding 4-year expansion, and several successive years of sluggish economic performance in the late 1950's increased the number of persons in poverty to about the level of 7 years earlier.[11]

Changes in the number of poor persons and in the incidence of poverty are shown in Figure 5-1. The recessions of 1948 to 1949,

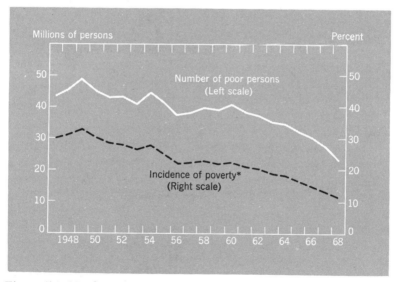

Figure 5-1. Number of poor persons and incidence of poverty, 1948 to 1968.

* Poor persons as percent of total noninstitutional population.

Source: *Economic Report of the President:* 1969, G.P.O., Washington, D.C., p. 154.

---

[11] *The Annual Report of the Council of Economic Advisers,* U.S. Government Printing Office, Washington, 1969, pp. 155-156.

of 1953, of 1957, and of 1960 all stand out clearly in Figure 5-1, manifested in increases in number of poor and, to a lesser extent, in increases in the incidence of poverty.

Not surprisingly, the poverty-reducing effects of buoyant aggregate demand are not the same for all poverty groups. Households led by working-age men benefit far more from buoyant demand than do households headed by working-age women, by elderly, or by disabled persons.

When aggregate demand rises, wages rise for the employed poor, some of the unemployed get jobs, some people with low-paying or part-time jobs get better jobs, and businesses expand training programs for skilled and semiskilled occupations. Working-age men and their families are the chief beneficiaries of these programs:

From 1964 to 1966, the number of poor households headed by a working-age man with work experience fell 400,000 a year; in contrast, there had been no decline from 1959 to 1961.[12]

Poor families headed by working-age women have benefited less from the high aggregate demand of the 1960s. Many of these women have small children; many who get work earn below-poverty incomes. During the 1960s, the incidence of poverty fell one fifth for households headed by women under 65, but the absolute number of poor households headed by women under 65 did not fall because there was a substantial increase in the total number of households headed by working-age women.

During the 1960s, the total number of households headed by persons past 64 rose rapidly. Prosperity cut the incidence of poverty in this category by 15% but reduced the total number only slightly. High aggregate demand helped this group by permitting more of its members to continue working after age 64 and by helping people accumulate more assets and larger pension rights before retirement.

As with the elderly, so—almost—with the disabled. Between 1959 and 1967, the incidence of poverty fell among households whose heads were under 65 and not working for health reasons, but the number did not fall. Instead, it rose slightly.

---

[12] *Ibid.*, p. 156.

VI. THE NEAR POOR

When evaluating the effects of prosperity and of other efforts to reduce poverty, it makes a difference whether the former poor move from poverty to a sticking point just above poverty, or whether they move far away from poverty. To be able to determine what is happening in the income category just above the poverty line the Social Security Administration has defined a "near-poor" income standard with criteria averaging about one third higher than the poverty criteria used for the various household categories. These near-poverty upper limits a third above poverty lines are, nevertheless, still less than half the median income of many types of households.

The prosperity of the 1960s reduced the number of near-poor households from 4.3 to 3.7 million—the number of near-poor persons from 15.8 to 12.0 million. Since the number of poor Americans dropped from nearly 40 million in 1959 to 25 million in 1968, most of those leaving poverty also left this category of near poverty; and although millions moved only from poverty to near poverty, other millions moved from near poverty in 1959 to above near poverty in 1968.

VII. RISING PRODUCTIVITY: NOT A CAUSE

Rising productivity is the chief instrument by which poverty has been reduced in the past in the United States and in the world. It is the chief instrument by which poverty will be reduced in the future. Yet, increases in productivity—in particular, increases in productivity brought about by technological change—often are cited as causes of poverty. How can the chief means for reducing poverty be blamed for causing poverty?

A. *For Example*

The following example of technological change and capital accumulation illustrates the four options opened up by every case of increased productivity. These four options explain how increased productivity serves to reduce poverty while exposing itself to the charge, "Poverty-creator."

Once upon a time, there were two men, Seth and Abel.[13] They were to pile up a great mound of earth on which priests would arrange stones for a temple to their god. The two men assembled a dirt-carrying platform by fastening 30-inch poles crosswise between the middle 36 inches of two 7-foot poles. Seth stood between the two long poles at one end, Abel at the other. On the platform between them, they could carry nearly their combined weight in dirt.

They had worked together before and had built an earth mound for another temple. One year had been required (24 man-months of work) with both men working 8 hours a day for 7 days a week.

The next earth mound was also to be completed in 24 man-months of work, but on the day they were to begin, Seth invented the wheel and axle and Abel invented the wheelbarrow. Temporarily, both men gave up earth-moving and worked on the wheel, axle, and barrow.

Construction of the wheelbarrow took one month of each man's time, but that time was well spent because experience would show that the use of the new wheelbarrow would permit one man to complete the earthen mound in 10 months of work of 8 hours a day, 7 days a week (after which the wheelbarrow suddenly disintegrated). The possibilities opened up by the introduction of the wheelbarrow can now be seen by developing the arithmetic assumptions that have already been made.

Before the wheelbarrow, the completion of the earthen mound required 24 months of labor. After the new inventions, completion required 2 months of labor to make the wheelbarrow plus 10 months using the wheelbarrow, a total of 12 months of labor. From 24 months before to 12 months after, productivity increased 100%.

Given a 100% increase in productivity, Seth and Abel could choose among four distinctly different ways of reaping the fruits of higher productivity. First, they could both continue to haul dirt 8 hours a day; they would have to work shifts so each could enjoy unrestricted access to the wheelbarrow during his 8 hours.

---

[13] My thanks to Charles W. Mann who originated this illustration in a junior thesis at Kenyon College.

In 5 months beyond the 1 month used to make the wheelbarrow, they would complete the dirt pile; in another 6 months (they would have to make a second wheelbarrow) they could complete a second dirt pile. Thus, their first choice was to continue the same amount of work and to double the number of earthen mounds thrown up during 24 man-months of labor.

Second, they could work 8-hour-a-day shifts 7 days a week and, after 5 more months, could finish the earthen mound in 12 man-months of labor; then they could use 12 months of labor to build houses, or to grow food, or to catch fish. Thus, their second choice was the same earthen mound in one half the work time with the other half devoted to producing other things. This option (and the first option when productivity increases occur in an activity more obviously connected with living standards than is temple building) is the chief means by which the output-to-population ratio is increased and poverty is reduced.

Third, they each could work 4 hours a day—again in shifts. Then the number of months of work required to complete the mound would be the same as before the invention of the wheel, axle, and wheelbarrow. Thus the third option was the same amount of earth moved with one half as much work and with more leisure daily.

Fourth, Seth could be laid off. In 10 more 8-hour-a-day, 7-day-a-week months, Abel could complete the mound of earth. Thus the fourth option was the same amount of earth moved with one half the labor force on that job, the other one half being laid off. This is the possibility that gives rise to the charge that increased productivity—that technological change—"causes" unemployment and poverty. It does not when aggregate demand is adequate and when labor is informed and mobile.

B. *Four Options*

Whenever productivity doubles, an economy must choose among (or some combination of) these four options:

1. Double the product (less poverty if population growth does not double).
2. The same product plus other goods and services (less poverty if population growth does not double).
3. The same product with one half the work per man.

4. The same product with one half the number employed (more poverty if aggregate demand is inadequate or labor is uninformed or immobile).

Of course, productivity never rises 100% so quickly. About 30 to 35 years are required for productivity to double in the United States, but a productivity increase of 20%, 2%, or 0.2% opens these same four kinds of options. The people working and buying in the market economy and participating in its government decide which option to take or, more often, they decide which combination of the four options to take.

Over the long run, the American economy has chosen a bit more daily leisure (option 3) and a larger quantity of output per person (options 1 and 2). Short-run fluctuations excepted, there has been *no* increase in unemployment (option 4) since 1900 or since 1800 or since 1776. Output per man-hour has gone up at least tenfold since 1800; yet the unemployment rate has not gone up at all; which is to say that, over the long run, rising productivity does not cause unemployment or poverty; over the long run, rising productivity reduces poverty.

But in the short run—and the short run extends over decades for some people—some Americans become poor when rising productivity throws them out of their jobs and inadequate aggregate demand, ignorance, immobility, or discrimination keeps them unemployed or in part-time jobs. The recent history of American agriculture illustrates how rising productivity can reduce national poverty while causing short-run regional poverty.

C. *1929 to 1969, American Agricultural Productivity Doubled*

Between 1929 and 1969, real product per man-hour rose more than 100% in American agriculture. If the Seth-Abel example were shifted from temple building to agriculture, their agricultural productivity increase would mean that Seth alone could produce more food and fiber in a 1969 hour than he and Abel together could have produced in a 1929 hour. This increase in agricultural productivity has contributed to the reduction in the incidence of poverty in America.

Responding to greater agricultural productivity, Americans took a bit more food per person, and a lot more of many other things (option 2), but they did not choose 100% more food per person (option 1) or anything near a 100% increase. Nor did population growth absorb the extra potential of the 1929 agricultural labor force; so very many former farmers became superfluous. To adjust to rising productivity by switching to the production of other products, many "Seths" had to leave farming for nonagricultural work. Many went to cities to manufacture the agricultural equipment that has increased agricultural productivity. Most took other city jobs.

When the first American census was taken in 1790, 5% of all Americans lived in urban areas (towns of 2500 or more people). The other 95% lived on farms. During every decade since 1790, the *percentage* engaged in farming has decreased. Since World War I, the *number* of people on American farms has decreased persistently. In 1920, the United States farm population was about 32 million; by 1960, it had dropped to 16 million, and by 1969 it was down to 10 million.

This decline has been rapid, but not rapid enough. Ignorance of choices, lack of access to education, unwillingness to change—especially among older farmers—and years of deficient demand have kept many Seths from leaving farming. These Seths experience unemployment or, more often, "underemployment" by working "poverty farms." What is "underemployment" on "poverty farms"?

Farms run by the "Abels" are big and well suited to the new equipment and the new techniques. Around these big farms there remains other farmland. But when this land is divided among numerous Seths, the resulting farms are often too small to permit use of the new farming equipment and techniques. Whether or not these Seths use modern farming methods, their superfluous numbers confine them to "poverty farms"—farms too small to yield outputs that would achieve the net incomes of the Abels who use the new equipment and the new techniques on large farms. It is as though Abel worked with the new wheelbarrow while Seth, after being laid off the wheelbarrow job, insisted on enlisting another man to help him carry dirt on the old two-man hand-carried platform. Alternatively, it is as though Abel used the wheelbarrow for full loads while Seth insisted on using it for half loads. Either way, Seth's income is only one half that of Abel's.

Some Seths are so limited by heredity or irreversible misfortune that their Intelligence C could never lift them above poverty incomes. But many Seths could earn their way out of poverty if they would leave their poverty farms for other work. Such men are underemployed when on poverty farms. If most of them gave up farming, the high Intelligence C Seths who remained could obtain enough land to become Abels.

In the meantime 45% of all farm families lived in poverty in 1959, 19% in 1968. However, because relatively few Americans lived on farms in 1968, less than 10% of all poor persons lived on farms.

Rural poverty can be reduced by decreasing the number of Seths on poverty-size farms. But the superfluous Seths can get out of farming only if aggregate demand provides a market large enough to absorb the increased quantity of goods and services they can produce if freed by rising productivity. This is true of agriculture, of coal mining, and of all industries in which rising physical output per man-hour enables workers to produce more.

Rising productivity adds to a nation's potential NNP. So does a growing labor force. If aggregate demand rises less rapidly than the labor force and productivity (or if ignorance, discrimination, or immobilities keep prospective workers from jobs), the incidence of poverty will rise. But it is not the growing labor force or the increase in productivity that is the cause of the rise in poverty. Inadequate demand, ignorance, discrimination, and immobility are the causes.

VIII. SUMMARY

This chapter considered the factors that cause some adults to be poor even though their Intelligence A is equal to or above that of their fellow citizens who are not poor. Six factors were considered here:

1. Malnutrition of pregnant women—more particularly of poor pregnant women—causing some individuals to be born with Intelligence B below that of others conceived with equal or inferior Intelligence A.
2. Malnutrition in children which impairs their mental capacity and limits their interest in learning and in achieving.
3. Underallocation of resources to education, misallocation of ed-

ucational resources as among individuals, and the inefficient use of educational resources, leaving individuals ignorant of job opportunities, lacking in ambition, or undereducated given the market and their Intelligence B.

4. Family obligations that keep women home caring for children although they would prefer to work.

5. The social minimum wage that keeps employers from hiring individuals whose productivity is below the minimum wage the employers are permitted or willing to pay.

6. Inadequate aggregate demand that inhibits all the forces that operate to raise the poor—especially working-age people—into productive nonpoverty.

During much of the 1960s, aggregate demand was sufficient. So much so, that it overcame much of the effects of poverty-creating factors and, as shown by figures for the nonpoor, lifted millions not only out of poverty but also out of near poverty.

Whenever productivity rises, an economy has three options: (1) increased output per capita, (2) the same output and more leisure per member of the labor force, or (3) the same output and more unemployment. When the first option is chosen—and it is the one usually chosen over the centuries, along with some amount of the second option—the incidence and severity of poverty are reduced. The third option is chosen only in the short run and then only because aggregate demand is insufficient or because of the immobility of resources.

6

White Power Discrimination

If consumer satisfaction is to be maximized, production must be efficient and oriented to consumer tastes. To attain this orientation and this efficiency, the market must provide individuals with the opportunity to spend their incomes as they want and to work where they want after obtaining training-education to develop appropriate Intelligence C's. These generalizations are economic commonplaces and are explained more fully in an introductory price theory text such as Haveman and Knopf's *The Market System*, or in intermediate price theory texts such as Watson's *Price Theory and Its Uses*, and Leftwich's *The Price System and Resource Allocation*.[1] The last chapter considered a number of factors that bring poverty to people with Intelligence A equal to or above the Intelligence A of others. Most of these factors operate by holding down Intelligence C and by keeping people out of jobs they want and are capable of doing. American white power has been used to enforce racially discriminatory practices that add to the force of those poverty-creating factors. The result is the exceptionally high incidence of poverty among black Americans, Indians, and Spanish-speaking Americans: in 1968, fewer than 9% of majority-group white Americans were poor, but almost one fourth of persons of Puerto Rican origin were poor, one fourth of white persons of Spanish surname in the Southwest were poor,

---

[1] Watson, Houghton Mifflin, Boston, 1968; Leftwich, Holt, Rinehart, New York, 1966.

one third of black Americans were poor, and at least 50% of Indians were poor.

If one is born in America without a large property inheritance, one escapes poverty by exercising choices that bring a high Intelligence C and that take one to jobs that pay wages or salaries proportional to the productivity of one's Intelligence C. White power has kept minority groups from participating fully in this process. The largest minority group thus affected is, of course, black.

I. SLAVERY

The first Negroes who arrived on land that was to become part of the United States were the 20 bound ("bound" to work to pay for the expenses of their passage) servants imported into Virginia in August 1619. Many of the white and most of the black immigrants to America in the first three quarters of the seventeenth century were to some degree unfree and were referred to indiscriminately as "slaves" or as "servants." During the last 30 years of the seventeenth century, the desire of the colonists to swell the labor force by attracting European immigrants (who often were preferred to the linguistically and ethnically strange Negro) and the absence of choice on the part of Negro cargoes led to a relaxation of the servile obligations of European immigrants and to a parallel hardening of the bonds on the Negroes. By 1700, the term "slave" had acquired a distinctive legal meaning defining the slave to be a chattel, and the Negro, in most cases, had become such a chattel slave.

During the eighteenth century, tobacco, indigo, and rice—not cotton—provided the principal employments for slave labor. In the North, the small farms did not permit the profitable use of crude gang labor; slavery created no vested interests and soon was abolished by laws that asserted moral imperatives. In the South, following independence, the tobacco, indigo, and rice plantations, hard hit by guerrilla warfare and shorn of their English markets, ceased to yield large profits. The abolition movement, citing the moral law, gained momentum, and many of the Founding Fathers anticipated the end of slavery within their lifetimes.

Then, in 1793, the invention of the cotton gin made upland

cotton profitable. In 1814, General James Wilkinson smuggled long-staple Mexican cottonseed into America, and cotton was on its way to being king. Between 1793 and 1940, there were no labor-saving innovations in cotton; and every increase in output required more land and more labor. The morality of slavery began to be viewed in a new light; Henry Ward Beecher described it thus to a friendly abolitionist audience:

Slaves that before had been worth from three hundred to four hundred dollars, began to be worth five hundred dollars. That knocked away one-third of our adherence to the moral law. Then afterwards they became worth seven hundred dollars, and half the law went— (cheers and laughter); then eight hundred or nine hundred dollars, and then there was no such thing as moral law—(cheers and laughter); then one thousand or twelve hundred dollars, and slavery became one of the Beatitudes.[2]

Of the 3,204,313 slaves in 1850, about 57 percent were growing cotton, 11 percent tobacco, and 12 percent other crops. Few of those in the fields had opportunities to develop a very productive Intelligence C. But not all slaves worked in the fields. The need for skilled labor and the availability of Negro talent induced antebellum planters to train slaves in the Intelligence C's highly valued in the Southern market. Black cabinetmakers, shipbuilders, gunsmiths, masons, blacksmiths, bookkeepers and other clerks and craftsmen were so numerous that the plantation owners' practice of supplying slave mechanics to do urban work provoked numerous petitions from white mechanics to the various Southern state legislatures in protest against slave competition. Those petitions were generally ignored because the legislators to whom they were addressed were the slaveowners who profited by hiring out slave craftsmen.

In Virginia, Maryland, and other border states, plantation agriculture limped, but whites profited by operating breeding farms that exported slaves to the Southwest. Despite the best breeding efforts of Virginia and other white slave growers, slave prices continued to rise, and the system of cotton, tertiary industry, and breeding worked so well

---

[2] *England and America: Speech at the Free-Trade Hall, Manchester,* Boston, James Redpath, 1863, p. 20.

. . . that slavery was apparently about as remunerative as alternative employments to which slave capital might have been put. . . . Slavery in the immediate antebellum years was, therefore, an economically viable institution in virtually all areas of the South as long as slaves could be expeditiously and economically transferred from one sector to another.[3]

The nineteenth century saw the accumulation of an enormous quantity of physical and human capital in America, but nearly all black Americans were kept from taking title to any of the physical capital, and those who acquired skills were denied the fruits of their skills. In the North, free blacks were excluded from crafts and were confined to service jobs. Few were able to acquire land.

II. FREEDOM?

After the war, black farmers were forced into debt by necessity to obtain first seed then food while their crops matured. Southern white honor and justice kept them in debt by a simple expedient:

Mr. Jones (storekeeper): "Well Joe, after buyin' yore cotton and matchin' that money off against yore debts to me, I find you start off the plantin' season owin' me $7 and 85¢."

Joe (suppressing smiles): "Mr. Jones, I done forgot, I got one more bale of cotton back to the house."

Mr. Jones: "Dagnabbit, now I got to figure yore debt all over again."

No matter how large the crop, the black farmers were never allowed to pay off their debts; and as long as they were said to be in debt (lynching immediately removed any black who said the white creditor lied), the white sheriff kept them from leaving the land. This system of debt peonage bound Southern blacks to the land almost as effectively as slavery had done.

After the Civil War, white planters had to hire craftsmen, white or black, and thus lost their economic incentive to favor blacks over whites. Under the banner of white supremacy, white mechanics began to displace blacks from skilled jobs and to keep

---

[3] Alfred H. Conrad and John R. Meyer, "The Economics of Slavery in the Ante Bellum South," *The Journal of Political Economy*, LXVI, April 1958, p. 110.

blacks from the training required for skilled work. As white Americans added to their skills, young blacks were kept from perpetuating the skills of their elders. The growth of AF of L trade unions in the 1880s and 1890s led to a further displacement of black Americans from the construction skilled trades, from the railroads, from stevedoring, from street railways, shipbuilding, hotel service, and barbering. In 1902, only the United Mine Workers admitted blacks without discrimination.

III. THE TWENTIETH CENTURY

The labor shortages of the two world wars pulled hundreds of thousands of blacks and their families to Northern and Western manufacturing activities to work with massive physical capital. Malcolm X described the process with rather more optimism than it could justify:

Around that time, 1939 or '40, or '41, they weren't drafting Negroes in the army or the navy. . . . They wouldn't take a black man in the navy except to make him a cook. . . . This is what they thought of you and me in those days. . . .

When the Negro leaders saw all the white fellows being drafted and taken into the army and dying on the battlefield, and no Negroes were dying because they weren't being drafted, the Negro leaders came up and said, "We've got to die too. We want to be drafted too, and we demand that you take us in there and let us die for our country too. . . ."

So they started drafting Negro soldiers then, and started letting Negroes get into the navy. But not until Hitler and Tojo . . . were strong enough to put pressure on this country, so that it had its back to the wall and needed us, [did] they let us work in factories; I'm talking about the North as well as the South.[4]

But even as late as 1955, the managers of most manufacturing plants would not allow blacks to learn to operate machines in their plants.

Even when white managers have been willing to hire blacks, labor unions have interfered—not only to prevent hiring but also to

---

[4] *Malcolm X Speaks*, Grove Press, New York, 1965, pp. 140-141.

obtain layoffs. In 1953, the International Brotherhood of Electrical Workers became the bargaining agent at the Bauer Electric Company of Hartford, Connecticut. The Union immediately demanded that all Negro electricians be laid off. Extensive unyielding discrimination by building trades and railroad unions continued into the 1970s.

A. *Agriculture*

As long as hand labor was required to weed and thin cotton, there was no incentive to replace hand labor in cotton planting or picking—although mechanical planters and pickers had been invented in the nineteenth century. The great change came in the early 1940s when thinning and weeding were mechanized. For the first time, hand labor could be replaced in *all* stages of cotton culture. During the next 25 years most Southern black farmers and agricultural workers were thrown off the farms as cotton growing was mechanized and as livestock and poultry raising and other crops supplemented and partly supplanted cotton farming.

To succeed in the new agriculture of the South, a man needed to learn a great deal about new tools, new crops, and new methods; and he needed more equipment and a larger farm than had been needed in the past. To obtain that needed equipment and land, farmers needed access to credit. To make effective use of the new equipment, they needed training. Through the Federal Home Board and the system of county agricultural agents, the federal government played a leading role in providing credit and instruction to farmers—to white farmers. The Federal Home Board made loans to whites to buy land and equipment; it made loans to blacks only for food and seed. The loans to whites increased their physical capital. Loans to blacks left their capital position unchanged. No statistics exist to show the extent to which white bankers were willing to lend to black farmers for expansion, but changes in farm size suggest a marked unwillingness. Between 1930 and 1959, the average size of Southern white farms grew 119 acres, or 91%, from 130 to 249 acres, although the average black farm grew only 9 acres, or 21%, from 43 to 52 acres.

The United States Department of Agriculture taught the white agricultural extension agents the new techniques as they evolved, and the white agents taught them to white farmers while black agents were left to teach the old obsolete techniques of hand-labor cotton culture.

In 1965 the United States Commission on Civil Rights focused national attention on Department of Agriculture discrimination. In a publication titled, "Equal Opportunity in Farm Programs," the commission reported home board and extension agent discrimination. In conclusion, the commission observed that "many thousands of Negro farmers are denied access to services provided to white farmers which would help them to diversify, increase production, achieve adequate farming operations or train for off-farm employment."

Following hearings in 1968 on 16 Black Belt counties of Alabama, the commission concluded that the pervasive pattern of racial discrimination in the policies and practices of federally assisted farm programs had *not* changed significantly during the three years following its initial report. Thus the United States Department of Agriculture continued to play a key role in keeping black farmers isolated from the agricultural mainstream and in accelerating their decline. In May of 1967, four white doctors made a team study of the health of black children in rural Mississippi. They found that there

are, in fact, children who are getting *absolutely no medical care.* In almost every child we saw . . . we observed one or another parasitic disease: trichinosis; enterobiasis; ascariasis; and hookworm disease. Most children we saw had some kind of skin disease: dryness and shrinkage of skin due to malnutrition; ulcerations; severe sores; rashes; boils, abcesses, and furuncles; impetigo; rat-bites. Almost every child we saw was in a state of negative nitrogen balance; that is, a marked inadequacy of diet has led the body to consume its own protein tissue. What we saw clinically—the result of this condition of chronic hunger and malnutrition—was as follows: wasting of muscles; enlarged hearts; edematous legs and in some cases the presence of abdominal adema (so-called "swollen" or "bloated" belly); spontaneous bleeding of the mouth or nose or evidence of internal hemorrhage; osteoporosis—a weakening of the bone structure—and, as a consequence, fractures unrelated to injury or accident; fatigue, exhaustion, and weakness.

These children would need blood transfusions before any corrective surgery could be done—and we found in child after child the need for surgery: hernias; poorly healed fractures; rheumatic and congenital heart disease with attendant murmurs, difficult breathing, and chest pain; evidence of gastro-intestinal bleeding, or partial obstruction; severe, suppurating, ear infections; congenital or developmental eye diseases in bad need of correction.

The teeth of practically every child we saw were in awful repair— eaten up by cavities and poorly developed. Their gums showed how severely anemic these children are; and the gums were also infected and foul smelling.

Many of these children were suffering from degenerative joint diseases. Injuries had not been treated when they occurred. Bleeding had occurred, with infections. Now, at seven or eight, their knee joints or elbow joints might show the "range of action" that one finds in a man of seventy, suffering from crippling arthritis.[5]

The report continues:

Frequently throughout the Mississippi Delta we heard charges of an unwritten but generally accepted policy on the part of those who control the state to eliminate the Negro Mississippian either by driving him out of the state or by starving him to death. At first, the charge seemed to me beyond belief. And yet reviewing now all that we saw and heard it becomes more and more credible.[6]

Without access to the growing stock of physical and human capital needed in the new agriculture, black farmers were forced to give up their small ill-equipped farms as the larger, efficient white farms pressed down on both costs and prices. With access to training and credit, whites became eager to dispossess black tenants and to buy distressed black farms. Blacks were given, and are being given, the choice: starve or move. Blacks have moved out. In 1930, there were 882 thousand black farms with about 4.7 million residents. By 1968, there were only 222 thousand of these farms with 1.1 million residents.

The rise of agricultural productivity has necessitated an enormous reduction in the number of American farmers, black and white. The special racial feature of the change has been the way

---

[5] "Hungry Children," Southern Regional Council, 5 Forsyth St., N.W., Atlanta 3, June 1967, pp. 6-7.
[6] *Ibid.*, pp. 26-27.

in which American institutions have operated to exclude blacks from accumulating capital to raise their productivity and to maintain their share in American agriculture. In 1900, 28 percent of Southern farm operators (14% of farm owners or part owners) were black; in 1964, only 13 percent of farm operators (9% of farm owners or part owners) were black.

B. *The Federal Government*

Throughout most of the century following the Civil War, the federal government either stood aside when white power suppressed black productivity or actually intervened to assist in that suppression—as in the case of the Federal Home Board just cited. Several more examples may make the point as effectively as would a longer discussion.

When Woodrow Wilson became President in 1913, one of the first initiatives of his "New Freedom" program was to segregate the previously unsegregated Washington employees of the federal government. To critics, President Wilson replied:

It is true that the segregation of the colored employees in the several departments was begun upon the initiative and at the suggestion of several of the heads of departments. . . . It is as far as possible from being a movement *against* the negroes. I sincerely believe it to be in their interests.[7]

Whether or not segregation was "in their interests," it was the American Way, and white power enforced it with a violence from which the federal government stood aloof. The following quotations from the *Macon Telegraph* and the *Birmingham Post* describe a fairly typical case.

This morning a mob seized Claude Neal, 23, from a jail in Brewton, Ala., . . .

At noon a "Committee of Six" representing the mob announced a timetable for the lynching which was given in newspapers and over the radio. . . .

"All white folks are invited to the party," said the announcement. . . .

---

[7] *Woodrow Wilson: Life and Letters,* by Roy S. Baker, Vol. IV, Doubleday, New York, 1931, p. 221.

As a result, thousands of citizens have been congregating all afternoon at the Cannidy farm. Bonfires have been started, piles of sharp sticks have been prepared, knives have been sharpened and one woman has displayed a curry-comb with which she promises to torture the negro.

The crowd is said to have been addressed by a member of the Florida State Legislature who, in a humorous vein, promised that no one would be disappointed if the crowd maintained decorum. . . . In Washington the Attorney General of the United States said that he was powerless to invoke the federal kidnapping law to rescue Neal because no ransom was involved.[8]

Then they sliced his sides and stomach with knives and every now and then somebody would cut off a finger or toe. Red hot irons were used on the nigger to burn him from top to bottom. From time to time during the torture a rope would be tied around Neal's neck and he was pulled up over a limb and held there until he almost choked to death, when he would be let down and the torture begun all over again. After several hours of this punishment, they decided just to kill him. . . .

A woman came out of the Cannidy house and drove a butcher knife into his heart. Then the crowd came by and some kicked him and some drove their cars over him. . . .

Photographers say they will soon have pictures of the body for sale at fifty cents each. Fingers and toes from Neal's body are freely exhibited on street-corners here.[9]

This was 1934, when Franklin D. Roosevelt's New Deal kept its attorney general as powerless as had preceding administrations. Many of the men and women lynched were innocent of any crime. Many were guilty. White families picnicked and joined in the torture without concern for the fine points of proof—much less of judicial process. Tuskeegee Institute recorded 4733 lynch victims (not all black) between 1882 and 1959. Black resentment had little political outlet because only a minority of black Americans were allowed to vote before the mid-1960s. President Johnson's Voting Rights Act of 1965 gave Southern blacks the right to vote. This newly obtained political power has begun to bring other changes.

---

[8] *Macon Telegraph*, 26 Oct. 1934.
[9] *Birmingham Post*, 27 Oct. 1934.

IV. WHY ARE SO MANY BLACKS POOR?

A. *Americans Do Not Become Poor*

Except in old age. That is to say, children born to nonpoor parents rarely become nonpoor—except in old age. Most poor Americans are poor because poor parents have poor children. This point has already been made in Chapter 2.

This is true for whites as well as for blacks (and reds). The last two chapters considered the factors that are immediate causes of poverty:

> Low intelligence A,
> Little inherited physical capital,
> Inadequate prenatal and obstetrical care,
> Malnutrition,
> Inadequate knowledge of opportunities,
> Failure to learn ambition,
> Inadequate education in marketable skills,
> Insufficient aggregate demand.

Black parents who live in poverty usually have had children who have grown up to live in poverty because most of these listed factors have applied with especially unfavorable force to blacks. Other minority groups have experienced similar effects.

B. *Banker, Realtor, John Doe Conspiracy*

Black immigrants to the North and West moved first, "naturally," to homes near people with similar backgrounds. Then an unyielding phalanx of white bankers, realtors, and men in the street drew together and conspired by furtive subterfuge and by open denial to keep blacks forever contained within their ghettos.

In 1790, 91 percent of black Americans lived in the South; in 1900, 90 percent of black Americans lived in the South, most on farms. In 1969, 48 percent lived in the North or West, and 70 percent lived in metropolitan areas—North, West, or South—instead of in rural nonfarm or farm areas. The National Advisory Commission on Civil Disorders found 12 million, of the 1966 black American population of 22 million, living in central cities (as distinct from suburbs) with the concentrating trend leading toward a central-city black population of 20 million in 1985. Pervasive racial discrimination alone accounts for these conditions; although they often are cited as a cause, economic factors are not important.

The persistence of the poverty explanation of racial residential segregation is puzzling. It is not necessary to resort to elaborate statistical models to dispute it; simpler statistics might suffice. In Cleveland City in 1960, the median monthly rent reported by non-white households was $82, by white households, $76. The median value of non-white-owned houses was $13,100, of white-owned homes $13,900. Racial segregation in central city housing clearly has little relation to ability to pay. . . . Simple observation reveals that poor whites are segregated from poor Negroes, and wealthy Negroes are segregated from wealthy whites. The ghetto exists.[10]

This increasing confinement within the central cities has intensified the effects on black Americans of the factors that are the immediate causes of poverty.

C. *Low Intelligence A?*

One of these factors begs a question. Is the incidence of poverty higher among blacks than among whites because of differences in Intelligence A? On average, blacks score lower than whites on tests for various Intelligence C's valued in American markets. Does this gap appear because the Intelligence A of blacks (and of Indians and of Spanish-speaking Americans) is lower than that of majority group whites?

No one has yet devised a means to measure Intelligence A. Perhaps someday men will be able to measure the productive potential of a newly joined sperm and egg. For the present, such a measurement remains almost inconceivable.

Some newly conceived whites have the potential to become physicists, theoretical mathematicians, novelists—and even economists—capable of superior achievements. Some newly conceived blacks have equally superior potential. This is known because some blacks and some whites have become great physicists, theoretical mathematicians, novelists, and economists. Defective

---

[10] Karl E. Taeuber, "The Effect of Income Redistribution on Racial Residential Segregation," *Urban Affairs Quarterly*, IV, No. 1, Sept. 1968.

genes limit some whites at the moment of conception to a life, usually mercifully short, of idiocy. Some blacks are similarly doomed from conception.

The market richly rewards members of the former groups if they realize much of their potential, but the market offers nothing to the members of the latter group who must depend on relatives, charity, or government aid. However, these are extremes; most persons enter life near the center. Presumably, the distribution of Intelligence A among whites ranges from retardate to genius following the shape of a nearly normal curve containing most persons near its center. The distribution of Intelligence A among blacks also ranges from retardate to genius—again, it is assumed, in a nearly normal curve.

How do these two curves compare? There are three possibilities, as Figure 6-1 shows. The means of the curves may be equal; the black mean may be inferior to the white mean; or the black mean may be superior to the white mean. No one, as yet, knows which of the three sketches is "right." If Possibility 2 comes closest to being accurate, one might ask: Why all the discrimination against blacks at the right-hand end of the distribution? In any case, much is known about other factors affecting Intelligence B, Intelligence C, and income.

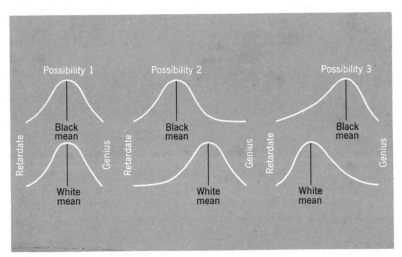

Figure 6-1. Distribution of Intelligence A among blacks and among whites.

D. *Little Inherited Physical Capital*

Many Americans with low Intelligence C, whether or not their Intelligence A was low, receive high incomes because they inherited large quantities of physical capital. In 1790, nearly one fifth of Americans were black. During the following century and a quarter, much of the land between the Alleghenies and the Pacific was given to homesteaders and other settlers who paid for it with work or with $2 or less per acre. The products of that land then provided, directly or indirectly, the seed capital for most of the manufacturing and commercial enterprise that since has been in the United States. The original settlers took title to hundreds of millions of acres of fertile land that have assured their heirs a volume of physical capital that has grown and grown. Most of the original settlers were white. Some were black. Most were poor. Whites took title to most of the land, and that land has yielded the wealth and income that have lifted most of their heirs into or above the comfortable middle class.

Black Americans lived here in large numbers throughout the time that federal land was being turned over to individuals, but disposition was in the hands of white power and, with few exceptions, blacks were kept from acquiring land—and with it the basis for incomes that eventually would permit acquisition of the nation's growing stock of manufacturing and commercial capital. Later, employment discrimination kept black Americans from labor incomes that would have permitted them to "buy in" to a share of the nation's growing stock of physical capital. Whites obtained land and escaped poverty. Blacks did neither.

Spanish-speaking Americans in the Southwest now charge that large areas of the Southwest were taken from them by better-armed English-speaking Americans during the decades before the Civil War. The now mostly landless Spanish-speaking Americans assert that the original Spanish titles antedate and supercede acts of force and that present titles should be invalidated. Conceivably, the courts could intervene; as yet none have done so. In the meantime, those with the present titles to the land have a much lower incidence of poverty than do those who claim that land.

Indians are obviously a special case. All of North America belonged to Indians (and Eskimos) until white power crushed red power by an overwhelming force of arms. Had Indian ownership been honored by the white and black immigrants, had the immigrants paid rent continuously for every acre of land used, the income position of Indians would be vastly different today.

E. *From A to B: Inadequate Prenatal and Obstetrical Care*

In general, inadequate prenatal and obstetrical care is associated with poverty. Since the incidence of poverty is much higher among blacks, Indians, and Spanish-speaking Americans than among the majority-group whites, inadequate prenatal and obstetrical care is peculiarly characteristic of those minority groups. It is the first of the factors considered here that cause minority-group individuals conceived with a particular Intelligence A to grow up to a lower productivity than majority-group individuals conceived with equal Intelligence A.

As a fetus develops, the brain cells increase both in size and number. Malnutrition can interfere with cell division, resulting in fewer cells in the brain; and the effects can be permanent. In addition to malnutrition, severe emotional stress and inadequate medical attention attending expectant mothers also erode the Intelligence B of babies below the potential afforded by their Intelligence A. When expectant mothers have access to proper food, shelter, security, and medical care before and during delivery, most of the potential Intelligence B is realized. A large percentage of minority group mothers, because of poverty of means and because of gross ignorance, are malnourished, in emotional turmoil, and medically unattended even during delivery.

In 1965, five of every thousand white babies and 82 of every thousand nonwhite babies were delivered by a midwife. In 1967, 14 of every thousand white, 26 of every thousand nonwhite babies died at birth. During 1967, the maternal mortality rate per 100,000 live births was 19.5 for whites and 69.5 for nonwhites. Psychiatrists find that the mental deficiency and neuropsychiatric disorders associated with prematurity and complications of pregnancy appear with inordinately high rates among blacks.[11] These unfavorable results for black, and presumably for other minority group Americans, result primarily because of malnutrition but also because of other inferior care received by minority-group mothers. Consequently, majority-group white mothers, on average, conserve more of their babies' Intelligence A potential for Intelligence B than do black mothers.

F. *From B to C: Malnutrition*

The 1967 neonatal and infant mortality rates for whites and for nonwhites are shown in Table 6-1.

Table 6-1. Neonatal and Infant Mortality Rates for Whites and Nonwhites in 1967 and Nonwhite-to-White Ratios

	Nonwhites	Whites	Nonwhite to White
Neonatal mortality rate per 1000 live births	23.8	15.0	1.6
Infant mortality rate per 1000 live births	12.1	4.7	2.6

Source: U.S. Bureau of the Census, *Statistical Abstract of the United States: 1969*, G.P.O., Washington, 1969, p. 55.

The neonatal mortality rate refers to deaths during the first 30 days after birth; the infant mortality rate refers to deaths during the next 11 months—until the child is one year old. The role of malnutrition shows up in the circumstance that the nonwhite-to-white mortality ratio is higher during the second through twelfth month of life than it is during the first month.

During the first few months of his life an infant has a slowly diminishing immunity to disease that has been acquired from the mother before birth. By the time of his weaning he must start replacing his immune substances by those that his body produces. For that he needs ade-

---

[11] Benjamin Pasamanick and Hilda Knobloch, "Epidemiologic Studies on the Complications of Pregnancy and the Birth Process," in *Prevention of Mental Disorders in Children*, G. Caplan, ed., Basic Books, New York, 1961, pp. 74-94.

quate body tissues and adequate nutrition to build them. This is vital between the time of weaning when a few months old and about two years of age.[12]

During the first month of life, the nonwhite infant's chances of death are sixty percent greater than the white infant's. But after neonatal immunity wears off, the nonwhite infant's chances of death are eighty percent greater than the white infant's. Referring to black and white poor together, the Citizens' Board of Inquiry into Hunger and Malnutrition in the United States observed:

Although nutrition is not the exclusive factor causing death, it is the primary factor *added* as a cause of death during the post neonatal stage. This marked divergence between rich and poor reflects the importance of nutrition which, after weaning, can only be supplied by prepared foods.[13]

Individual blacks may be no worse off than individual whites, but the incidence of malnutrition is much higher among black than among white children. For some, the effects are fatal; for others, the effects appear as restrictions on physical and mental growth.

Differences in medical care also contribute to the gap between white and black average Intelligence C. Table 6-2 contrasts white and black in physician and in dental visits per year. The contrast is most marked for the 1- to 15-year-old age group, where, on average, whites, rich and poor, visit doctors and dentists twice as

Table 6-2.　Number of Physician and Dental Visits per Person per Year, by Age Group, by Color

| | | Physician Visits | | | | | Dental Visits | | |
	All ages	Under 15	15 to 44	45 to 64	65+	All ages	Under 15	15 to 64
Nonwhite	3.3	2.1	3.6	4.7	5.6	0.9	0.7	1.0
White	4.7	4.0	4.5	5.1	6.7	1.7	1.4	1.9

Source: *Health, Education, and Welfare Trends,* 1966 to 1967 Edition: Part 1, "National Trends," Washington, G.P.O., p. S-34.

---

[12] Dr. Joseph Brenner, quoted in *Hunger, op. cit.,* p. 33.
[13] *Ibid.,* p. 34.

often as nonwhites, rich and poor. Between poor blacks (many of whom have *never* seen a doctor) and nonpoor whites, the contrasts are, of course, much more marked.

Obviously children receiving medical attention to help make and keep them well will learn more than those who do not get that help.

G. *From B to C: Inadequate Knowledge of Opportunities*

Isolated in racial ghettoes, many black children have little knowledge of opportunities in the "outside" American economy.

The image of success in this world is not that of the "solid citizen," the responsible husband and father, but rather that of the "hustler" who promotes his own interests by exploiting others. The dope sellers and the numbers runners are the "successful" men because their earnings far outstrip those men who try to climb the economic ladder in honest ways.

Young people in the ghetto are acutely conscious of a system which appears to offer rewards to those who illegally exploit others, and failure to those who struggle under traditional responsibilities. Under these circumstances, many adopt exploitation and the "hustle" as a way of life, disclaiming both work and marriage in favor of casual and temporary liaisons. This pattern reinforces itself from one generation to the next, creating a "culture of poverty" and an ingrained cynicism about society and its institutions.[14]

Raised in ghetto ignorance of the large world, black youths of any particular Intelligence B aspire to different Intelligence C's than do whites of equal Intelligence B raised in the outside world.

Black boys are often deprived of adult male models because so many black children are raised in homes headed by women, and in many other black homes women earn more than men. In 1968, women headed approximately 32 percent of black families but only 8 percent of white families with children. In most white families, masculinity means being the financial pillar of the family. Poor black children daily observe a different system. Majority-group white children eat two or three meals a day with

---

[14] *Report to the National Advisory Commission on Civil Disorders*, Washington, G.P.O., 1968, pp. 129-130.

fathers who are part of the national economy. These children learn at their supper tables what many black children never have an opportunity to learn about industries, occupations, and jobs.

H. From B to C: Inadequate Education and Training

Education and training, as noted above, begin at home. Poor urban black families—crowded because of relatively high housing costs (10 to 25% higher than for whites in similar quarters) and many children per family—lack books, pencils, and a safe outdoors to explore. Few adults read very much for pleasure. Most adults have a small vocabulary and use it with diction judged very poor by the white majority. Most of these adults want their children to "get ahead," but the adults are ill-equipped to help. Formal education has been of modest help.

Reconstruction introduced public school systems into most Southern states. The Redemptionists viewed Yankee schoolmarms as subversives to be expelled, and public education stagnated, especially in rural areas, until the turn of the century. Since 1900, public school systems have expanded, but until recent months most Southern blacks have been segregated in facilities that have barely qualified for the title, "schools."

The official reports of Mississippi's Department of Education tell that, in 1900, Mississippi school districts spent $8.20 per white child and $2.67 per black child for educational costs other than buildings. For these same purposes, Mississippi spent $31.23 per white and $6.69 per black pupil in 1940 (in 1940, the amount spent per black pupil was still less than 80% of the amount spent per white pupil in 1900). In 1961, the figures were $173 for whites and $116 for blacks. In 1931, Mississippi schools operated 165 days for white and 119 days for black children. In 1931, Mississippi had 706 white and 64 black high schools, although there were 30% more black than white children of high school age.

The 1933 to 1935 *Biennial Report* of Mississippi's State Superintendent of Education reported:

Negro teachers in the lower grades frequently have in their charge from seventy-five to one hundred and fifty pupils. . . . Of the 3735 Negro schoolhouses in Mississippi . . . 1440 schools are conducted in churches, lodges, old stores, tenant houses, or whatever building is available. . . . In hundreds of rural Negro schools there are just four blank, unpainted walls, a few old rickety benches, an old stove propped up on brickbats, and two or three boards nailed together and painted black for a blackboard. In many cases, this constitutes the sum total of the furniture and teaching equipment.[15]

Southern black pupils shared discarded textbooks but had no erasers, crayons, library books, maps, or charts. Black children were confined within this system and were taught by teachers themselves miseducated in segregated schools. Black children did not acquire Intelligence C that white children acquired in public schools. Yet, when black children grow up, they must complete with better educated whites, and they must do what they can to help their children get ahead.

In the winter of 1970, the Supreme Court insisted on an end to public school segregation forced on blacks by Southern white power. But urban ghettos seem likely to perpetuate segregation in Northern and Western cities. What happens in ghetto schools has been described recently in an

honest and terrifying book by Jonathan Kozol, a young teacher fired from his job by the Boston school system for using a poem by Langston Hughes that was not on the prescribed list of "reading materials." . . .

"Death at an Early Age" is not a long book. Its content can be easily summarized . . . Mr. Kozol entered the Boston schools as a substitute teacher in 1964, and the next spring he was summarily dismissed . . . His "classroom" was the corner of an auditorium in which other classes were also held. . . . Not only was the school a disgraceful hovel . . . the children were relentlessly and at times brutally tyrannized. . . . All day long the children learn rules and regulations—to the point that whatever is original in them, whatever is *theirs* by virtue of experience or fantasy, becomes steadily discouraged and denied. What is even more awful to contemplate, boys and girls are taught by men and women who refer to Negroes as "black stuff" and worse.

The reader will find out about the cynicism, condescension, outright racism, and severely anti-intellectual attitudes that Mr. Kozol quite easily and openly encountered as a teacher among teachers. The city of Boston may someday (when is anyone's guess) tear down its already crumbling school buildings and provide its poor children with the best

---

[15] Quoted in the Senate Committee on the Judiciary, *Voting Rights Hearings*, 23 March-5 April 1965, 89th, 1st, U.S. G.P.O., Washington, D.C., p. 1044.

imaginable "facilities" and "materials." But it is quite another question whether any American city is ready to look into its own soul, and admit to the subtleties of hate and terror that persist in the disguise of "education" or "law-enforcement."

Eventually—inevitably we only now know—Jonathan Kozol slipped and brought down upon himself the self-righteous wrath of what emerges in his book as a hopelessly insensitive bureaucracy. The charges leveled against him were absurd: he taught Langston Hughes and Robert Frost to Negro children; he showed them pictures by Paul Klee, and read to them from Yeats—with surprising responses from his "disadvantaged" class.

Like so many of us, he can move on, obtain another job—and write this book. What of the children he describes, and their cousins and parents and neighbors? At the end of this book we are taken to a meeting of the Boston School Committee, to meet up with the vulgar, tricky and abusive comments of those "leaders" who control and direct the education of thousands of American children.

In the strongly worded title he has given his book, Mr. Kozol charges the Boston School Committee and the system they run with spiritual and psychological murder. Nothing in what they say, some of it supplied word for word in the book's notes, makes the accusation seem excessive.[16]

Ghetto schools cannot be improved very much unless many of the present teachers, administrators, and school boards are replaced.

I. *Maternal Responsibility*

Some households are poor because they lack adult males and their female heads are unable to work because they must stay home to care for their small children. Although black households average more children than white households, a larger percentage of black than of white women choose—or feel compelled—to join the labor force. Table 6-3 compares labor force participation rates for nonwhites and whites during the childbearing years, 20 to 44. Within each of the age divisions, the labor force participation rate is higher for nonwhites than for whites.

Although many nonwhite women work, many earn so little that their families remain poor. Because many work while the fathers

---

[16] Robert Coles in a preface to *Death at an Early Age* by Jonathan Kozol, Bantam Books, 1967, pp. vii-ix.

also are absent, many ghetto children are left to run in the streets of a crime-ridden, violence-prone, poverty-stricken world. Because their mothers work to escape poverty, many of these children are left to learn the kinds of Intelligence C most likely to keep them in poverty.

Table 6-3. Percentage of Women in the Labor Force, Nonwhite and White: 1967

Age group	Nonwhite	White
20 to 24	58	54
25 to 34	57	41
35 to 44	59	48

Source: *Statistics on Manpower: a Supplement to the Manpower Report of the President: 1969,* G.P.O., Washington, March 1969, p. 5.

J. *Insufficient Aggregate Demand*

Table 6-4 shows unemployment rates for nonwhite men and for white men and the ratio of nonwhite-to-white unemployment rates for the years 1948 to 1969. Adjacent years with very similar unemployment rates have been grouped together to shorten the table.

The table shows the law of the 1950s and 1960s to have been that the unemployment rate for nonwhite men has been, at least, twice as high as that of white men.

When white unemployment rises from 3.0 to 6.0 percent, the increase is 3.0 percentage points, but nonwhite unemployment is rising from more than 6.0 to more than 12.0 percent, an increase of over 6.0 points. In this sense, nonwhites have twice the stake that whites have in full employment.

Because of buoyant aggregate demand during the 1960s (and to a lesser extent, because of government antidiscrimination efforts), black men accumulated human capital and increased their access to physical capital during those years. Between 1960 and 1969, the median income of married black men in blue collar work rose 44% while the median income of married white men in blue collar work rose only 27%. After decades of exclusion, able black men began to be hired for the better skilled and semiskilled jobs.

Table 6-4.   Unemployment Rates for Nonwhite Men and for White Men
and Ratio of the Two Rates: 1948 to 1969

Years	Nonwhite Men	White Men	Ratio of Nonwhite to White Rates
1948	5.8	3.4	1.7
1949 to 1950	9.5	5.1	1.9
1951 to 1953	5.0	2.5	2.0
1954	10.3	4.8	2.1
1955 to 1957	8.3	3.6	2.3
1958	13.8	6.1	2.3
1959 to 1960	11.1	4.7	2.4
1961	12.8	5.7	2.2
1962 to 1963	10.7	4.3	2.5
1964	8.9	4.1	2.2
1965	7.4	3.6	2.1
1966 to 1967	6.1	2.7	2.3
1968 to 1969	5.4	2.5	2.2

Source: *Manpower Report of the President, 1970*, G.P.O., Washington, 1970, p. 229.

K. *Racial Discrimination Distinguishing Black Poor*

If all the poor of this generation were to have inherited more property, there now would be fewer white poor and fewer black poor. If nutrition and prenatal and obstetrical care had been better for all American poor in the past, there would be fewer majority-group white, and fewer black, and fewer Indian, and fewer Spanish-speaking poor today. If nutrition had been better for all poor children, if knowledge of opportunities, if education in ambition, if education in marketable skills had been better for all poor children, had aggregate demand been less often inadequate during the 1950s, there would be fewer majority-group white poor, and fewer blacks, and Indian, and Spanish-speaking poor today, since the causes of poverty for the white majority are also the causes of poverty for minority groups. Put differently, any program that reduces the incidence of poverty in the white majority also reduces the incidence of poverty among minority groups.

Nevertheless, racial discrimination intensifies the impact on blacks of each of the general causes of poverty.

Rural Southern whites born of mothers ill cared for during

pregnancy, malnourished in infancy, and educated in shacks nevertheless have access to housing and to urban jobs that are out of the reach of blacks with similar backgrounds. In the South, *and* in the North and West, these poorly educated whites are more readily accepted by employers—and by labor unions—than are blacks of equal Intelligence C. Discrimination by unions and by employers keeps blacks from working with physical capital in quantities that would raise their productivity and incomes out of poverty. Discrimination by bankers, realtors, and John Q. White, has forced blacks to live in ghettos out of reach of many jobs.

Federal law is now uniformly opposed to racial discrimination, but its effects must be applied by individuals, and these applications have only begun. Between 1950 and 1960, as physical capital piled up in urban areas, Southern manufacturers added 944,000 employees; 20% of Southerners were black in 1960; yet of the 944,000 added employees only 12,000 were black women, and *none* were black men. The 1950s cannot be repeated; but hiring and promotion remain in large part the prerogatives of white individuals who can evade the law.

During Autumn 1969, blacks demonstrated against construction union discrimination in several cities. The facts, in 1969, were that the locals of AFL-CIO President George Meany's plumbers' union and locals of iron workers, electrical workers and other building trades unions still exclude blacks totally and unreservedly from apprenticeship and from journeyman membership. The demonstrations brought promises of change in some cities, but for every actual change, there remain dozens of whites in influential positions determined to resist change. The certain continuation of housing discrimination for many more years assures that ghetto isolation will be perpetuated for many more years. Thus, discrimination will continue to raise the incidence of poverty among blacks (and other minority groups):

1. By excluding qualified or potentially qualified individuals from work, training, or both to which majority group whites of lower Intelligence B are admitted.

2. By discouraging youths who otherwise would exert themselves to achieve higher Intelligence C's.

3. By burdening black adults with the inferior preparation received in Southern schools and in Northern ghetto schools.

L. *Self-Image*

One other consideration.

Writing of his personal odyssey in self-understanding, Eldridge Cleaver tells how he

went on to notice how thoroughly, as a matter of course, a black growing up in America is indoctrinated with the white race's standard of beauty. Not that the whites made a conscious, calculated effort to do this . . . but since they constituted the majority the whites brainwashed the black by the very process the whites employed to indoctrinate themselves with their own group standards. It intensified my frustrations to know that I was indoctrinated to see the white woman as more beautiful and desirable than my own black woman.[17]

Charles Silberman observed that blacks "learn in earliest childhood of the stigma attached to color in the United States . . . Negroes are taught to despise themselves."[18]

In 1939, psychologist Kenneth Clark asked a group of Northern Negro children to choose the "nice doll" as between white and brown dolls; 68% of the black children identified the white doll as the "nice" one. In 1967, Stephen R. Asher and Vernon L. Allen repeated the experiment with 186 black and 155 white children aged 3 to 8 in Newark, New Jersey; 76% of the white children picked the white doll and 76% of the black children picked the white doll as the "nice" one.[19]

To succeed in the American economy, one must believe in oneself, in one's ability to get ahead. The kind of self-rejection that persisted in 1967 stands immensely in the way of ambition. "Black Power" and "Black Is Beautiful" have very recently appeared to oppose and perhaps to replace the old assumptions. To the extent that these new visions give black children a more confident self-image, they will contribute to the kind of self-image that includes belief in personal ability to succeed that leads to concentrated efforts to achieve success in the economy outside the confines of the ghetto.

---

[17] Eldridge Cleaver, *Soul on Ice,* Dell, New York, 1968, p. 10.
[18] Charles E. Silberman, *Crisis in Black and White,* Random House, New York, 1964, p. 11.
[19] "Racial Preference and Social Comparison Processes," *Journal of Social Issues,* Vol. XXV, No. 1, 1969.

V. LABOR SUPPLY AND DEMAND

Figure 6-2 summarizes the effects of past and present discrimination on the relative incomes of black and white Americans. The supply and demand sketches of Figure 6-2 make the simplifying assumption that there are only two degrees of Intelligence A—high and low—and that there is but one labor market for each —one using the high Intelligence C permitted by high Intelligence A, and one using the low Intelligence C permitted by low Intelligence A or resulting from unfulfilled high Intelligence A. (The general conclusions following this assumption of only two markets and only two degrees of Intelligence A are the same as the ones that follow the realistic recognition of the diversity of markets and of man's Intelligence A.)

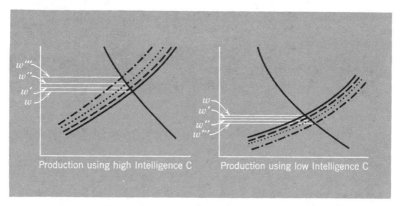

Production using high Intelligence C   Production using low Intelligence C

Figure 6-2. The effects of the heritage of racial discrimination on labor supplies and wages.

The solid lines show labor supply and demand in each market if every person is provided with human and fiscal capital to that point at which marginal capital costs equal the value of the marginal product from that capital. Black and white persons of high Intelligence A then qualify for the market using high Intelligence C where the equilibrium wage of black and white persons is W. Blacks and whites of low Intelligence A end in the low Intelligence C market with equilibrium wage, w.

The dashed lines show supply in each market when inadequate

prenatal and obstetrical care for black Americans restricts some to low Intelligence B and consequent low C even though they enjoyed high Intelligence A. The consequence is fewer black people in the high Intelligence C market and the higher equilibrium wage W' and more black people in the low Intelligence C market and the lower equilibrium wage w'. (Some whites of high Intelligence A will fail to reach high Intelligence C; their numbers are many, the consequences are large—and easily can be shown in these sketches as larger departures from the solid supply lines; these people are ignored here because the portion of black Americans thus affected is relatively so large.)

The dotted lines show supply in each market when malnutrition and inadequate education keep some black Americans from realizing high Intelligence C, permitted by their high Intelligence B. The consequence is even fewer black people in the high Intelligence C market and the even higher equilibrium wage W''; even more black people in the low Intelligence C market and the even lower equilibrium wage w''.

The supply lines of dots and dashes show supply in each market when housing discrimination, inhibiting mobility, and employment discrimination keep black Americans with high Intelligence C from jobs in the high Intelligence C market. The consequence is even fewer black people in the high Intelligence C market (not long ago, almost none) and the still higher equilibrium wage W'''; still more black people in the low Intelligence C market and the even lower equilibrium wage, w'''.

One simplification used here obscures a favorable aspect of the effects of reductions in discrimination. The same demand (marginal physical product) curves were assumed throughout. This is unrealistic. When discrimination holds down the Intelligence C of black Americans, labor demand in *all* markets is less than it would be otherwise. The relevant D for each S', S'', and S''' is lower, therefore, than the D shown. As discrimination is reduced the low Intelligence C supply will move down, the high Intelligence C supply will rise, and both demand curves will rise as the macroeconomy expands with rising productivity based on the increasing stock of human capital. Blacks surely will be better off relatively and absolutely; whites will be better off absolutely if demand rises relative to supply in the high Intelligence C labor market.

VI. INDIANS

Allowing for differences in history, most of what has been said here about black Americans applies in some important degree to Americans of Spanish surname and to Indians. Together, the general causes of poverty and racial-ethnic discrimination have caused a higher incidence of poverty among Spanish-surname Americans than among majority-group whites, a still higher incidence of poverty among black Americans, and a much higher incidence of poverty among Indians of whom something more will be added here.

Before the Revolution:

. . . the belief had been comfortably expressed that the Indians . . . would merge with the new settlers

. . .

. . . [but] the Indians had not, in time, shown the inclination to adopt the standards of civilization accepted by other Americans

. . .

By the end of the [nineteenth] century the pattern of racist practices and ideas seemed fully developed: the Orientals were to be totally excluded; the Negroes were to live in a segregated enclave; the Indians were to be confined to reservations as permanent wards of the nation.[20]

Indians have remained wards of the nation confined to reservations. Some millions of Americans who claim Indian ancestry do not consider themselves Indians. About 600,000 Americans do consider themselves Indians; about 400,000 live on upward of 300 reservations. More than one half of the 600,000 are poor. The average income of an Indian family is about $1500; 80% of Indian dwellings are substandard; 70% of Indian children do not finish high school; only 1% go to college, and of that 1%, 60% drop out.

Many people in the world are poor because they live by low-productivity traditional subsistence methods. Many among those

---

[20] Oscar Handlin, *Race and Nationality in American Life*, Doubleday Anchor, Garden City, New York, p. 26, p. 27, and p. 38.

groups enjoy the multiple satisfactions of life in accord with ancient traditions. Indian Americans, in contrast, have been torn away from the ancestral environment and now are cut off absolutely from ancestral practices and satisfactions. Everett E. Hagen has reported the following about the Sioux before they were confined to reservations:

Their hunting-fighting life required certain types of behavior for its success and their survival.

. . .

. . . it was essential that the men be always free to fight or hunt at short notice. They thought any form of labor demeaning. . . .

Mobility also required that the goods of the band be held to a minimum . . . any tendency to accumulate was regarded as a sort of perversion. . . . The words *my* and *mine* denoting possession apparently do not exist in the Dakota language.

. . .

To Sioux parents, love of children demanded that children receive all they desired of everything they desired.

. . .

This paradise of receiving and of plenty must have provided the basis for the individual's lifelong unconscious assumption that one will always get things from those who have them; that therefore one not only does not need to accumulate for oneself but also can always safely share all that one has.

. . .

During childhood and adolescence, while the boys were learning the skills needed for hunting and warfare . . . they were also learning that hunting and fighting are the roles of the man and that other activities are beneath him.

. . .

Like all social-cultural systems, this one did not work perfectly.[21]

It did work well enough for centuries of survival.

Indian Americans confined on reservations have remained so near their ancestral environments, that they have been unable to abandon traditional value systems. But men have had no opportunity to earn the traditional satisfactions of hunting and

---

[21] Everett E. Hagen, *On the Theory of Social Change*, Dorsey, Homewood, Illinois, 1962, pp. 473-479.

fighting, and few men on the reservations have found a satisfying place in the outside economy.

Several Indian communities have formed in big cities with Indians earning above-poverty incomes and retaining tribal attachments to other people in the city and to those remaining behind on the reservations. To attract manufacturing plants to Indian reservations, the Bureau of Indian Affairs, especially since 1962, has been offering a variety of financial aids: financing feasibility studies, reimbursement for a large portion of training costs, labor recruiting services, construction assistance, and no property tax on reservation land. Between 1962 and 1967, the number of manufacturing plants built on or near reservations rose from 9 to 113; but even in 1967, they employed only 5500 Indians.[22]

The general rule remains. Indians (expecting the few with oil or other royalty income) escape poverty only by leaving their reservations and by abandoning Indian culture. Those that remain on reservations, on those fractions of their original land, remain poor. Recently evolved urban Indian communities and recent efforts to bring manufacturing to the reservations hold forth the possibility that some Indian Americans will be able to escape poverty and also to retain much of traditional Indian culture. Perhaps the new trend away from white control and toward Indian control of Indian affairs will lead to more effective means by which Indians will be able to escape poverty.

VII. SUMMARY

The incidence of poverty has remained highest among Indians, black Americans, and Spanish-surname Americans because these groups have had least access to the means for the accumulation of Intelligence C and least opportunity to acquire title to and to work with accumulating physical capital. Slavery, sharecropping, trade unions, the United States Department of Agriculture, and the American school system have all placed obstacles between capital and the members of particular minority groups.

---

[22] Niles M. Hansen, *Urban and Regional Dimensions of Manpower Policy,* U.S. Department of Labor Manpower Administration, Multilith, June 1969, pp. 241-242.

The original state of man was poverty. People leave that condition by acquiring capital, either Intelligence C through learning or physical capital by developing land or constructing buildings and machines. The factors that inhibit acquisition of capital by members of minority groups are the same factors that inhibit acquisition of capital—human and physical—by members of the majority: these factors include inadequate prenatal and obstetrical care, malnutrition, inadequate knowledge of learning and work opportunities, inadequate education and training, and insufficient aggregate demand. Minority groups are special in that these factors inhibit their capital accumulation especially severely. In addition, minority groups have been and are the objects of discrimination that excludes them from learning and from work that would utilize their ability. Finally, discrimination by America's white majority has scarred the self-image of many members of particular minorities and has, thereby, restricted their belief in the possibility of and their interest in reaching for success in the national economy.

7

Transfer Programs Now Operating

He that hath mercy on the poor, happy is he.

Proverbs 14:21

It is more blessed to give than to receive.

Acts 20:35

Give to the poor, and thou shalt have treasure in heaven.

Matthew 19:21

When the nonpoor give to the poor, whether through private charity or via government taxes and transfers, poverty is less severe and less widespread than it would otherwise be. Some poor people—children, the aged, the infirm, the mentally retarded, some with mental illness—can be kept out of poverty only by transfers of income from the nonpoor to them. Others, those able to work at above-poverty productivity levels, may escape poverty by an alternative route—the one that is traditionally judged the better of the two. Here speaks the medieval scholar Moses Maimonides (A.D. 1135-1204):

There are eight degrees in the giving of charity, one higher than the other. The highest degree, than which there is nothing higher, is to take hold of a man who has been crushed and to give him a gift or a loan, or to enter into partnership with him, or to find work for him, and thus to put him on his feet so that he will not be dependent on his fellow men.[1]

---

[1] Moses ben Maimon quoted in Jacob S. Minkin, *The World of Moses Maimonides*, Thomas Yoseloff, New York, 1957, p. 369.

Among the million poor in 1968, some could never earn their way out of poverty. Their only route of escape is transfer payments (that is, payments for which no work, goods, or services are received in exchange) from the nonpoor through either private or government channels. Others among the 1968 poor could not earn their way out of poverty in the short run. Their only route of escape in the short run is transfers. In the long run they could work their way out of poverty after putting small children into school or day care centers, after healing ailments, or after acquiring more education. The rest of the 25 million 1968 poor could escape poverty immediately by moving into work in which they could use their existing potential.

This chapter describes existing transfer programs. The next chapter describes trends and current programs that raise the productivity and earning ability of the poor. These two chapters merely describe. Controversy is deferred until Chapter 9. It surveys issues raised by the prospect of changes in transfer programs and in various other activities that affect the incidence of poverty in the United States.

I. PRIVATE TRANSFERS: WITHIN FAMILIES

Left to support themselves, most children would die of want. Few American children die of want because the biggest transfer flow in the United States is from adults who earn to children who do not earn income. Each year, tens of billions of dollars worth of the national product are transferred from relatives to children through the family. This system may be succinctly termed "mother-care."

Perpetuation of any society requires that some institution provide for people—at least, for children—unable to care for themselves. In the United States, the family fulfills this role. Americans take for granted this role of the family, although other arrangements could be used, such as the communal nurseries of the kibbutzim.

Family mother-care begins in infancy. Children old enough to work (age 16, 12, or 6?) do not require it, but in the United States these older children, nevertheless, receive tens of billions of dollars in transfers from their families. Even college students, unquestionably old enough to produce, receive summer home care plus money for tuition, room, board—and even for convertibles—while they are attending college. Many, although not all, of these transfers are used to increase human capital and productivity by educating youth; thus, these transfers reduce poverty and increase the total product later.

Mother-care transfers may go much further. In extreme cases, sons taken into family businesses or law firms live out their entire lives in the womblike security of extended mother-care.

The institution of the family gives additional billions of dollars to elderly relatives. Some elders, like small children unable to work, would be poor without transfers. Others could work, but choose leisure instead because they are permitted to do so by family transfers.

The family aids a third group: persons rendered unproductive or of low-productivity because of physical or mental imperfection, injury, or disease. Many of these individuals are kept from poverty by the millions of dollars worth of national product transferred to them each year by their families.

If each person in the nation received an income proportional to his contribution to output, most young, most old, and most infirm Americans would be left poor. However, the institution of the family provides transfers of several hundred billion dollars a year, and these transfers keep most American young, elderly, and nonfirm out of poverty.

A. *Other Private Transfers*

Poverty also is reduced when individuals and families donate to persons unrelated to them. Poor families and individuals receive gifts of food, clothing, and money from people who know them and who feel able to give. If the country's 40 million nonpoor families averaged $10 worth of such gifts a year, the total annual amount would be $400 million. Is the actual figure larger or smaller? One can only guess.

Partly because of the prodding of the National Jewish Welfare Board's associated agencies, the incidence of poverty is much lower among Jews than among gentiles. During 1967, Jewish charities raised approximately $125 million for expenditure within the United States. Roman Catholic agencies, for instance, the National Conference of Catholic Charities (a coordinating agency), the National Council of Catholic Men, the National Council of Catholic Women, the National Catholic Rural Life Conference, the Society of St. Vincent de Paul, and other affiliated groups, raised between $150 and $200 million during 1967.

American Protestant churches transfer smaller sums per member from nonpoor to poor than do Jewish and Roman Catholic agencies. During 1969, approximately $300 million was transferred by Protestant social welfare agencies from nonpoor Protestants to the poor.

Individual churches also make transfers from nonpoor to poor through the minister's contingency fund. There were about 274 thousand Protestant churches in the United States in 1968. If their transfers to the poor averaged $1000 a church, the total amount transferred would have been $274 million.

The Salvation Army and the Volunteers of America operate independently of other religious denominations. They spend about $200 million a year and most of this money goes to help the poor. A host of other agencies and individuals sometimes help the poor: the YMCA, YWCA, Goodwill Industries, individual doctors, the Red Cross, fraternal lodges, service clubs, foundations, the American Cancer Society, and other health groups. Table 7-1 shows figures on "giving" in the United States in recent years.

Table 7-1. "Giving" in the United States: Selected Years 1955 to 1968 (Billions of Dollars)

	1955	1960	1965	1968
Health	0.6	1.1	2.1	2.7
Welfare	1.4	1.3	.9	1.1
Religion	3.1	4.5	6.0	7.4
United Funds	0.3	0.5	0.6	0.7

Source: *Statistical Abstract of the United States: 1969*, G.P.O., Washington, D.C., 1969, pp. 305 and 303.

The statistics are not comprehensive and are somewhat ambiguous (for example, when one gives $100 to a church-related medical school, is it for religion, education, health, or research?). What portion goes to the poor? In the 1969 edition of *Giving USA*, the American Association of Fund-Raising Counsel, Inc., estimates that private donors contributed $1.8 billion during 1968 for "programs for development of human resources," that is, for programs concerned with poverty, race relations, and disadvantaged persons. Most of that $1.8 billion must have been of some help to the poor. But $1.8 billion was only 0.002 of 1968 GNP.

B. *Hiding the Poor in Cities*

In short, private transfers, apart from those within families, are relatively unimportant today. This is in part because the nation has changed from its mostly rural-small-town antecedents to its mostly big-city present. This change has reduced contact between poor and nonpoor and has changed the attitude of the nonpoor regarding the poor and regarding charity and government transfers.

As long as the frontier lasted in America, the poor and dissatisfied, if adventuresome and physically strong, could move to fresh, new land. By enjoying the satisfactions of land ownership they could, in the short run, obtain a minimal amount of food, clothing, and shelter from their land while they anticipated a far greater yield in the future. Adventurers thrust the frontier across the breadth of the continent, and by 1890 the frontier was gone. Population movements thereafter were from farm to city, and the poor became increasingly urban and landless.

Access to land ownership may have been a great comfort to many nineteenth-century poor (youth especially). They were in the position of twentieth-century graduate students who spend years in poverty with the prospect of greater affluence not far ahead. The closing of the frontier narrowed the range of opportunities for the twentieth-century poor and sent many to cities where few owned land and where the relationship between the poor and nonpoor was markedly different from their relationship when they lived together in small towns and rural townships. Before massive urbanization, every rural township had both poor and nonpoor families, as did every small town. In small towns and rural townships, each family knew every other family in the vicinity. Although a minority of Americans live this way today, it was not so long ago when a majority lived in rural areas. As late as 1900, the rural population of the United States was 50%

greater than the urban population, and much of the population classified as "urban" in 1900 lived in towns of 2500 to 7500 people. Large cities were then exceptional. The typical living arrangements in the United States were those of Thornton Wilder's *Our Town.*

After 1900, technological changes in manufacturing and agriculture accelerated rural outmigration. The nonfarm population grew rapidly, but the farm population decreased in absolute as well as in relative numbers (the rural nonfarm population grew) during every decade after 1910. By 1920, the rural farm *and* rural nonfarm population was only 2% greater than the urban population; and by 1960, the urban population was 131% greater than the rural farm and the rural nonfarm populations combined.

In small towns and rural townships, the farms or lots of the poor adjoined the ones of the nonpoor. Small towns had right and wrong sides of the tracks, but the best and the worst sections consisted of only a few blocks so that each touched blocks with families in quite different income groups. The children of the poor and nonpoor played together. Emergencies and holidays brought rich and poor together. In the country, many poor and nonpoor cooperated in havesting seasonal crops. The nonpoor of a town or township knew the poor by name, knew where each poor family lived, knew how many children it had and what its special problems were. Knowing the poor, the nonpoor extended charity on a family-to-family basis or, at its most remote, on a family-to-church-to-family-basis. In those townships and "Our Towns" the nonpoor tailored charity to fit their means and the needs of poor neighbors.

In the 1970s, most "Our Towns" have been superceded. Approximately 64% of the population lives in 212 metropolitan areas of 75 thousand or more people. The Boston, Cincinnati, Nashville, and Seattle metropolitan areas typify American residential environments. Poor and nonpoor are no longer neighbors. This is partly because the poor are relatively fewer in number but it is mostly because each urban area is divided into large residential sections by income groups. Most nonpoor workers commute from home to work with no more than a glimpse of the poor. This circumstance keeps most nonpoor from knowing any poor people. If one asks a suburban husband to list the names of the fathers, mothers, and children he knows in poor households, he is unlikely to know more than the names of a few men. The nonpoor know of the poors as a mass, not as individuals. Presumably, feelings of charitable obligation are thereby reduced; surely, occasions for family-to-family aid are less numerous.

The nonpoor learn less about the poor today than in the past. Also, to the disadvantage of the poor, the poor learn less about the nonpoor. The splendid isolation of the nonpoor keeps most poor children from observing the behavior of the nonpoor, especially the behavior of nonpoor fathers. In small towns, the youthful poor know both the town's leading citizens and their children. Metropolitan areas isolate poor youth and leave them to learn the high-productivity characteristics of nonpoor adult behavior—if they learn at all—from books, movies, or television.

The behavior of Protestant churches has been affected by these changes in residence patterns. In middle-sized towns, Protestant churches have stratified economically—Episcopal and Presbyterian with the highest income groups, evangelical sects with the lowest. In these denominations, nonpoor meet nonpoor, poor meet poor. In big cities, each Protestant church serves the economic group of its area. In suburban churches, nonpoor Methodists meet nonpoor Methodists. In downtown churches, poor Methodists meet poor Methodists. Similar economic segregation exists in the other denominations in big cities. In this system, most charity must be between strangers.

In contrast, most Jewish congregations and Catholic parishes encompass wider and, therefore (usually), more diversified congregations. Poor and nonpoor meet together to worship. Charity then passes among people who meet on the Sabbath.

Outside the Jewish and Roman Catholic religious communities, the impersonalization of private transfers has culminated in the Community Chest and the United Fund drives. In these drives, recreational, educational, and medical research agencies take most of the receipts but leave some money for agencies that make transfers to the poor. Here, the splitting of the pot is decided not by contributors but by the community fund directors. One commentator concludes as follows:

The great changes in voluntary welfare in the twentieth century . . . have been its centralization, mechanization, and ever increasing subordination to those who are masters of its financing. No longer is the small agency serenely independent as it works for humanitarian causes entirely of its own choosing, financed by its friends. More than most Americans would care to admit, the former motivating spirit of charity and mercy has been replaced by competitive spirit, desire for progress, and obsession with efficiency—all bearing the aspect of being ends in themselves. Economic aid to individuals has been almost entirely depersonalized; the person being helped cannot even be sure that the giver intended that a person with his problem be helped. . . .

The act of individual charity (has been) increasingly dehydrated by the united fund-raising technique. The contributor often feels little or no thrill as he gives to "the one big cause." On the whole, he has little sense of accomplishment as he signs a pledge form . . . to him it is likely to be almost like a tax—"just another tax." . . . Clearly, Americans are not living the kind of life in their sanitary suburbs that facilitates much contact with the world of pain and strain. We may not be enthusiastic about depersonalized giving, but few of us would have the slightest idea where to begin a new personal routine of person-to-person direct charity.[1]

Table 7-1 shows the amount that United Fund drives have been collecting in recent years. (To the extent that United Fund monies go to "health" and "welfare," they are included twice in Table 7-1.) How much of United Fund monies go to the poor must be guessed at; the proportion is small.

The Citizens' Board of Inquiry into Hunger and Malnutrition asked each of more than a hundred organizations if it was doing anything to alleviate hunger and malnutrition. Only one half answered. Of those answering, only a few said that they distributed food, and they stated that they did so only to meet exceptional short-term crises. The board cited this reply as typical:

To the best of my knowledge, the health and welfare services related to the Episcopal church do not engage in the direct distribution of food nor do they normally make financial contributions in lieu of contributions in kind. This is not an appropriate role for the private voluntary agency to fulfill. . . . As you also know, there are a great number of parishes which, regrettably, distribute Thanksgiving and Christmas baskets to the deserving poor. We have not been successful

---

[1] Vaughn Davis Bornet, *Welfare in America*, University of Oklahoma Press, Norman, 1960, pp. 139-141.

in discouraging this practice w.
self-worth of persons.

The board's report then comme.

Roughly three out of five agencies c.
fund-raising organizations, thus not
the same time these agencies could n.
undertaken in their communities to f.
how much, if any, of the funds raised v.

Perhaps one may reasonably con
Fund agencies have had many worth
scarce funds; the poor have been b
and only a fraction of United Fund ⸳ ⸜⸜⸜ⅼ chan-
neled to the poor.

146 Transfer Programs Now

the number of benef
and the estimate
under each of

Table 7-2

II. GOVERNMENT TRANSFERS

A variety of government programs transfer portions of the
national product to the poor. Table 7-2 shows the size of the
largest of these programs in terms of dollars paid in 1960 and in
1969, and in terms of the number of beneficiaries in January
1970. These government transfer programs originally were designed to provide income to persons who might otherwise be
made poor by the operation of the market system. However, the
following is true:

1. A large portion of transfer funds (about 40%) go to people who
would *not* be poor in the absence of these programs.
2. A large number of people are poor but are not helped by these
programs ("one half or even two thirds of the 15 million children in
poverty [in 1964] live in poor families that receive no benefits" from
government transfers).[3]
3. Many poor people remain poor after receiving government
transfers.

Table 7-2 shows the amounts paid out under each of 11 government programs during 1960 and during 1969. Table 7-2 also shows

---

[2] Citizens' Board of Inquiry into Hunger and Malnutrition in the United
States, *op. cit.*, pp. 45-46.
[3] Michael S. March, "Poverty: How Much Will the War Cost?" *Social
Service Review*, XXXIX (1965), p. 149.

...ciaries under each program in January 1970
... of the portion of payments going to the poor
...everal programs in 1965.

Government Transfer Programs: Dollars Transferred, 1960 and
1969; Beneficiaries, January 1970; Portion to Poor 1965 (Only
Dollar Transfers Shown; the Administrative Costs of the Programs Are Excluded)

Program	Dollar Transfers[a] (Billions)		Number of Beneficiaries[a] (Millions) January 1970	Portion to the Poor[b] 1965
	1960	1969		
Old age, survivors, disability, health insurance[c]				
Cash	$14.9	$33.3	25.5	63%
Medicare	0.0	6.6		33%
Veterans pensions				
Cash	3.5	5.2	5.3	46%
Medical	0.8	1.6		
Unemployment insurance	3.0	2.4	1.9[d]	36%
Workmen's compensation	1.4	2.6		
Temporary disability insurance[e]	0.4	0.7		
AFDC	1.0	3.6	7.5	
Old-age assistance	1.6	1.7	2.0	
APTD	0.2	0.8	0.8	80 to 95%
General	0.3	0.5	0.9	
AB	0.09	0.09	0.08	
Medical assistance	0.5	4.7		

[a] **Source:** Tables in any late issue of the monthly *Social Security Bulletin*.
[b] **Source:** Robert J. Lampman, "How much Does the American System of
Transfers Benefit the Poor," in *Economic Progress and Social Welfare*,
Columbia University Press, N.Y., 1966, p. 136.
[c] Including railroad and public employee programs.
[d] Average weekly number.
[e] Four states: California, New Jersey, New York, Rhode Island.

A. *Transfers Alleviating Poverty Associated with Old Age*

1. *Old-Age, Survivors, Disability, and Health Insurance,*
OASDHI. This program, operated exclusively by the federal
government, was begun in 1935, and usually is referred to simply

as "social security." The original act excluded all self-employed persons and all agricultural and household workers. Today, almost all gainfully employed workers are covered by OASDHI or by similar, although separately administered, railroad or government employee pension programs (all of them are lumped together under OASDHI in Table 7-1). The program is compulsory in that every person employed in a "covered" industry *must* pay the "social security" tax. On retirement or disability, payments are an earned right (there is no prerequisite "means" test of need), and the amount of benefits a worker and his or her family receive is larger the greater the individual's lifetime earnings in "covered" employment. People now young will not be eligible for benefits until they have worked for 10 years in covered employment, but older people are now retiring who had no opportunity, in their particular industry, to be covered for 10 years; these people receive benefits if they have worked at least one and one-half years in "covered" employment.

At irregular intervals, Congress raises contribution taxes and benefit payments. At present, the tax is 9.6% on only the first $7800 in earnings. An employee earning $7800 or more, pays a social security tax of $374; his employer must pay an additional $374 a year on this employee. A self-employed person pays $538. In 1971, the tax will go to $468 on employee and on employer and to $675 on a self-employed person. The minimum annual benefit payment is now $768; in February 1970, the average annual payment was:

$100.76 to a retired worker, and
$87.42 to an aged widow.

Full retirement benefits are payable at age 65 (or at actuarially reduced rates from age 62) to a retired insured person and to that person's spouse. Additional benefits are paid for any dependents under 18. A lump-sum benefit is payable on the death of an insured worker.

Medicare benefits began to be paid in 1966. Medicare has two parts: (1) a compulsory program of hospital insurance that provides for costs of inpatient hospital services and related post-hospital care (including up to 100 days in a skilled nursing home) for all persons who are covered by social security or railroad retirement; and (2) a voluntary program of supplementay medical insurance for which participants must pay $4 a month premium (matched from federal funds) and from which payments are made for physicians', surgeons', and some other medical services that are not covered by Medicare's compulsory hospital insurance. Because of deductibles, benefit limits, exclusions, and coinsurance provisions, Medicare pays only about 40 percent of an elderly person's health-care costs.

Of all persons who will reach age 65 this year, more than 92 percent will qualify for OASDHI benefits. Of all persons aged 65 or over, 85 percent now receive OASDHI benefits. Of all American households, one in five receives monthly OASDHI benefits.

In 1965, the Social Security Administration counted 4,120,000 poor households headed by persons over 64. Another 2,950,000 aged households would have been counted poor had they not received OASDHI benefits. Of all cash transfers by OASDHI and railroad and government employee insurance programs during 1965, about 60 to 65% went to households that would have been poor without those benefits. Without social security payments, two thirds of aged households would have been poor in 1965; with these payments, only one third were poor.

Annual benefits are about $8 billion more than an actuarially based insurance program would permit. General revenue subsidies to the program and a growing labor force provide the $8 billion extra for beneficiaries.

Sixteen percent of persons past 64 are not covered by OASDHI. They are excluded because they were chronically unemployed, institutionalized, or otherwise unemployable during their working years or because they worked in agriculture, service, or other industries not yet covered at the time of their retirement.

2. *Old-Age Assistance.* The Social Security Act of 1935 originated the federal social security system and also provided for matching federal grants to the states for three Public Assistance Programs: (a) old-age assistance, (b) aid to the blind, and (c) aid to low-income families with dependent children. In 1950, Congress added a fourth Public Assistance Program: aid for the totally disabled. In social security insurance programs, benefits are related to work and earnings ("need" is not a criterion); in

Public Assistance programs, benefit amounts are related to need —although the amounts are not supposed to be enough to cover "needs."

Old-age assistance is financed about 40% from federal and about 60% from state and local money. The program is administered by the States, and they have considerable latitude in deciding eligibility standards and the amount of payments. Individuals must be past age 64 to qualify for assistance.

The number of people drawing old-age assistance reached a peak of about 2.8 million in 1950, then fell 1 to 2% a year to 2.0 million in 1965 as recipients died and as a larger and larger share of workers reached retirement age eligible for OASDHI benefits. Despite population growth, the number of recipients has stayed about the same since 1965. The portion of persons over 64 receiving OASDHI benefits was 1.6% in 1940, 36.6% in 1954, 76% in 1965, and 85% in 1970.

Because many elderly blacks worked all their lives in agriculture, services, or casual labor when these areas were not covered by OASDHI, blacks are overrepresented on old-age assistance roles and underrepresented on OASDHI roles. In 1965, blacks comprised 11% of the population, 6.2% of persons drawing OASDHI, and 38% of persons receiving old-age assistance.

Nearly all aid-to-the-aged transfers go to persons poor by SSA criteria, but the payments are so small that most people receiving old-age assistance remain poor despite OAA checks. In 31 states, applicants with property are given assistance only if they give the state a lien on their property permitting the state, to the extent permitted by the individual's estate, to recover assistance given.

Each state determines standards for the assistance "needed" and then determines what fraction of those unmet needs the assistance will finance. Most Southern states pay only 50 to 70% of "needs"; for example, Idaho: need, $132; benefit paid, $132; Florida: need, $111; benefit paid, $75.

B. *Transfers Alleviating Poverty Associated with Youth*

1. *Aid to Families with Dependent Children.* The 1935 Social Security Act authorized federal grants to states to aid children who are needy because of the death or continued absence from

the home of a parent. Later, aid was authorized to parents and guardians as well as to their children. As a rule, states do not provide aid unless the federal government will bear a portion of the costs. For years, Congress authorized federal cost-sharing of Aid to Families of Dependent Children (AFDC) only when one parent was dead or absent. That rule gave members of a family an incentive to decide that they would be best off with the father on "continued absence." One day the family is ineligible for aid because the father is present; the next day, the family is on its way to eligibility because the father has absented himself. Unfortunately for the accumulation of Intelligence C, the children must then grow up without a father in view. He may sneak back occasionally, but this is discouraged by state welfare administrators who spend many nights sneaking up on the homes of women drawing aid and then searching each home, looking for a man or, at least, a man's pants. If a man is found, the women and her children lose their AFDC eligibility.

In 1961, to remove the incentive for an unemployed father to desert, Congress authorized aid to children and adults in families with unemployed fathers present. By March 1970, only 25 states had adopted this option, but only 100,000 families are now admitted to the program under this provision. The other 25 states continue to encourage fathers to desert and continue 2 A.M. bed checks.

The number of AFDC beneficiaries rose from 3 million in December 1960 to 7,500,000 in January 1970. One of every six persons reaching the age of 18 during the 1960s was a recipient of AFDC benefits at sometime during his childhood.

Within the limits set by federal law, each state sets its own eligibility and benefit provisions. In the past, 41 states required residence in the state for a year or more before granting eligibility. All states, at local option, could deny aid to children if the mother (or parents) failed to maintain a morally "suitable home" —local welfare investigators were the sole judges of morally "suitable." In 1969, the Supreme Court declared both of these eligibility obstacles unconstitutional. AFDC payments have been rising during the past decade because of the urbanization of the rural poor (who cannot have city gardens) and because Congress, the Supreme Court, and local authorities have eased eligibility requirements.

Benefits vary greatly from state to state. In January 1970, the average payment was $45.81 a month, $549.60 a year per recipient ($2198.40 a year for a four-person family). As among states, benefits ranged from $12.00 a month in Mississippi to $70.90 in Massachusetts. Benefits are based on state estimates of need. At least one need provision is odd:

It is unlikely that the food requirements of an active adult female raising children are less than those of an aged person, yet the AFDC mother is allotted $26.50 for food per month against $39 for a recipient of Old Age Assistance.[4]

In three fourths of the AFDC cases, the father is absent. Two thirds of the AFDC families have three or fewer children. Eleven percent of Americans are black; 42% of the AFDC recipients are black. Sixty percent of AFDC mothers have not finished high school. Almost 20% of AFDC cases receive some income from earnings.

A 1967 social security amedment established a work-incentive program, WIN, under which adult AFDC beneficiaries judged "appropriate" by local authorities are referred to work and training projects. In some areas, women who refuse to accept these referrals are declared ineligibile for benefits.

2. *OASDHI Payments.* OASDHI makes payments to children of deceased workers.

3. *Veterans' Administration Payments.* The Veteran's Administration makes payments to children of deceased veterans.

C. *Transfers Alleviating Poverty Associated with Injury, Disease, or Congenital Handicap*

1. Workmen's compensation is America's oldest form of social insurance. Before the establishment of workmen's compensation programs, most begun during the decade of 1909 to 1919, a worker injured on the job could sue the employer; but the

---

[4] President's Commission on Income Maintenance Programs, *Poverty Amid Plenty, The American Paradox*, G.P.O., Washington, D.C., Nov. 1969, p. 117.

employer could escape legal penalty if he could show the injury was due to (a) the "normal risks" of such work, (b) a fellow worker's negligence, or (c) the plaintiff's negligence. Workmen's compensation is an insurance program operated by each state (and by the federal government for its own employees, the District of Columbia employees of private firms, and harbor workers). Cash benefits and medical care are provided when a worker is injured in connection with his job, and cash payments are made to his survivors if he is killed on his job.

About 80% of employed Americans are covered. Most agricultural, domestic, and casual workers are excluded. Most employees of charitable and religious institutions also must look to a higher authority for protection.

Workman's compensation programs are financed by employers, thus making the costs of on-the-job accidents a part of production costs. Rates vary with the hazards of the industry, sometimes modified by the "experience rating" of the particular company (an incentive to employ safety experts). The rate may be less than 0.1% of payroll if nearly all employees are clerical or as much as 20% of payroll where risks are very high. The average rate is about 1% of payroll.

Disability payments are higher the higher the individual's earnings when well. In 1968, South Carolina's weekly payments ranged from $5 to $50, California's from $25 to $70, and the federal government's from $59 to $345.

In 43 of the programs, medical aid is provided with no limit other than need. The other 11 programs limit duration, or amount, or both.

When men die from a work injury, 22 of the programs provide monthly payments throughout the widow's unmarried lifetime and during the minority of any children. Thirty programs limit these payments to 300 to 500 weeks. Two programs provide only lump sum death payments. All except the Oklahoma program pay burial expenses.

2. Temporary disability insurance in Rhode Island (the pioneer in 1942), California, New Jersey, New York, and the railroad industry provides transfers during unemployment that is caused by inability to work because of any disease or accident (pregnancy makes working women eligible for benefits in Rhode

Island and New Jersey). Approximately 14 million employees are covered by these five government programs. Another 20 million employees are protected through company group disability insurance or formal sick-leave employer programs.

3. Aid to the permanently and totally disabled was authorized by a 1950 social security amendment. All states except Nevada operate an APTD program with federal assistance. Eligibility requires a medically verified physical or mental impairment that is likely to continue indefinitely and that is severe enough to keep the individual from earning wages *or* being a homemaker. Of the 700,000 APTD recipients, one half suffer from chronic diseases of the aging, and one fourth suffer mental illness. Of those who have worked, more than half of the men were laborers and more than half of the women were domestic servants.

Benefit levels differ as among states, $51 a month in Alabama, $135 in Iowa. In January 1970, the national average was $91.40 a month.

4. Aid to the blind helps only 90,000 people. To qualify, vision must be less than 20/200 in the better eye with correcting lens. Three fourths of AB beneficiaries are 50 years old or older. Benefit levels ranged from $658 a year in Mississippi to $1917 in California. The national average was $100 a month in January 1970.

5. Veterans' disability benefits are paid when individuals are disabled by injuries or illnesses incurred during or aggravated by military service. Disabilities are rated by percent of impairment and the benefits are roughly proportional to percent of impairment. Veterans with 50% or more impairment receive extra benefits if they have dependents. Some 2 million veterans received disability benefits in 1968.

6. Medical Assistance programs (called Medicaid) were authorized by a 1965 social security amendment to replace the several programs then in effect to provide medical care to persons drawing OAA, AFDC, APTD, and AB assistance. Persons not receiving any of these forms of public assistance may also receive Medicaid if their income level is less than 133% of AFDC assistance in the State. By July 1969, 44 states had Medicaid programs that were helping about 10 million people. Beneficiaries are not given cash; instead their doctors or hospitals send bills to the

state agency that operates old-age assistance programs, and it pays with funds roughly one third state and two thirds federal.

D. *Transfers Alleviating Poverty Associated with Unemployment*

During 1969, average monthly unemployment was 2.8 million. Because the people unemployed during December were in large part different than the ones unemployed in January, the total unemployed at sometime during the year was more than 11 million.

Eighty percent of nongricultural employees (more than 55 million workers) are now covered by state unemployment insurance. Wisconsin initiated the first program in 1932 and paid the nation's first unemployment insurance benefit check in August 1936; the federal Social Security Act of 1935 introduced incentives for all states to provide unemployment insurance, and all have done so since 1937. Coverage, benefits, and taxes vary from state to state; 60% of North Dakota's and 100% of Hawaii's workers are covered. Many states exclude agricultural workers, domestic servants, and employees of nonprofit and government agencies. In August of 1970, Congress passed a bill that reduced these exclusions.

Benefits are a matter of right for people who are laid off after a minimum length of time or after earning a minimum amount in covered employment. A candidate for aid must register in a state employment office and must be prepared to accept "suitable" employment if it is offered.

Workers on strike or fired for misconduct are ineligible. Persons also are disqualified if they fail to appear at their local employment office once a week with evidence of job hunting, or if they refuse to accept a job offer "suitable" to their experience.

The program is supported by an employer's tax that varies according to "experience rating" and is higher the higher the employer's record of past layoffs. The average tax is about 1.6% of payroll, but rates range from 0% for some employers to 5.4% for others. Minimum and maximum benefit levels are higher the higher the individual's past wages. In 1939, weekly unemployment compensation benefits were about 50% of the average wages in each state. In 1969, benefits were $41.25, or about 35% of the

average wage in covered employ[...]
tional benefits for an unemployed [...]
so for a nonworking spouse.

Only four laws permit benefits [...]
ployment. All states limit the num[...]
ments can be made; 26 weeks is the[...]
During periods of national recessio[...]
been increased, typically, by 13 wee[...]

Table 7-2 shows that, according [...]
employment compensation goes to [...]
of—and in many cases after—UC be[...]

E. *Food*

The United States Department of Agriculture was created and is maintained to promote the interests of farmers—especially of the more efficient farmers. The department's concern with efficiency and farm income promotes more output per acre and lower prices per unit, but acreage restrictions tend to raise prices. The net effect on consumers has been lower prices, but the department has been reluctant to exercise initiative to get food to hungry Americans. This reluctance has been shared by the agricultural committees of Congress. In early 1969, Representative W. R. Poage, Chairman of the House Agricultural Committee, sent a letter to county health officials that said:

From my limited knowledge of nutrition I would assume that it was true that many Americans suffer from an improper diet, but the problem there is one of education and of personal decisions. It differs greatly from the inability of citizens to secure either through gainful employment or public relief enough nutrients.[5]

In Representative Poage's eleventh Texas district the following obtains:

1. It has approximately 400,000 inhabitants, among whom about one third are poor.

2. It received $5,318,892 in agricultural payments from the federal government in fiscal 1968, paid to producers receiving $5000 or more each (smaller sums were paid to other farmers); the $5,318,892 went to about 00.1% of the district's population.

---

[5] Grand Rapids, Michigan, *Times,* 26 April 1969.

24,000 in food assistance moneys from the
nt during fiscal 1967, the $224,200 went to some
or so (33.0 percent of the population) who were

ture Department priorities place farm income first.

able 7-3. Government Programs for In-Kind Transfers: Cost and Number of Beneficiaries, 1969

	Value of Transfers (Billions of Dollars)[a]	Number of Beneficiaries (Millions)
Surplus commodity distribution	0.14	3.6
Food stamps	0.30	2.9
School lunch and extended school lunch	0.50	18.0
Breakfasts	0.01	n.a.[b]
Milk program	0.10	n.a.[b]
Elementary-secondary Education act	n.a.[b]	2.5
Public housing	0.34	2.5
Leased housing	0.10	0.5
Rent supplements	0.02	0.1

[a] Program administrative expenses are not shown.
[b] n.a. = not available.

Sources: Food transfers, *U.S. News and World Report*, 28 April 1969, p. 100; 19 Jan. 1970, pp. 24-25; housing, *Poverty Amid Plenty*, G.P.O., Washington, D.C., Nov. 1969, pp. 128-130.

The House and Senate Agriculture Committees have produced food-for-the-poor programs for the Department of Agriculture to administer. But these programs have been incidental to the main purposes of federal agriculture agencies.

The Southern Democrats and conservative Republicans who control the [House Agriculture] committee are torn between their philosophy and practical political realities. They fervently want to expand aid for farmers and limit food stamps for the poor. But their legislative judgment tells them they should recommend just the opposite, or else risk having a farm bill crippled or even killed on the House floor while the food stamp program is expanded anyway.[6]

---

[6] Norman C. Miller, "Fading Farm Block," *The Wall Street Journal*, 19 Feb. 1970, p. 1.

Seven food-for-the-poor programs are now operating. Table 7-3 shows the value of food transferred and the number of beneficiaries of these programs in 1969.

1. The Surplus Commodity Distribution Program pays the cost of food and the cost of delivering it to county warehouses. Each county pays for warehousing and distribution. During the late 1960s, about 20 commodities were "surplus"; the Department of Agriculture buys "surplus" commodities to help raise their prices. It then gives away to participating counties a portion of what has been bought. In 1968, 1240 of the nation's 3100 counties participated. About 3,600,000 people received surplus food during 1969. Recipients must satisfy their county's need test. The total cost of the program in 1969, as Table 7-3 shows, was $140,000,000.

2. The Food Stamp Program was reactivated in the early 1960s. Participants—meeting their city or county needs tests—pay cash for food stamps that are redeemable in grocery stores for much more than the purchase price. The purchase price varies with a family's ability to pay. For example, a 5-person household

> with $480 monthly net income
> pays $116 for stamps worth $144;
> with $0 monthly net income
> pays $2.50 for stamps worth $68.

A county may participate in either the Surplus Commodity or the Food Stamp Program but not in both. In 1968, 1200 counties participated in the Food Stamp Program; 2,600,000 people benefited.

When counties first shifted from the Surplus Commodity to the Food Stamp Program, the number of participants dropped sharply even though the food stamps might appear more attractive in that they gave their recipients a range of choice that was denied to surplus commodity recipients. Homer Bigart reported in the New York Times of February 18, 1969:

It had taken former Secretary of Agriculture Orville L. Freeman several years to solve the mystery of why the number of participants in food programs always dropped sharply whenever a county switched from free distribution of Federal surplus commodities to food stamps.

Finally, some of his aides went to Mississippi and brought back the startling news: "There are families existing with no discernible income."

Food stamps must be bought all or nothing once a month; a household cannot buy half an allotment (or one quarter). If the household does not have all the money needed on one of the few days the local welfare office offers the stamps, then no food stamps can be bought. If a household misses buying stamps during one month, it loses its eligibility and must reapply for admission to the program.

This present Food Stamp Program was designed to serve people who are poor but have a regular income. The poorest poor benefit least. Funding is being expanded rapidly in order to reach more people. Table 7-3 shows that $300 million was spent in fiscal 1969, $103 apiece for 2.9 million people; $600 million is to be spent during fiscal 1970, $175 apiece for 3.4 million people; $1.2 billion is to be spent during fiscal 1971. Several hundred counties offer neither food stamps nor surplus commodities. Those that offer one or the other usually limit distribution to about 25% of the poor.

3. The School Lunch Program provided a 4½ cent to 11 cent discount to about 16 million nonpoor children and free lunches to about 2.5 million poor children during 1969. The other five million school-age poor children were not affected by this program. Its main purpose is not lunches for the poor, or even lunches for children. "The National School Lunch effort primarily serves to consume foodstuffs having a soft price in a glutted market."[7] Schools without cafeterias cannot take advantage of the program.

4. In 1968, Congress enacted The Extended School Lunch Program to provide free or subsidized lunches to poor children in camps and day care centers.

5. The Child Nutrition Act of 1966 provides $9 million a year

---

[7] Robert Choate, "Hunger and Malnutrition among the American Poor— Background Data for Constructive Action in 1969," *Economic Opportunity Amendments of 1969, Hearings,* United States Senate Committee on Labor and Public Welfare Subcommittee on Employment, Manpower, and Poverty, April 23 to June 6, 1969, p. 178.

for children who must travel long distances to school and for children who do not get any breakfast at home.

6. The Milk Program provides half pints of milk to poor and nonpoor alike. The reduced price costs the federal government about $100 million a year.

7. The Elementary and Secondary Education Act provides for free lunches for poor children. Robert Choate reports that as many poor children may be fed by this program as by the School Lunch Program.[8]

8. A million dollars a year is now available for supplemental feeding for about 225,000 pregnant women.

F. *Housing*

Table 7-3 shows 1969 value and beneficiary figures for three major housing programs operated by the federal government.

1. The Public Housing Program provides financial backing to independent local housing authorities. Approximately 2.5 million people now live in the 700,000 units of public housing. The federal subsidy averages about $40 per month per family.

Very poor people are excluded from public housing by a rule that each family must pay at least 30 percent of the cost of its housing unit. Each housing authority also limits the number of public assistance recipients it will admit. The median 1968 income of families in public housing was $2800; their median rent was $54 a month. Elderly persons occupy one third of public housing units.

2. Leased housing began in 1968. The federal government subsidizes local housing authorities that sign leases with private owners. Low-income families are admitted to the leased homes and pay part of the rent, but the authority pays the rest. By 1969, 62,000 units had been leased.

3. Rent supplements offer incentives to private individuals or to organizations to build low-rent housing. The owners rent to whomever they please. Low-income renters need pay only 25% of their income for rent, and the federal government pays the difference. The federal subsidy averages $80 a month (compared with

---

[8] *Ibid.*, p. 176.

$40 on new public housing); yet costs and rent maxima have restricted the program to lower-cost southern and southwestern cities. By the end of 1970, 45,000 housing units will be completed and occupied under the provision of the rent supplement law.

4. Urban renewal makes room for some public housing and subsidizes other housing for low-income people, but the net effect of urban renewal has been to reduce the housing stock. *Twice* as many housing units were destroyed as were built by urban renewal between 1950 and 1963.

G. *Social Service*

Social service is supposed to provide low-income households with free useful information. The 1962 amendments to the Social Security Act provided subsidies to the states for social services that would help people to qualify for work that would get them off of welfare. In February 1969, the California State Legislature examined the effectiveness of its social service program and found few positive results. Social workers saw recipients only once every two months. The social workers spent two thirds of their time determining eligibility. This California study concluded:

There is a tendency to offer social services, especially counseling, in a well-meaning but fruitless effort to compensate for inadequate aid grants.[9]

H. *General Assistance*

Table 7-2 shows that 800,000 people benefited (at $500 apiece) from $400,000,000 in general assistance during 1968. General assistance is financed by the states and localities and is the last resort of people who do not qualify for assistance under any other program or who remain in great need despite help from other programs.

Eligibility is narrowly proscribed in most states and the benefit amounts are small. One third of the states permit no aid if a family includes an employable person. Some states authorize help only for emergencies. Limited funds bring limits on individual grants and on the length of time for which assistance may

---

[9] California Assembly Committee on Social Welfare, *California Welfare: A Legislative Proposal for Reform,* February 1969, p. 53.

be given. The need for help must yield to the small means appropriated by state and local governments. In December 1967, the monthly payment per recipient ranged from $4 in Arkansas to $80 in the District of Columbia; the national average was $39.

I. *The Philosophy Behind Government Transfers*

The basic character of most of the present government transfer programs was shaped in the early 1930s when 20% of the labor force was unemployed. Given the perspective of those times, policy makers anticipated that unemployed poor persons would leave poverty when they obtained jobs. Transfer payments then were designed (a) to tide the employable over between jobs, (b) to help a family whose breadwinner retired, died, or became disabled, and (c) to aid individuals and families unable to participate in the labor force.

The following social insurance programs:

Unemployment compensation
Workmen's compensation
Temporary disability insurance
Veterans' pension
Old age, survivors, disability and health insurance

were introduced to accomplish the first two objects by providing benefits in amounts that were related to the size of contributions made during the years of work.

These public assistance programs:

Aid to families of dependent children
Aid to the aged
Aid to the partially and totally disabled
Aid to the blind
Medical assistance
Food assistance
Housing assistance
General assistance

were introduced to accomplish the third objective by providing benefits that were related to the size of the needs of people cut off from participation in the labor force and from sharing the earned incomes of people in the labor force.

The social insurance programs operate simply: (1) What has

been paid in for an individual? (2) What is his present circumstance? (3) What benefits—if any—is he entitled to? Administrative expenses are 3% of the value of transfers.

Public assistance programs are more than five times as expensive to operate; administrative expenses are 15.6% of the value of transfers. Administration effort is devoted to sneaking up on women's beds to look for unauthorized men and to all the other labors required to check and recheck eligibility.

The bed checks and other investigations are not principally efforts to determine needs. Instead, they are efforts to determine whether people in need satisfy the eligibility requirements for specific categories of aid. Needy persons who qualify in a particular category receive aid; needy persons who do not qualify in any of the legislatively defined categories receive no aid. More precisely, since public assistance administrators have wide discretionary authority, needy persons who, in the opinion of an administrator, qualify in a category receive aid, needy persons who, in the opinion of an administrator, do not qualify do not receive aid.

Until recently persons were disqualified if they had lived in the area less than one, or five, or some other minimum number of years time period and if, in the opinion of an administrator, a woman failed to keep a "suitable home." Those restrictions were ruled unconstitutional in 1969.

Needy people are now denied help because they fail to meet all legislated criteria. Many poor people are denied aid because they have low-paying work (for example, a man working full time year-round for $1.50 an hour earns $3150 a year. If he has four children, the family would be better off in many states if he would desert the family or would, at least, quit his job; yet such a family can get very little aid so long as the man works).

Under the present system, as observed in the introduction to this chapter:

1. A large portion of the nation's government transfers go to people who are not poor.

2. Many poor people receive no government transfers.

3. Many poor people remain poor after receiving government transfers.

J. *Portion Helped, Portion Left Poor*

Table 7-4 shows the number and the portion of households helped by public assistance, social security, and by other government transfer programs; it shows for each of the three program categories the portion of beneficiaries who were poor before receiving these transfers; it shows for each of the three program categories, the portion of the poor helped who, although poor beforehand, were lifted out of poverty by such help. In each case, a distinction is made between households with heads under 65 and those with heads past 64.

Table 7-4. Households with Head under 65 and with Head over 64, Number and Portion Receiving Public Assistance, Social Security, or Other Government Money Transfers; of Households so Aided, Portion Poor Beforehand; of such Poor Households so Aided, Portion Lifted out of Poverty: 1965

Government Transfers to	Number Receiving Each Kind of Transfer (Millions)	Of Such Households, Portion Receiving These Transfers (Percent)	Of Such Households, so Aided, Portion Poor Before Such aid (Percent)	Among Such Poor Households so Aided, Portion Lifted Out of Poverty (Percent)
Households with head under 65:				
Public assistance	1.8	3.6	77	14
Social security	3.9	8	41	40
Other	5.0	10	21	50
At least 1 of the 3	9.6	20	38	33
Households with head over 64:				
Public assistance	1.1	10	87	24
Social security	9.1	78	67	48
Other	1.8	15	50	68
At least 1 of the 3	9.9	86	72	50

Source: Calculated from Mollie Orshansky, "The Shape of Poverty in 1966," *Nutrition and Human Needs,* part 2, *Hearings,* Senate Select Committee on Nutrition, Jan 1969, G.P.O., Washington, D.C., pp. 662-663.

A large portion of American households receive government transfers; one in five of nonaged and seven of eight aged households receive money transfers under one of the three categories of aid distinguished in Table 7-4. For aged households, most transfers are from social security; nonaged households receive most transfers from "other" programs; for example, workmen's and unemployment compensation and veterans' pensions.

Government transfers to households with nonaged heads go mostly to the nonpoor; this is especially true of "other" transfers. The fact that public assistance goes to many nonpoor households is mostly a result of Social Security Administration poverty income standards being so high that families without children can qualify for assistance, although classified as nonpoor by SSA criteria.

Government transfers to households with aged heads go mostly to the poor. This is especially true of public assistance.

Many are helped by government transfers; many of the poor are helped. But government transfer payments are so small to households with nonaged heads that only one third of those helped during 1965 were lifted out of poverty. Payments are so small to households with aged heads that only one half of those helped were lifted out of poverty in 1965.

Table 7-5 summarizes the extent to which (a) government

Table 7-5.   Government Money Transfers[a] to Nonaged and to Aged Households: Nonpoor Beneficiaries, Poor Not Aided, Assisted Poor Left Poor, Poor Made Nonpoor, Poverty Number without These Transfers: 1965 (Millions)

Households with Head	Nonpoor Beneficiaries	Poor Not Assisted	Poor Assisted but Left Poor	Raised from Poverty by Transfers	Poor after Transfers	Poor if No Transfers
Under 65	5.9	4.7	2.4	1.3	7.1	8.4
Over 64	2.8	0.4	3.7	3.4	4.1	7.5
Total	8.7	5.1	6.1	4.7	11.2	15.9

[a] Public assistance, social security, unemployment compensation, workmen's compensation, veterans' pensions.

Source: Same as Table 7-4.

transfers go to nonpoor households, (b) poor households receive no government transfers, and (c) poor households receiving government transfers are (I) left poor, and (II) lifted out of poverty. Eight million seven hundred thousand households that received government transfers were not poor in 1965 by SSA criteria; 5.1 million poor households received no help from the transfer programs covered in Table 7-4. Of the 10.8 million otherwise poor households receiving such transfer help, 6.1 million remained poor and 4.7 million were thereby lifted out of poverty, thus reducing the 1965 count of poor households from 15.9 to 11.2 million.

Transfers are much more effective in lifting aged households out of poverty than in lifting nonaged households out of poverty. Of the 8.4 million nonaged households poor in the absence of these government transfers, 3.7 million received government transfer aid; of the 3.7, 1.3 million were lifted out of poverty. Of the 7.5 million aged households poor in the absence of these government transfers, 7.1 million received government transfer aid, and almost one half of the 7.1 million were lifted out of poverty.

Transfers lift relatively more of the aged households out of poverty. Nonaged households (averaging twice the members of aged households) are supposed to escape poverty through the work of one or more household members.

III. TAXES ON POOR AND NONPOOR

To the extent the poor pay as taxes the monies coming to them as government transfers, they receive no net benefits from those transfers. What portion of their *post*-transfer income do the poor pay in taxes? *Note:* if a household pays taxes equal to one third of its earned plus transfer income and if transfers comprise one third of its earned plus transfer income, it breaks even vis-à-vis government cash flows.

American taxes can be grouped under these three heading

(a) State and local
(b) Federal excise, social insurance, and corporation
(c) Federal personal income

Among these three categories, federal

accounted for 27% of 1969 tax receipts of local, state, and federal government; 34% came from state and local taxes, 39% came from "other" federal taxes.

A number of economists have undertaken to estimate the "incidence" (percent of income paid) of particular taxes on families in various income ranges. The results at best are good estimates, since no certain evidence exists to show who bears what portion of corporation taxes, of property taxes on rented homes, or of gasoline taxes paid by truckers.

Table 7-6 shows in simplified consolidated terms W. Irwin Gillespie's estimates of the incidence in 1960 of state and local taxes. For selected income groups, this table shows Gillespie's estimates of the portion of its money income paid by the typical family in state and local property, sales, income, gasoline, social insurance, and other taxes.

Table 7-6. Incidence of State and Local Taxes

If Family Money Income Was:	Then State and Local Taxes, as A Percentage of Income, Were:
Under $2000	12
$2000 to $3999	14.5
$4000 to $7499	15
Over $9999	6

Source: Adopted from W. Irwin Gillespie, "Effect of Public Expenditures on the Distribution of ⟶ ᵒme," in R.A. Musgrave, ed., *Essays in Fiscal Federalism,* The P⟋ ⟍stitution, Washington, 1965, p. 136.

The ⟋ in such taxes is lowest when incomes ⟍ ℩e families pay a higher percentage t to property tax) than do high- ℩e families have little insurance 'irect part of their income into ᵗouched by sales and excise

of the 1960 incidence of and other federal taxes. gressive because they lual's income. People

with higher incomes pay federal social in
percent on income in excess of $7800.

Table 7-7. Incidence of Federal Social Insurance,
"Other" Taxes: 1960

If Family Money Income Was:[a]	Then, as a percent of money i		
	Social Insurance Taxes Were:	Personal Inco Taxes Were:	..e:
Under $2000	6	2	10
$2000 to $3999	9	5	11.5
$4000 to $7499	7.5	7	10.5
Over $9999	1.5	18	11

[a] Includes employers' payroll social insurance taxes as part of individuals' money income.

Source: Same as Table 7-6.

The Federal personal income tax charges everyone—rich and poor exactly alike—the same 14% on their first $500 in taxable income and exactly the same 15% on their second $500, and so on for added increments of income. The rates are the same for rich and poor on any given increment but high-income families have increments (taxed at higher rates) that low-income families do not have. The many deductions allowed under federal tax law permit individuals—especially high-income individuals—to avoid tax obligations on much of their income. Nevertheless, the personal income tax is a progressive tax.

All other federal taxes bring in somewhat more revenue than the personal income tax ($95.6 billion in 1969 for personal income; $106 billion for the others). Taken together these others are nearly proportional to money incomes.

Table 7-8 sums the tax incidence of all federal and of state and local taxes. Federal income taxes are progressive, but the regressivity of state and local taxes and of federal social insurance taxes makes the total tax burden progressive only over the lowest range of incomes. At higher incomes, taxes are regressive.

These figures are dated, since tax legislation changes each year, but the overall incidence may not have changed much during the ᴗ. Incidence of All American Taxes, 1960

If Family Money Income Was:	Then Taxes, as a Percent of Income, Were:
Under $2000	30
$2000 to $3999	40
$4000 to $7499	40
Over $9999	36.5

Source: Tables 7-6 and 7-7.

1960s. In *Income Distribution and the Federal Income Tax*,[10] Benjamin A. Okner examined the effects of the 1965 federal income tax amendments and showed why, contrary to general opinion, the federal income tax law does not greatly affect the distribution of American income.

The benefits from government expenditures are more unequal as between low-income and high-income families. Table 7-9 shows Gillespie's estimates of the distribution of benefits that are received from expenditures by the federal, state, and local governments.

Table 7-9. Estimated Benefit Rates, Incidence, and Net Effects of American Taxes, 1960

If Family Income (Money) Was:	Tax Benefits as Percent of Income[a]	Tax Incidence[b]	Benefit Rate Minus Incidence
Under $2000	85	30	55
$2000 to $3999	71	40	31
$4000 to $7499	38	40	− 2
Over $9999	23.5	36.5	−13

[a] Source: Same as Table 7-6, p. 162.
[b] Source: Table 7-8.

For the assumptions underlying Gillespie's estimates, one must study his short and quite readable essay cited under Table 7-6. According to these estimates, benefits are very regressive, which is to say, benefits as a percent of income are much larger for low- than for high-income families (this is not to say that benefits are

---

[10] Institute of Public Administration, University of Michigan, Ann Arbor, 1966.

larger for a low-income family, for example, 85% of an $1800 income is $1530; 23.5% of a $20,000 income is $4700).

Table 7-9 repeats the tax incidence figures of Table 7-8 and shows the net of tax-benefit rates and of tax incidence for the four listed income groups. Transfers to the poor are not simply a return to the poor of their own tax payments. The net effects do favor low-income families. The American well-to-do are taxed to help Americans less well off.

IV. SUMMARY

"Transfers" are payment—cash or in kind—for which no work or goods or services are received in exchange. In the United States, the family provides the transfers that keep most of its young, aged, and infirm out of poverty. Private charity alleviates or prevents poverty in many cases, but private charity has become less and less important as the nonpoor have increasingly isolated themselves from the poor.

Government transfers (not counting subsidies) now move about $65 billion a year from the nonpoor—and poor—to the poor—and nonpoor. Between one third and one half of government transfers go to people who would not be poor even if they received no transfers. Of households that would be poor in the absence of government transfers, about one third are lifted out of poverty, one third are helped but left poor, and one third are not helped at all by government transfers. Excepting general assistance and the food and housing programs, transfers are "categorical" in that aid is offered only to people in particular categories; that is, the aged, the blind, children, veterans—and then, usually, for limited time periods. People outside those categories (for example, mentally defective nonaged adults) or beyond the authorized time periods must rely on the limited resources of general assistance programs, on private charity, or on themselves.

Since the poor pay nearly one third of their gross income to governments in taxes, their net gains from government are much smaller than they would be if the poor were exempt from taxes. To some as yet unmeasured extent, the poor who do not receive government transfers are paying taxes that, in part, finance transfers to other poor households and to nonpoor households.

8

Reducing Poverty Through Increases in the per Capita Productive Contribution of the Poor

Transfers can increase the income of the poor only by subtracting from the income of the nonpoor. In a country with a high output-to-population ratio, transfers can keep poverty to zero—if the nonpoor are willing.

Alternatively, poverty can be reduced by increases in the per capita productive contribution of the poor. This chapter considers trends and programs that raise their per capita productive contribution. First, the average product curve must be reconsidered.

Figure 8-1 is a typical average product curve, given a particular state of technology, given particular quantities of natural resources and physical and human capital, and assuming full employment with maximum efficiency. The essential characteristic of the curve is its slope downward to the right. If the population is ON and if resources are used with maximum efficiency with people paid in proportion to their productive contribution and working the full number of hours they want to work, given the real wage structure permitted by the stock of other resources, average product will be OT.

If insufficient demand, resource immobilities, or other factors prevent the full and fully efficient employment of resources, the

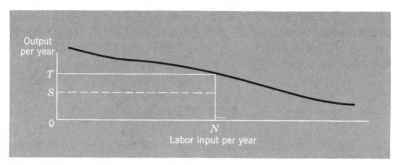

Figure 8-1. Typical average product curve for a nation.

average product will be less than *OT*, say, *OS*. Given initial average product *OS*, poverty can be cut by raising average product in the following ways:

1. By fuller more efficient use of existing resources (moving from *OS* toward *OT*).

2. By improving technology and adding to the stock of physical and human capital (raising the *AP* curve).

3. By reducing population size (producing at a point on the *AP* curve to the left and above points attainable with larger population).

This chapter considers each of these means to reduce poverty.

I. INCREASING PER CAPITA PRODUCT USING EXISTING RESOURCES

If realized average product is *OS*, the short fall below *OT* will be because of these reasons:

1. Some people or some other resources are unemployed.

2. Some people are employed fewer hours than they would like to work.

3. Some people are employed in jobs beneath their skill level.

The society can move from *OS* toward *OT* through some combination of the following:

1. Increased aggregate demand.

2. Improved knowledge among workers of job opportunities.

3. Increased resource mobility.
4. Reduced obstacles to labor force participation and
5. Reduced racial discrimination.

A. *Increased Aggregate Demand*

In March 1961, when the recession that had started in 1960 began to ebb, 6.9% of the civilian labor force was unemployed, 5% worked short hours (although desiring full time), and only 78% of factory capacity was utilized. By 1969, unemployment was down to 3.5% (a drop of almost one half), short-hour work for people seeking full-time employment was down to 3% (a drop of more than 40%), and factories were running at 85% of capacity. Thus workers and factories idle in early 1961 were at work in 1969, and people employed part time in early 1961 were working full time in 1969 because aggregate demand rose during the intervening nine years. Conceivably, these changes could have excluded the 1961 poor from their effects. They did not; instead these changes were largely responsible for the fall in incidence of poverty from 22% of the population in 1961 to 12.8% in 1968.

The decline in unemployment rates during the 1960s benefited black Americans even more than whites. Between 1961 and 1968, black employment rose 20% as white employment rose 15%. Of all the net increase in black employment, 1961 to 1968, 67% was in white-collar work; between 1961 and 1968 black employment rose 80% in clerical occupations and doubled in professional and technical occupations. Despite these developments, 44% of blacks but only 19% of whites worked in service, farm, or unskilled jobs in 1968.

The 1962-69 growth in aggregate demand occurred in three phases:

> 1962 to 1964. Modestly expansive monetary and fiscal policy kept unemployment rates in the 5.2 to 5.7% range.
>
> 1964 to 1965. The 1964 tax cut and permissive monetary policy reduced the unemployment rate to 4.1%.
>
> 1966 to 1969. The Vietnam War and a very expansive monetary policy cut the unemployment rate to 3.4%.

In 1969 the growth of aggregate demand was curtailed. The money supply was held constant from April 1969 until March

1970. Unemployment rates started up in January 1970. The 1961 to 1969 growth of aggregate demand reduced the incidence of poverty and cut the width of the black-white employment and occupation gaps. Last hired, blacks were in line to be first fired by restrictive monetary-fiscal policies that would slow the rate of decline in American poverty.

B. *Improved Knowledge About Job Opportunities*

Ignorance of the job market and obstacles to geographic movement prevent workers from moving into jobs that would maximize their productive efficiency. Consequently, some workers are left poor. Improvement in knowledge of employment opportunities and reductions in the obstacles to geographic movement help some poor to work their way out of poverty, even when aggregate demand stagnates. Year-to-year improvements in American education furnish better information regarding employment and investment opportunities, and some of the poor benefit from this knowledge by moving into jobs that they would not have reached without this information.

Private and government employment agencies exist as alternatives to the buddy system in bringing job hunters and vacancies together. In 1961, about 4% of all job placements occurred through fee-charging private agencies, and about 16% were made through state employment agencies. The state employment offices are administered entirely by the states but are financed exclusively by the federal government. State employment offices were begun in 1933 as part of the New Deal program to get the unemployed back to work. Their initial primary responsibility was to channel workers into the New Deal public works and relief programs. When unemployment insurance became operative in 1937, the unemployment insurance system was integrated administratively with the state employment offices. The image soon emerged that the combined agencies were *unemployment* offices.

This situation changed during the 1960s. The employment service has: (1) increased the percentage of applicants interviewed and tested in order to measure the productive potential of individuals; (2) moved unemployment-compensation claims offices into buildings separate from the ones that house employment service offices; (3) doubled counseling and placement work with high school seniors; and (4) made more aggressive efforts to induce companies to list their job openings with it.

A computerized job bank was begun during the months of 1969 to 1970. In October 1970, job banks were operating in 66 cities and were printing out an up-to-date list of available jobs appropriate to each job applicant. In the summer of 1970, national job vacancy statistics were first published by the Census Bureau to provide current information with respect to job openings in America.

The employment offices—public and private—are becoming more efficient at collecting job information, but workers remain reluctant to use them:

A survey of workers affected by plant shutdowns in five communities revealed that from 31 to 51 percent of those who had been successful in finding new jobs had relied on informal information. In a sample of young labor force entrants, as many as 60 percent reported reliance upon friends or relatives. Workers covered by these studies made relatively little use of the State Employment Service.

A nationwide survey of the 1962 graduates of vocational high schools showed the Negro youth to be more dependent than the whites upon informal sources of assistance in their job search. Half of all Negro students, as contrasted with about one-third of the white students, depended upon friends or relatives to assist them in finding jobs. The Negroes received less help from the schools' job placement facilities than the white students. Though they relied more than whites on the State Employment Service, the importance of this service to them as a source of job referrals was limited, compared with their dependence on friends and relatives.[1]

Because many poor remain ill-formed about employment opportunities, more aggressive placement efforts by state employment offices can move more poor people into jobs in which they will be more productive. Because many poor remain ill-informed as to their own productive potential, a greater use of interviews and aptitude tests can move some poor into "antipoverty" education-training programs (discussed below) that will raise their productivity and put them into jobs and out of poverty. Will

---

[1] *Manpower Report of the President: 1968,* G.P.O., Washington, D.C., April 1968, pp. 90-91.

many poor be involved? That is up to the local employment offices.

C. *Increased Resource Mobility*

The poor also may benefit from a reduction in obstacles to geographic movement. Many poor people remain in areas where there is no work capable of yielding them above-poverty incomes. Some remain because personal handicaps, for instance, age, keep them from moving to better jobs. Others stay because they are ignorant of work opportunities elsewhere or because, although aware of other opportunities, they are unwilling or are financially unable to move.

The automobile has made a difference by permitting workers to move more freely to jobs offering the highest pay. Some government programs also have made a small difference. Congress has considered a number of proposals that would provide federal money to help move the able-bodied poor and their families from high-unemployment to low-unemployment areas. Most of these proposals have been defeated because of a concern that much of this aid would go to people who would have moved anyway, and because elected officials do not want to lose voters in their districts and merchants do not want to lose customers—not even customers on relief.

Some modest experimental programs are operating. Since 1952, the Bureau of Indian Affairs has been providing an occupational training, job placement, relocation assistance package that has moved several thousand families each year from reservations to work in cities. The program has been expanded steadily and now helps more than 10,000 families a year, but one third to one half later return to their reservations (an even larger proportion of those who move without bureau help soon return to their reservations).

A labor mobility demonstration project was begun in Texas in 1968 to assist Mexican-American migrants. The beneficiaries receive basic language and mathematics training. Many receive federally subsidized on-the-job training.

About three dozen other mobility demonstration projects were launched between 1966 and 1969. Relocation assistance costs have averaged $750 per move including transportation, settling-in allowance, and counseling and placement expenses. One fourth of the people moved have returned home. Those who stayed have been earning more than control groups that remained behind.

The programs just discussed have moved labor to capital. Other federal programs have moved capital to areas of high unemployment. In 1961, the Area Redevelopment Administration was created to increase private employment in areas of chronic high unemployment.

The ARA made grants and low-interest loans to: (1) depressed-area plants planning expansions, (2) plants locating in depressed areas, and (3) depressed area governments for public facilities (water, sewage, roads) needed by employers. ARA also provided money for labor training programs. Between 1961 and 1965, ARA spent $322 million ($169 million in rural areas), trained 43,000 people, and took credit for bringing 65,000 new jobs to depressed areas.

In 1965, the Appalachian Regional Development Act and the Public Works and Economic Development Act were passed. The expenditures authorized by these acts are, in general, the same as the ones authorized by the Area Redevelopment Act. The special innovation in the 1965 legislation was its emphasis on regional and multistate cooperation and planning to obtain a broader perspective and, thereby, more efficient resource allocation than was usual under ARA aid to individual communities. Appalachia, the Ozarks, Upper New England, and the Upper Great Lakes, thus far, have been the chief beneficiaries of federal expenditures to attract capital to low-income areas. In Appalachia, far more than in the other assisted regions, highway building has been emphasized and 60% of Appalachian aid has been for roads. About one half billion dollars a year has been spent under these programs. Most of them were due to exxpire in 1970.

The extent to which the public as a whole does or does not benefit from these programs is not clear. They do not create jobs; they change the location of jobs. When Appalachian residents must move to Cleveland to find work in a new plant, Cleveland must provide housing, sewage, water, police and other services for the staff and for the plant; if the new plant locates in Appalachia, local people can stay in their old homes. Whether Cleveland or the Appalachian residents or taxpayers, in general, are better off in the long run if federal subsidies attract capital to depressed areas are questions that have not yet been answered.

D. *Reduced Obstacles to Labor Force Participation*

More than 40% of American women past 16 are in the labor force —most to supplement their husbands' incomes. When women have children and do not marry or are deserted, divorced, separated, or widowed, their income is more often primary than supplemental, but with the responsibilities of fathers as well as of mothers, they may have more difficulty arranging for outside care of their children so that they can work.

The Federal Economic Opportunity Act of 1964 (the original War-on-Poverty legislation) and the 1967 Social Security Act amendments provided funds to urban areas for day-care centers so that mothers of preschool children can go to work after leaving their children where they will be well fed and well cared for. Since 70% of all poor families headed by a woman have children under age 6, these centers may help many families to escape poverty by a means that is an alternative to higher aid to dependent children.

In 1968, 1,755,000 poor families were headed by women:

> 1,144,000 of these families had children under 6.
> 131,000 of the 1,144,000 female heads worked full time all year.
> 32,000 of the 1,144,000 female heads worked part time all year.
> 383,000 of the 1,144,000 female heads worked part of the year.

Almost one half of the poor female family heads with small children worked at least part time. But few among the 1,144,000 had access to child-care facilities.

The total capacity of licensed child-care facilities in the United States is less than 400,000. In 1965, only 3% of low-income (under $3000) families used these facilities.

E. *Reduced Racial Discrimination*

Discrimination keeps trained blacks in poverty when they are not hired or are not promoted because they are black, but this effect of prejudice is sharply reduced when aggregate demand presses unemployment rates below 4% of the labor force. The effects of prejudice also are reduced when effective legislation prohibits employment discrimination. Statutory prohibition of racial discrimination in employment went into effect in New Jersey and New York in 1945. Later, other Northern and Western states and municipalities followed. Many individuals were helped, but the general effects of these laws have been modest. In July 1965, the Federal Employment Opportunity Commission came into being to mediate *but not to prosecute.* Aggrieved individuals received the right to seek injunctions halting discrimination, and the United States Department of Justice received authority to prosecute companies, unions, and employment agencies for denying work or membership to persons qualified but rejected on the basis of race, color, or national origin. Although the threat of government intervention hangs over many employers, unions, and employment agencies, government act in only a few hundred cases a year. Employment and promotion decisions are made by hundreds of thousands of different people—many of whom are whites prejudiced against blacks; antidiscrimination agencies can reach only a few of these people at a time. High aggregate demand acts more pervasively to give blacks a chance. Government purchasing has also had wide-ranging effects; in particular, under President Johnson, the Defense Department's Office of Contract Compliance insisted that defense contractors show "positive action" to employ and ungrade minorities. Those aggressive initiatives have been ended by President Nixon.

Given the quantity of labor, the quantity of capital, and the state of technology, the changes just discussed (increased aggregate demand, improved job knowledge and resource mobility, greater access to the labor force, and reduced racial discrimination) can move output up and nearer to labor's average produce curve, up, for example, in Figure 8-1 from OS toward OT. Other forces can raise the average product curve.

II. RAISING THE AVERAGE PRODUCT CURVE

The average product curve of labor moves up with every increase in the stock of the "other" inputs with which labor works.

Thus labor's average product curve rises with every:

1. Improvement in technology.
2. Increase in the stock of physical capital.
3. Increase in the stock of human capital.

Technology provides the rules whereby all other productive inputs are combined. Over the centuries, improvements in technology have reduced the incidence of poverty as the introduction of the moldboard plow, the horse collar, the steam engine, the electric motor, hybrid grain and all the other innovations have raised the average product of labor.

What is happening to technology now? Do we seem to be running out of opportunities for invention? What are the prospects for the future?

One measure of technological change is the number of patents granted annually by the United States Patent Office. Not all patents affect labor's average product. Many, perhaps most, introduce only minor changes; some are mere gimcracks. Yet the portion permitting significant increases in labor productivity may remain about the same year to year. If so, the increases in productively significant patents are proportional to the increases in total patents.

Table 8-1 shows the number of new patents issued by the United States Patent Office during selected years. The number of new patents issued during 1950 was 16% more than in 1920; the number issued during 1968 was 46% more than in 1950. The rate

Table 8-1. Number of Patents Issued: Selected Years 1880 to 1968

Year	Patents Issued
1880	12,903
1920	37,060
1950	43,040
1962	55,691
1963	45,679
1967	69,098
1968	62,713

Source: U.S. Department of Commerce, *Historical Statistics of the United States,* U.S. Government Printing Office, Washington, D.C., 1960, p. 607, and *Statistical Abstract of the United States: 1969,* G.P.O., Washington, D.C., 1969, p. 532.

of invention has not declined. Many future innovations will raise labor's average product curve; and with population growth checked, the higher average product of labor will reduce the incidence of poverty.

A. *More Physical Capital per Worker*

Additions to the stock of physical capital can occur with or separately from improvements in technology. Technology is improved without change in the stock of physical capital when a new and better tractor replaces one that has worn out. Physical capital is increased without technological change when additional tractors like the old ones are produced. The construction of additional tractors of improved quality brings improved technology and added physical capital (as did the first wheelbarrow of Seth and Abel in Chapter 5).

As noted in Chapter 3, a nation consuming everything produced in a year adds nothing to its stock of capital. A nation consuming less than it produces, allowing for replacement of depreciation, adds to its physical capital. When the stock of physical capital increases, labor's average product curve rises.

Table 8-2 shows the recent growth of America's stock of producers' physical capital. This is the stock of producers' durables (tools and machinery), business inventories, and commercial, manufacturing, and farm buildings. These asset figures all have been valued in 1948 prices.

Table 8-2.   Reproducible Business Assets in Constant (1947 to 1949) Dollars: Total and per Worker, 1929, 1958, 1967

	1929	1958	1967
Producers' durables (billions)	$ 70	$ 140	$ 200
Business inventories (billions)	65	90	120
Business structures (billions)	115	170	220
Total (billions)	$ 250	$ 400	$ 540
Per worker	$5000	$6300	$7300

Source: Calculated from U.S. Department of Commerce, *Statistical Abstract of the United States: 1969*, U.S. G.P.O., Washingon, D.C., 1969, p. 334.

The figures in the table are shown both in total and on a per worker basis. Between 1929 and 1958, the per worker figure rose

25%. Between 1958 and 1967, it rose another 16%. This growing stock of physical capital raises the average physical product curve of American labor.

Improved technology and the growth of physical capital can raise output per labor hour even though individuals remain unchanged. A productive and complicated machine can be made to be operated by an illiterate; this has been done extensively in American agriculture, on manufacturing assembly lines, and in basic industries, for example, steel. But present engineering efforts concentrate on machines to be run by high school graduates. Labor's average product curve is rising because of improved technology, a growing stock of physical capital, and a growing stock of human capital accumulating in individuals through cultural conditioning, formal education, and on-the-job training and production experience.

B. *Increase in Human Capital: The Home*

To repeat a point made earlier, few Americans born nonpoor become poor. Persons born poor may become nonpoor, but are unlikely to become nonpoor unless they receive education that gives them an above-poverty productivity.

The first grade—sometimes kindergarten, sometimes nursery school—marks the beginning of "formal" education, but an individual's education begins at birth. By six, a child can be so miseducated as to be unlikely ever to benefit from formal schooling. If taught to hate school or to be indifferent, he is unlikely to gain much from school.

Most American education occurs in the home and with peers. This portion of education tends to teach the child to be like the people he knows. For children of the poor, this means learning to behave in ways likelier to keep them poor than in the ways taught by the example of suburban white, Protestant, Anglo-Saxon, certified-public-accountant fathers.

Much is being done with poor children to bend the twigs the other way. Given the state of technology and the amount of physical capital in any year, a poor child can begin to move slowly away from poverty if he has the Intelligence B required and is exposed to home and neighborhood influences that lead on to above-poverty productivity.

C. *Increase in Human Capital: Public Schools*

America's chief instrument of formal education is the public school system, supplemented by parochial and other private schools. Elementary and secondary schools, in addition to making life more fun, build the human capital required to run the American economy efficiently. Free public schools are available to all American children, except in Mississippi where children are denied free admission to public schools if their parents are dead or live in another state. In Mississippi, these children can go to school only if someone is willing—and able—to pay tuition for them. But even in Mississippi, the American school system is *the* agency likeliest to provide the means by which the children of the poor can escape the poverty of their parents.

In 1969, $59 billion, 7% of net national product, went into public and nonpublic schools (kindergarten through graduate and professional schools). Most of this schooling went to children of the nonpoor. Some went to children of the poor—but only to those in school. Of children aged 14 to 17 in 1967, 94% were in a school (83% in 1950); of children aged 18 to 19 in 1967, 48% were still in school (29% in 1950). Most of the dropouts were children of the poor who were on their way to remaining unproductive and in poverty. Increasingly, blacks are staying in school. In 1960, 36% of black men aged 25 to 29 had high school diplomas; in 1969, 60% of them did.

The 7% of net national product used for schooling was not divided equally for children in school. As among different age groups, the teacher-student ratio is about 1 to 8 in graduate schools and 1 to 30 or 35 in primary schools. As among children of the same age, school boards and geography cause differences. School board members usually come from nonpoor neighborhoods and represent the interests of the middle class. They are primarily involved with and concerned about the education of their children, boys and girls bound for college. School boards North, South, and West provide better buildings, better teachers, better equipment, greater course variety and, of course, more money per pupil for schools in nonpoor neighborhoods than for schools in poor neighborhoods. The differential has been reduced, but it persists in most localities; one has only to check the expenditure differences among schools in one's own city to observe that differential.

State governments and local school boards have arranged the large intrastate and intracity differences in expenditures per pupil. But conservative state governors have been pulling the states out of school financing. During the 1960s, many governors were elected on the "No new taxes" platform. Elected, these governors and their supporters have cut state support for public education and have invited the federal government to replace the state reductions.

The federal government has done so and also has attempted to reduce the size of the differences among schools in dollars spent per student. In 1951, the federal government paid about 1% of public school costs; in 1969, it paid about 16%. Congress has tried to provide the most assistance to schools with many children from poor families.

In the Elementary and Secondary Education Act of 1965, Congress "declared it the policy of the United States to provide financial assistance to local education agencies serving areas with concentrations of children from low income families."[2] Money appropriated under this legislation is divided among school districts in proportion to the number of children aged 5 to 15 from families with annual incomes under $2000 (*net* of any public assistance receipts).

One Congress committed itself to helping poor children close part of the gap between themselves and nonpoor children of equal Intelligence B. Local school boards sometimes have defeated that congressional effort by reducing allocations of state-local money to schools that receive federal help, thereby, leaving per-pupil expenditure differences among schools as large after federal help as they would have been in the absence of federal aid.

Vocational education can give a boost to the Intelligence C of students who do not go to college. In the past, a large portion of vocational education has been confined to cooking, plows, simple shop work with lathes and band saws, or experience on obsolete machines donated by local industries. Earning power was not increased much by these time-fillers.

---

[2] *Congressional Quarterly Weekly Report*, 2 April 1965, p. 574.

During the 1960s, state, local, and federal efforts combined to raise the productivity quality of vocational education. The Vocational Educational Act of 1963 and the 1968 amendments to that Act raised the federal share of vocational education costs (from 15% in 1962 to 23% in 1967) and brought federal assistance to office skills courses. Vocational education enrollments grew much more rapidly than the school-age population, and the relative importance of home economics and agriculture enrollments fell (numbers rose), but health and technical course enrollments grew more rapidly than any others. Table 8-3 shows the growth, 1962 to 1967, of vo-ed enrollments.

Table 8-3. Enrollments in High Schools and Vocational Education Courses by Field of Study: Fiscal 1962 and 1967 (Thousands)

	1962	1967
High School	12,433	13,790
Vocational education		
total	4,000	7,000
Agriculture	823	935
Distributive	321	481
Home economics	1,726	2,187
Trades and industry	1,005	1,491
Health and technical	198	381
Office	?	1,572

Sources: *Statistical Abstract of the United States: 1964,* pp. 109 and 142; and *1969,* pp. 103 and 131.

The 1968 amendments to the 1963 Vocational Education Act stressed aid to the disadvantaged and handicapped. Ten percent of basic vocational grants from federal to state governments now must be reserved for the physically and mentally handicapped (presumably they need more help if they are to become productive), and nearly 20% of basic grants must be used to aid the disadvantaged.

President Johnson's War on Poverty introduced educational programs designed to help children from poor families to get more out of school. Head Start, the Neighborhood Youth Corps, and the Job Corps have endured and expanded.

Head Start annually serves about 700,000 preschool children

in full-year or in summer programs. Head Start graduates have attitudes, values, habits, and skills that give them an advantage over non-Head Start graduates when they begin first grade. The differential is cut over time. Head Start is now a national program, although the portion of children enrolled is highest in the Southeast and lowest in the West. Most Head Start children are from minority groups:

> 43% are black.
> 12% are Spanish speaking.
> 4% are Indian.

The Neighborhood Youth Corps combines formal education with part-time work in its three programs. The Summer Program provides jobs in parks and recreation facilities and guides high-school-age youth back to school in September. The In-School Program provides part-time work (up to 15 hours a week) to help students remain in school. The Out-of-School Program provides work, remedial education, counseling, and encouragement to 14- to 18-year-olds to return to regular schools full- or part-time. In January 1970, 104,000 were enrolled in the In-School, and 32,000 in the Out-of-School Programs.

The Job Corps moves underprivileged youth out of their home environment and into camps where they can receive remedial education and vocational training. The Job Corps program has embraced youths least likely to become productive on their own. About 30,000 youths at a time were enrolled during the early years of the program at a cost of about $6700 a year. They have averaged 17.5 years of age with only 9 years of schooling and fifth-grade reading and arithmetic skills. Neighborhood Youth Corps and Job Corps enrollment figures are shown in Table 8-4.

President Nixon shifted the Job Corps from the Office of Economic Opportunity to the Labor Department, and the Labor Department has been closing rural Job Corps "land conservation centers" and expanding urban residential centers. In the summer of 1970, the capacity of the 53 Job Corps centers was about 20,000. The corps purpose remains unchanged: to move teenage boys and girls out of homes that discourage acquisition of Intelligence C and into youth centers that will encourage learning.

Table 8-4.　Estimated Number of First-Time Enrollments in Federally Assisted Manpower Programs: Fiscal Years 1963, 1965, 1967, 1968 and Total Enrolled in January 1970 (Thousands)

Program	Fiscal Year				
	1963	1965	1967	1968	1970
Neighborhood Youth Corps		138	556	467	133
Job Corps		12	71	65	20
MDTA					
OJT	2	12	115	125	45
Institutional	32	145	150	140	52
JOBS				100	200
Work Experience (WIN)	16	111	97	42	88
Other[a]	15	15	15	39	78

[a] Area Redevelopment Act 1963 to 1965, New Careers 1967 to 1970, Bureau of Indian Affairs 1963 to 1970, Operation Mainstream 1967 to 1970, Concentrated Employment Program 1968 to 1970, and Special Impact 1968 to 1970.

Source: *Manpower Report of the President, 1969* Government Printing Office, Washington, January 1969, p. 140. U.S. Department of Labor, Office of Information, *News Digest*, Washington, 20 July 1970.

D.　*Increase in Human Capital: Adult Training and Education*

Elementary schools, secondary schools, and colleges provide the principal instruments that aid children of the poor to escape poverty. In addition, a variety of programs offer access to higher personal productivity (Intelligence C) for adults. The chief thrust of President Johnson's War on Poverty was through educational programs: Head Start, Job Corps, Neighborhood Youth Corps, and adult training. The Johnson programs continue to provide hundreds of thousands of federally aided training opportunities not previously available.

1. Other adult training programs have been in operation for a long time. On-the-job training (OJT) has always been important. When unemployment is high, OJT is minimal; since employers, if hiring at all, can hire experienced workers for all but the newest kinds of occupations. But when aggregate demand is high (unemployment low), employers seeking labor and faced with inexperienced workers pursue two tacks:

(1) Jobs are adapted (meaning simplified) to suit the available workers.

(2) Inexperienced workers receive OJT to learn how to handle the work.

Employers unhappily mourn this situation because they must "scrape the bottom of the labor barrel," but they do succeed in fitting workers to jobs when the market is sufficiently large that it justifies the inconvenience and higher costs required to adapt inexperienced workers and complex jobs so that they fit together. The most spectacular barrel-scraping by employers occurred during World War II when millions of women, previousy unable to fasten nut to bolt, went to work as welders, riveters, and assemblers of guns, tanks, and airplanes. The assembly of *airplanes,* a highly technical task in 1940, was adapted to adaptable women in 1942. OJT raises the productivity and income of tens of thousands of the poor when aggregate demand justifies the expense to employers of running such programs. When unemployment drops below 5%, about 3% of the employed labor force participates in formal OJT programs.

The other side of the coin appears when aggregate demand is low. Then the bottom of the labor force barrel is not scraped, and the people at the bottom remain untrained, unemployed, and poor.

2. Apprenticeship involves fewer people but provides much more training per person than does OJT. In December 1969, 255,000 apprentices were enrolled in programs registered with the Federal Bureau of Apprenticeship and Training. Of the 255,000, about 1% were Indian, 3.4% black, and 3.4% had Spanish surnames. Most apprenticeship programs have been run as instruments of monopoly power by unions that admit only sons or nephews of incumbents, while they seek to restrict the supply and to hold up the prices of their service. Apprenticeship has not often helped the poor; until the 1960s, children of the poor were rarely admitted. The poor do pay the high prices that are caused by the supply restrictions imposed by union apprenticeship policies.

3. The United States Department of Defense spends hundreds of millions of dollars each year training service men in occupa-

tions that they will pursue after returning to civilian life. Most of military training is not helpful after discharge, but every year the military takes in tens of thousands who are poor and have little Intelligence C when sworn in but who are able to work their way out of poverty after discharge.

This training has not been offered to every man of draft age because the military has had admissions criteria that have excluded the men who are most in need of occupational training. During 1968, 42% of all draftees were rejected (54% of blacks): 30% were medically disqualified; 10% failed the mental test (30% in Mississippi); 2% were disqualified by both criteria (3% in Missisippi). Most of the mental flunkouts were poor and in need of training. Since October 1966, The Department of Defense has lowered entrance requirements and has accepted about 70,000 men a year who failed the standard armed service mental, physical, or educational requirements. These men have been given remedial reading and other supplemental instruction, and 96% have completed basic training. The military records of men in this group have been "satisfactory."

Since 1967, the public Employment Service has been trying to contact every veteran personally shortly after his discharge (about 800,000 men a year are being released from active duty). The Employment Service offers job counseling and referrals to suitable training opportunities. Many servicemen discharged since 1966 have participated in Project Transition during their last six months of active duty. The transition program offers counseling, training, education, and placement services during those last six months. Eligible personnel are the combat disabled, those with no civilian work experience, those without high school diplomas, and those without civilian skills. Several hundred military installations offer this help, but no figures have yet been released respecting the number of beneficiaries or the extent to which they have been helped.

4. The Federal Manpower Development and Training Administration (MDTA) began operations in 1963. Initially, adult occupational training in vocational schools was emphasized. Gradually, the emphasis has shifted to on-the-job training. From 1963 through fiscal 1969, about a million and a quarter people

participated in the MDTA program. Table 8-4 shows the annual figures and the increasing importance of on-the-job training.

As unemployment rates fell between 1963 and 1969, the character of MDTA trainees changed. At first, a majority were heads of households with at least three years of previous work experience. By 1968, program emphasis had shifted to more disadvantaged groups: the black, less educated, and the young. Some of the contrasts in MDTA enrollments between fiscal years 1963 and 1968 were (in percent):

	1963	1968
Nonwhites	24	49
Less than 12th grade education	41	60
Under 22 years of age	25	38

MDTA now seeks to fill 65% of its openings with disadvantaged persons while it uses the rest of its spaces to train to fill skill shortages.

To provide training and "development" appropriate to the "disadvantaged" (culturally impoverished, poorly educated, unemployed and past age 45, minority, rural), MDTA programs have evolved diversity and flexibility. Legal counsel and medical care are offered; training allowances are paid and are bigger for men with families, transportation costs are paid, "employment orientation" training is provided to help "disadvantaged" trainees develop acceptable work habits and work attitudes and to teach them how to look and to apply for jobs.

The institutional training courses cost about $1600 a trainee a year. While enrolled in courses and out of work, trainees receive an allowance equal to local unemployment compensation. Course offerings are supposed to match prospective local job needs. With experience, the administrators have loosened up on the formal arrangements and open-end courses have been replacing fixed-length courses. With open-end provisions, a trainee stays in a course until his needs have been met; some stay briefly; others stay long enough to repeat portions of their courses. Since 1966, part-time upgrading training has been offered to help unskilled workers qualify for better jobs. A $10-a-week "training incentive" has been paid, but the program thus far has had only modest results. Few people have been willing to spend two or three hours in training after an eight-hour workday.

The MDTA-financed OJT projects usually prepare workers for semiskilled jobs of various kinds—airplane subassembler, nurse's aid, welder, typist; but some participants have been trained for such occupations as draftsman and licensed nurse. The cost to the government has been about $650 per trainee.

With the decline in unemployment rates after 1964, MDTA policy set a goal of 65% "disadvantaged" in both the institutional and the OJT programs. The portion of "disadvantaged" in the institutional programs rose rapidly to 60% in 1966, 64% in 1967, and 68% in 1968. In the OJT programs, employers have to accept candidates, and the "disadvantaged" were less easily scheduled into factories than into classrooms during 1966 and 1967. But the falling unemployment rate eventually pressed employers to meet the MDTA goals, and the portion of "disadvantaged" among OJT trainees rose from 41% in 1967 to 49% in 1968 and 65% in 1969.

As the portion of "disadvantaged" grew, the need for supplemental education grew. To overcome trainees' severe educational and cultural handicaps, "coupled projects" have been introduced. Trainees receive classroom training in basic education, communication skills, and "good" work attitudes in addition to OJT. Some beginners must spend a number of weeks in classroom work before they can begin to learn on the job; but even these people are introduced to the factory work situation at the very beginning because motivation is usually much greater when trainees can see the jobs that can be theirs.

5. "Job Opportunities in the Business Sector" (JOBS) is the program launched in 1968 to apply this a-job-is-motivation principle to the hardest-core unemployed, to people who employers, at first contact, consider unemployable for even the least-demanding jobs. In the JOBS program, cooperating companies first hire "unemployables" and then train them, with the federal government bearing all above-normal recruiting and training costs. The National Alliance of Businessmen, a voluntary organization, promotes employer participation in the JOBS plan.

President Johnson publicly announced the beginning of the JOBS program in January 1968 when seasonally adjusted unemployment ,was 3.5%. That timing followed from the accumulated

MDTA experience with respect to training for the disadvantaged and from the barrel-scraping that was forced on employers by a 3.5% unemployment rate.

The JOBS program serves only "disadvantaged" workers (as vaguely defined above). The Department of Labor contracts with corporations to provide money and counsel, but the companies hire and, from their own facilities, arrange for job orientation, basic education, transportation assistance, and health care as well as for more narrow job training. The Department of Labor and the AFL-CIO have, in a few cases, cooperated to train rank and file workers to pair off in a buddy system with the JOBS trainees in order to help them meet the requirements of regular work schedules.

Costs have been running between two and three thousand dollars per worker (for comparison, the costs to taxpayers are about $9000 per student in three-year state university law schools), and the people included have come from far down in the labor barrel. Of 54,000 JOBS employees in November 1968:

(a) Unemployment averaged 24 weeks during the previous (low-unemployment rate) year.

(b) Family average annual income was $2790: 75% were black; 10% had Spanish surnames.

(c) Average educational attainment was below 11th grade.

By 1970, President Nixon had embraced the JOBS program and had made it the major government-industry program to hire and to train the hard-core unemployed. By the spring of 1970, about 380,000 hard-core unemployed had been hired, 95,000 under government-subsidy contracts, 285,000 without subsidies; and, at least, 200,000 were still on the job. The National Alliance of Businessmen had a goal of 614,000 on the job by June 30, 1971.

In March of 1970, an unpublished Labor Department study rated the program "a qualified success." The study also offered some criticisms:

"Many employers," the study concludes, "may be participating in JOBS as a convenient means to assure compliance with equal employment opportunity regulations." The study says it's impossible to ascertain how many companies may be in this category, but they're generally large employers and "may account for a significant proportion of total slots being made available."

The study observes that relaxing these regulations could reduce the number and type of jobs offered by employers under the program. On the other hand, the report asserts that stronger Federal requirements for the hiring of the poor could help the growth of the JOBS program.

Specifically, the study suggests that the Government might extend minority-hiring goals similar to those it has already imposed on Federally funded construction projects to such Federally regulated concerns as banks, savings and loan associations and airlines.

"Reliable information concerning the number of people actually placed under the program and the number currently at work is, for all practical purposes, impossible to obtain," the study says of the noncontract portion of the effort. There weren't any complaints in the report about the statistics covering the Federally funded part of the programs in the nine cities.

The study assails the performance of state employment services, which were generally the major source of JOBS referrals in the nine cities.

The report states: "Generally, employment service offices have few minority staff members and don't fully utilize their capability to recruit hard-core; nor do they normally have much experience with the frequently unique problems of the hard-core in preparing for and adjusting to a work situation."

"One of the most significant impacts of the JOBS program is that participation has caused many employers to lower entry-level standards, many of which were historically—if unnecessarily—high," the study observes. These requirements have been changing during recent years, the report notes, "and the JOBS program is speeding up this process as companies discover, through their hard-core hiring experience, that many potentially productive employees are excluded by unrealistically stringent entry level standards."[3]

    6. The Work-Experience Program (WEP) of 1965 has evolved into the Work Incentive Program (WIN) of 1969. In all its forms, this program has been directed toward people on welfare. At present, WIN concentrates employable (immediately or after training) people in families drawing AFDC. Basic education, work orientation, skill training, and work experience are offered.

---

[3] "Heavier Rights Laws Use Would Prompt More Firms to Join JOBS, Study Says," *The Wall Street Journal*, March 9, 1970, p. 4.

The ultimate objective is to put to work every employable person benefiting from AFDC—or to stop benefit payments to persons reluctant to work, although deemed "employable" by their local welfare worker. A special post-1967 WIN incentive is the provision that an AFDC beneficiary may retain the first $30 of earnings each month plus 30% of all additional earnings (a 70% "tax"). In the past, an AFDC recipient lost $1 in AFDC benefits for every $1 earned (a 100% tax on effort). For people who require training before employment, WIN adds $30 per month to welfare benefits during the training period. Table 8-4 shows the fluctuation in WEP-WIN enrollments since 1965. During the 21 months January 1969 through June 1970, WIN placed 27,000 persons in jobs.

7. Table 8-4 lumps a number of programs under "other." Each of them is described briefly here. Area redevelopment training was mentioned earlier in this chapter in the section on "Increased Resource Mobility"; the program ended in 1965. The Bureau of Indian Affairs trains about 7000 people a year. Operation Mainstream employs about 12,000 workers, aged 55 and over, in community service; Project Green Thumb was the component first in operation; its participants landscape parks and highway right-of-ways. Concentrated Employment Programs (CEP) operate under Community Action Agencies to coordinate other programs; CEP's usually refer prospective trainees to other programs for help but also contract for the training of about 50,000 a year. Special Impact Programs use approximately $20 million a year to train and to counsel about 3000 people in Bedford-Stuyvesant, Watts, Hough, Washington, D.C., Eastern Kentucky, and a few other areas of exceptionally concentrated poverty.

III. THE RATIO OF POPULATION
TO OTHER RESOURCES

In Figure 8-2 *AP*-1 is an average-product-of-labor curve for a nation for some particular year. Again, the essential characteristic of this curve is its downward slope to the right. As explained in connection with Figure 3-3, the height of the AP curve of labor depends on the state of technology and on the stock of physical and of human capital. But average product is not *one* value, it

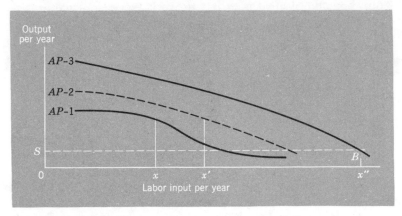

Figure 8-2. Shifts in labor's average product curve following increases in the stock of capital and improvements in technology.

is a range of mutually exclusive possibilities. Only one can be realized and that one will depend on the size of the labor force. If, for example, the labor force is *0x*, labor's average product can be almost twice as large as it can be if the labor force is *0x'*. Because labor's average product curve slopes down to the right (because of diminishing average returns to a variable factor combined in increasing amounts with fixed factors), the larger the population and labor force, the smaller the possible average product of labor. This is a universal rule from which there is no escape.

If *AP-1* holds constant and population rises persistently, eventually the ratio of population to other resources must be so high that everyone—or nearly everyone—must be poor.

But labor's average product curve does not hold constant. It rises as the stock of physical and of human capital grows and as technology develops. Yet the fixed quantity of the earth restrains the rise of labor's average product curve. Air, water, and land— and, more especially, clean air, water, and land—are in limited supply.

Despite earth's restraints, America's average-product-of-labor curve and the world's average-product-of-labor curve continue to rise year after year after year. As a result of the rising curve, a growth of labor force from $0x$ to $0x'$ does not cut labor's average product when the new curve is $AP\text{-}2$ for the labor supply $0x'$.

But no matter how rapidly a nation's AP curve rises, if the nation's population always rises more rapidly still, then eventually all the people in the nation must be reduced to poverty. Given $AP\text{-}3$ and a sufficient increase in population, for example, to $0x''$ in Figure 8-2, consumers will be reduced to the subsistence-level average product represented by the height of the horizontal line SB.

Thus far, America's average-product-of-labor curve has risen more rapidly than America's population. Yet, even in America, part of the rising per capita real GNP has been misleading, for a "GNP-net" calculation (as described in Chapter 3) of goods plus services *plus bads* would show smaller annual increases. Population growth has been responsible for a large share of the pollution and congestion included in the "bads" (for example, if America contained only 100 million people, Lake Erie would still provide a pleasant place to swim). Even in America, population growth can outpace the rise of goods plus services plus bads. However, we shall remain unable to tell how we are doing in this respect until we obtain accurate measures of the bads that can be added algebraically to the goods and services in GNP.

In some part of the world, population growth has already out-stripped the rise of labor's AP curves. Such disproportionate population growth may become more common in the future as disease control and free-breeding customs exert their combined effects. Latin America may be a case in point if its population rises from 400 million in 1969 to the 1,000,000,000 predicted for the near 2000. By the end of this century, the victims of unre-stricted population growth may agree that the worst villains of the twentieth century were those persons who opposed pop-ulation restraint.

For the United States as a whole, population growth brings further pollution and congestion now, but the threat of nation-wide poverty appears far into or even beyond the next century. For individual American households, population growth aggra-vates poverty now.

In 1960, the Survey Research Center of the University of

Michigan and the Scripps Foundation together surveyed "White-Nonwhite Differences in Family Planning in the United States."[4] They did not collect income statistics but did show that many unwanted babies are born each year in America—especially to nonwhites. The survey found:

Total children wanted by wife:	white	3.3
	nonwhite	2.9
Average number of births:	white	2.3
	nonwhite	2.7
Unwanted pregnancies:	white	17%
	nonwhite	31%

The unwanted babies came in disproportionate numbers to the poor because, until the 1960s, birth control information was available to few poor people, and government policy, typified by President Eisenhower's unyielding assertion, was that governments should not provide birth control information. Without birth control, poor families have unwanted babies whose needs intensify their families' poverty.

Change came during the 1960s. In 1964, 470 public birth control clinics operated in 11 states; in 1965, there were 689. In 1968, 181,000 persons, in 1970, over 600,000 persons received federally subsidised family planning services. In the past, poor families have had to make do with the maximum conceivable misinformation about birth control. Their poverty has been aggravated and perpetuated by unwanted pregnancies. Dissemination of birth control information will reduce the number of unwanted children in America, and that reduction will bring a parallel reduction in the incidence and severity of poverty.

IV. SUMMARY

Whereas Chapter 7 described existing arrangements that reduce poverty by transferring part of the nation's output from nonpoor to poor households, this chapter describes the existing arrangements that reduce poverty by raising the average product of the poor. If actual average product is below potential (given tech-

---

[4] See the article by that name in *Health, Education and Welfare Indicators*, February 1966.

nology and the stock of other factors), the actual can be lifted by increasing aggregate demand, by improving workers' knowledge about job opportunities, by increasing the mobility of capital and labor, by reducing obstacles to labor-force participation, and by reducing racial discrimination in hiring and promotion.

The average productivity curve can be raised by improvements in technology, by addition to the stock of physical capital and by increases in the stock of human capital. These latter increases can arise in homes, in schools, or in adult education and training programs. The Kennedy-Johnson War on Poverty consisted almost entirely of educational and training programs that have raised labor's average product curve by adding to the stock of human capital. These programs have been continued by the Nixon administration.

Because labor's average product curve slopes down to the right, labor's actual average product is a function of the degree of resource utilization, of the height of the AP curve, and of the ratio of population to other resources. The larger the population, the lower labor's average product possibility. Technological change and additions to the stock of physical and human capital in America and in the world can raise labor's average product curve, but they *cannot* raise labor's average product if population growth is more rapid than the rise of labor's AP curve. When realized average product rises, poverty is likely to decline. When population growth retards or prevents the growth of realized average product, the reduction of poverty is slowed or prevented.

9

Policy Issues

This final chapter is concerned with policy issues about which each individual must form his own judgments. The first section provides a brief history of poverty as an introductory perspective for the issues that must be faced in the future.

I. THE "CHANGELESS RACE OF THE POOR"

Europe's medieval gentry referred to their own offspring as *liberi* (children) and to the children of serfs as *sequelae* (litters), the same word used for baby cats, dogs, pigs, and other lesser creatures. The European gentry dismissed the serfs' *sequelae* because of the unquestioned assumption that God, nature, and justice made the gentry superior, a race apart.

In medieval times, 95% of the European population was poor. The 5% who were not assumed that their God-given superiority entitled them as a matter of natural right to be nonpoor while the God-given inferiority of the poor consigned them and their children to poverty forevermore.

Over the centuries, Europe's technology and stock of capital increased and the education and training of Europeans steadily improved. As a result of these changes, the portion of the population living in poverty fell century by century. Yet within each generation most of the nonpoor continued to view the poor as a naturally inferior race whose poverty was mostly unchangeable.

Poverty continued to be viewed as divinely ordained. Early in the seventeenth century, Robert Herrick wrote:

> God could have made all rich, or all men poor;
> But why He did not, let me tell wherefore:
> Had all been rich, where then had Patience been?
> Had all been poor, who had his Bounty seen?[1]

By the nineteenth century, only 65 to 75% of the English and American populations were poor. But there were still some among the 30% or so nonpoor who were convinced that the 65 to 75% were poor by irremedial heredity and would leave children equally poor. The English nonpoor mournfully described the English poor as the "dirtiest, laziest, most debased" people whose natural character would keep them poor.

By the beginning of this century the fraction of nonpoor had grown in the United States, but America's nonpoor were concerned about the innate poverty characteristics of the races of people then coming to the United States. This concern culminated in support for legislation to curb the influx of "new immigrants," the people coming not from northwestern but from southern and eastern Europe: the Greeks, Italians, Spanish, Hungarians, Russians, and other Slavs. In 1920, the chief investigator for the House Committee on Immigration spoke for the native-born group when he summarized the findings of his study of the new immigrants:

> The outstanding conclusion is that, making all logical allowances for environmental conditions, which may be unfavorable to the immigrant, the recent immigrants as a whole, present a higher percentage of inborn socially inadequate qualities than do the older stocks.[2]

This conclusion that the new immigrants (with names like Agnew, Volpe, Celebrezze, and Lausche) were unchangeably inferior followed by 60 years an earlier conclusion of the then contemporary native-born people that the Germans and Irish (with names like Shultz, Wirtz, Kelly, and Kennedy) were unchangeably inferior. This conclusion also led to the expectation

---

[1] "Riches and Poverty," *Poetical Works,* Oxford, 1915.
[2] Cited by Oscar Handlin, *Race and Nationality in American Life,* Doubleday Anchor, Boston, 1957, p. 105.

that the economy either must prepare to live with a growing number of doomed inferior poor and their children or to exclude the new immigrants. The consequence was legislation to exclude the "new immigrants." But the Greeks, Italians, and Slavs already here (like the Irish and Germans before them) moved gradually out of poverty and became attorneys, governors, CPA's, doctors, and bank presidents; and the percentage of the new immigrants living in poverty, like the percentage of old immigrants living in poverty, continued to decline with each decade.

As the Slavs, Greeks, and Italians became nonpoor, their conviction grew that black Americans "present a higher percentage of inborn socially inadequate qualities than do" the children of the "new immigrants." The old pattern continues to be repeated. Perhaps in 25 years black Americans will be protesting in Cicero, Illinois, against the use of tax money to assist the "irredeemable poor" of Mexico.

II.   POLICY ISSUES

Most of the long-term reductions in the incidence of poverty are because of the changes that have raised the average product curve of American labor. Part of the reductions have resulted from the increases in transfers from nonpoor to poor, but even these reductions have been politically possible only because the nonpoor have been earning from work with a rising average product of labor. Technological change, the accumulation of physical capital, and improvements in education and training will continue. Their continuance is not an issue, but many policy decisions yet to be made will affect the rate of changes, and will determine who is to receive the benefits and who is to bear the costs of changes. Earlier sections of this book have given an analysis of the whys of poverty and the hows of changes in the extent of poverty. In general, this analysis has been noncontroversial.

Now policy issues are to be considered, but choices will not be urged here. Each reader must choose for himself by combining an analysis of the economics of poverty with his personal system of value judgments regarding good and bad. This could mean looking for all-or-nothing choices; accept a program whole or reject it entirely. Sometimes programs are indivisible and must be accepted all or nothing. More often, utility maximization means cutting back when marginal costs exceed marginal benefits or trying to expand operations until marginal benefits fall to equal rising marginal costs.

The following issues are considered:

    A. With respect to people who might earn more:
        1. Should there be lower unemployment or greater inflation?
        2. How much more, or less, government spending should be provided?
            (a) to increase labor mobility
                (i) by helping people to move to obtain work?
                (ii) by subsidizing transportation between ghettos and jobs?
            (b) to remove barriers to labor force participation by subsidizing child day-care centers?
            (c) to provide jobs for people seeking but unable to find work?
            (d) to add to the stock of human capital
                (i) by upgrading the education of poor children?
                (ii) by providing education and training for adults?
            (e) to affect population growth?
        3. How should tax legislation be revised?
        4. What modifications should be made in government legislation and in activities affecting racial discrimination?

    B. Respecting people unable to earn more, what changes should be made in the system of programs that transfer money from the nonpoor to the poor?

III. LOWER UNEMPLOYMENT OR LESS INFLATION?

Unemployment rates are positively correlated with the incidence of poverty. In the short run, this correlation can be explained simply by differences in opportunities to earn income. But unemployment levels also influence business decisions regarding investment in physical capital and expenditures on research leading to technological improvements, which raise labor's average product curve and increase the output-to-population ratio in the long run. When unemployment is high, research and expenditures and net investment are low. During the 1956 expansion, net private domestic investment was $36 billion; during the 1958 recession, it was $22 billion (in 1932, at the depth of the Great Depression, it was minus $6.4 billion, for depreciation exceeded gross investment). Unemployment levels also affect the accumulation of human capital. During the 1930s, many Americans failed to obtain the on-the-job training, the apprenticeship training, the general work experience, the college or even the high school education they would have obtained if unemployment rates had been lower.

A. *The Dilemma*

There is a policy issue to be resolved because the United States can have

1. lower unemployment and more inflation *or*
2. less inflation and higher unemployment.

Given present business, labor, and government practices, the United States cannot simultaneously·experience

> low unemployment and
> small inflation.

The dilemma is shown in Figure 9-1 where the civilian labor force's yearly unemployment rates are compared with year-to-year percentage changes in the GNP price index (which, officially, is called the "GNP price deflator"). The consumer price index is the price index most familiar to Americans, but it applies only to goods and services in the ordinary budget of average urban wage and salary workers. Needed here is the GNP price index that applies to everything produced in America. The line sloping downward to the right through the graph shows the approximate year-to-year price changes associated with particular unemployment levels in America. For example, an unemployment rate of about 7½% to 8% would be associated with stable prices. An unemployment rate of 8½% would bring slightly falling prices. An unemployment rate of 5½% would be associated with price increases of about 1¼% a year. An unemployment rate of 3½% has recently been associated with annual 4%+ increases in the GNP price index.

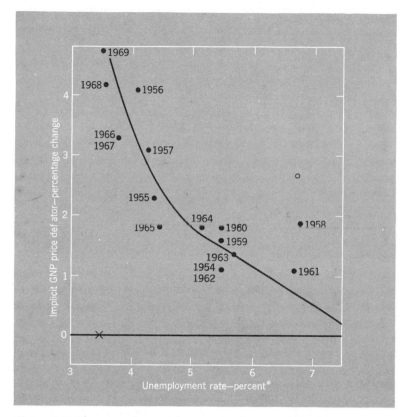

Figure 9-1. The unemployment-level, price-change relationship.

* Average for the year.

Source. *Calculated from the Economic Report of the President: 1970,* G.P.O., Washington, D.C., 1970, pp. 180, and 202.

B. *Who Gains, Who Loses, and Why*

Whether the nation is at a point to the lower left in Figure 9-1 or at a point to the upper right makes a great difference to a great many people. The consequences of higher or lower unemployment may be obvious; the total effects of inflation or of deflation are less apparent.

Inflation means buyers pay higher prices to sellers who distribute their higher incomes in wages, salaries, rent, interest, and profits. Whatever is paid in higher prices is received by someone as higher income. If an inflation is so great that prices double and the national product of one year costs twice as much as the national product of *equal quantity* of an earlier year, then incomes will also be doubled. If prices double and incomes double, who cares? Who is hurt?

In this example, prices double—on average—and incomes double—on average. But not all prices would double; some would rise more, some less. Neither would all incomes double; some would rise more, some less. If all prices rose equally, if all incomes rose equally, *and* if there were no creditors, inflation would injure no one. But there are creditors and there are fixed-income families, and they are hurt by inflation.

Creditors (a term embracing all savers-lenders) who store $100 in banks, in cash, in life insurance, or in bonds or other loans before prices double do so expecting possession of a future $100 (plus perhaps $6 a year interest). When, following a doubling of prices, the creditor spends his money, the $100 (and the $6 a year interest) buys only one half as much as when the $100 was saved. Thus, creditors lose. But their loss is exactly equal to the gain of borrowers. When the borrowers agreed to repayment, they anticipated a sacrifice of purchasing power fully double that required after the inflation. Although borrowers do nothing to "deserve" the gain, borrowers do benefit from inflation, and their gain is exactly equal to the loss of the lenders—who did nothing to "deserve" the loss.

A deflation—a drop in prices—has an exactly opposite effect. Deflation robs borrowers, the booty going to saver-lenders. But deflation is not an imminent prospect for the United States; hence it is not considered further here.

Inflation robs creditors to benefit debtors. Inflation also robs fixed-income groups to benefit variable-income groups. During inflation, the sum of price increases equals the sum of higher incomes, but some people's income rises more than the average price increase. Thus inflation enables these people to buy more goods and services in an amount equal to the loss of those whose income rises less than prices. The latter make up the "fixed income group," those whose income does not rise at all *as well as* those whose income rises but by a smaller percent than prices rise. The "variable-income group" is made up of those whose income rises more than prices (all these comparisons refer to *percentage* change). The variable-income group does nothing to "deserve" its gain in purchasing power; yet it receives whatever the fixed-income group loses. As it does with debtors and creditors, deflation reverses inflation's effects by robbing the variable-income group in order to aid the fixed-income group.

Newspaper cartoons sometimes suggest that everyone—or at least the average John Q. Public—loses during inflation. This cannot be, since inflation changes the prices of output not the quantity (with few exceptions, quantity of output rises during periods of inflation). What anyone loses, someone else must gain.

The poor gain when unemployment rates are cut by high aggregate demand, but the poor lose from rising prices caused by that same high aggregate demand. What is the net effect on the poor? Have the poor more or less to fear from inflation than have other groups?

In a recent study of the impact of inflation on the poor, the authors conclude:

that price rises have hurt the poor *less* than the non-poor . . . the benefits of tight labor markets which normally accompany inflationary pressures are very important to the poor . . . the gains to the poor from tight labor markets go beyond those strictly related to lower unemployment . . . the poor gain relatively *more* than other groups probably because of increases in hours worked and narrowing of wage differentials. Public transfer payments . . . have risen more than . . . the rise in the Consumer Price Index . . . The assets of the poor are found to be small in total value . . . thus negative wealth effects of inflation are extremely small . . . while the "tax of inflation" does not fall heavily on the poor, it is clear that the "tax of unemployment" which is likely to result from anti-inflationary policies does indeed fall very heavily on the poor . . . this study indicates that the cure for inflation is likely to impose a far heavier burden on the poor than does inflation itself.[3]

The poor do gain from high aggregate demand and low unem-

---

[3] R. G. Hollister, J. L. Palmer, "The Impact of Inflation on the Poor," multilith, Institute for Research on Poverty, University of Wisconsin, Madison, 1969, pp. i-ii.

ployment. But if the statistics shown in Figure 9-1 can be believed, low unemployment is inevitably associated with rapidly rising prices. Can these statistics be believed?

C. *The Statistics*

The Census Bureau's unemployment statistics accurately measure unemployment as defined by the bureau. Some critics argue that additional people should be counted among the unemployed; other critics argue that some people now counted as unemployed should be excluded from the count. Inclusions or exclusions of this kind would not affect Figure 9-1 beyond shifting the dots and curve a bit to the left or the right.

The GNP price index may show an upward bias because of failure to allow adequately for improvements in quality. When automobile tire life is increased from 15 to 30 thousand miles, a change in single-tire price from $25 to $50 would not represent any increase in tire-mileage price. The Bureau of Labor Statistics collects prices per tire and makes some allowances for quality change, but critics assert that these allowances do not adjust fully for quality improvements so that, should there be a case like the one just described, the GNP price index would show—incorrectly —some increase in tire-mileage prices.

Sellers of medical services have complained that price-index calculations have made inadequate allowances for quality improvements. Between 1950 and summer 1970, the GNP price index rose 56%, and the medical care portion of the price index rose 126%. No one believes that a 1970 appendectomy and a 1950 appendectomy are the same product, but statisticians are hard put to determine how much of the higher price of the 1970 appendectomy is the result of higher quality and how much is because of price inflation.

Both the unemployment and the price-index statistics are widely accepted. One can safely assume that both are imperfect; beyond that, the degree of doubt is a matter of opinion.

D. *Why the Dilemma?*

Why do price averages rise when unemployment rates are below 7%? One reason may be that the price index overstates price increases. A second reason is employer reluctance to hire able members of minority groups except when labor costs are rising. A third reason is labor immobility that leads to a bidding up, first, of wages and, then, of product prices when businesses seek to attract particular kinds of employees away from other employers or other areas. A fourth reason is the monopoly power possessed and used by some businesses and some unions; one thinks immediately of the brutal use of monopoly power by the plumbers' and electricians' unions. A fifth reason is the post-World War II custom that manufacturers do not cut prices when their productivity goes up. Instead, they use the fruits of higher productivity to increase the income of their laborers, managers, and owners; service industries, which have fewer and smaller increases in productivity, have responded by raising prices to approach the increases in income that manufacturing labor, management, and stockholders receive from rising productivity. If Kennedy's wage-price guideposts, described in the next section, were followed, this fifth reason would no longer apply.

E. *Easing the Dilemma*

The Figure 9-1 line showing unemployment level-price change relationships applies to post-World War II America. The location of that line is not unchangeable. It could move farther left or farther right; it could become steeper; it could flatten out.

If institutional conditions were to change so that the line passed through point *X*, then America could experience price stability and low unemployment simultaneously. Improvements in the education of the least-educated portion of the labor force, improvements in labor-force knowledge of work opportunities, improvements in geographic mobility, reductions in racial discrimination, and reductions in monopoly power would move the line farther to the left.

In an attempt to move the line to the left, the Council of Economic Advisers, in 1962, urged labor and management to observe "wage-price guideposts." The general guidepost for wages was the premise that the annual rate of increase of total employee compensation (wages *and* fringe benefits) per man-hour worked should equal the 3.2% national trend in rate of increase in man-hour output. The guidepost for prices carried a different instruction for each of three kinds of firms.

1. In firms where output per man-hour rises 3.2% a year, prices should be held *constant* while profits, salaries, and wages rise 3.2%.

2. In firms where output per man-hour rises more than 3.2%— for example, chemicals—wages, salaries, and profits should rise only 3.2%,[4] while the rest of the increase in productivity is passed along to buyers in *lower* prices.

3. In firms where output per man-hour rises less than 3.2% a year—for example, medical services—prices are to *rise* just enough to permit profits, salaries, and wages to rise 3.2%.

The guideposts admitted a host of exceptions regarding growth industries and declining industries but would have resulted, in general, in an across-the-board increase of 3.2% a year in wages and salaries, the average annual increase in labor's productivity, while average prices remained perfectly level even at low levels of unemployment. Roughly, this *is* the way American firms did behave during the 1920s.

No one expected the guideposts to yield that neat an outcome, but they may have edged the line of Figure 9-1 a little to the left. The Nixon Administration explicitly renounced the guideposts and adopted programs of restrictive monetary-fiscal policy to move the nation to the right in Figure 9-1 to an unemployment rate above 5% and to less rapidly rising prices.

F. *Where Should We Be?*

Where should we be in terms of Figure 9-1? To the right or left? Weighing the merits of left and right, one astute commentator observed:

From a welfare standpoint, one also remembers the probable upward bias of measured price indexes. Very possibly the average price rise of 1.5 per cent in 1958-1963 was matched by or even exceeded by improvements in product quality, so that the value of money did not decline. This assumption would greatly improve the outlook for reconciling full employment with stability in the value of money. Some economists argue in favor of a more vigorously expansionary policy even if the price level does rise more. They feel the harm done to

---

[4] These wage and salary increases are across the board and are separate from increases associated with movement up the escalator of responsibility as older men retire and are replaced by promotion from below.

the unemployed by unemployment is at least as great as the harm done by inflation to those who actually lose by it. And they note that a more expansionary policy means more total output, benefiting many more people than those who might be unemployed. There seems little doubt, however, that American public opinion tends to react strongly against price increases when they pass (roughly) the 3 per cent level. This was apparent in the political campaign of 1952, for example. Such an attitude may reflect an incomplete balancing of burdens and benefits, but it cannot be ignored.[5]

The farther the nation moves to the right, in terms of Figure 9-1, the higher will be the incidence of American poverty; the farther left, the lower the incidence of poverty. Each individual must decide for himself. Where should we be?[6]

IV. GOVERNMENT SPENDING TO RAISE THE PRODUCTIVITY OF THE POOR

By spending more, government can earn a "social profit" for the nation whenever the marginal social benefit of an additional expenditure exceeds the marginal social cost. Policy making is controversial because the values of social cost and of social benefit are subjective. The following issues invite personal judgments concerning the value of marginal social costs and of marginal social benefits.

A. *Moving Workers to Jobs and Jobs to Workers*

In Sweden, an unemployed worker in the far north can obtain government financing to move himself, his family, and his household effects to the south of Sweden if there is a job for him there. America might expand the experimental programs now in operation to move the unemployed and their dependents: the people from Appalachia, the Ozarks, the rural South or other areas. Should government funds be used for this purpose? If so, should grants as well as loans be used?

---

[5] Paul B. Trescott, *Money, Banking, and Economic Welfare,* 2nd ed., McGraw-Hill, New York, 1965, pp. 171-172.
[6] For a more detailed analysis of the relationships between aggregate demand and prices, see Arnold Collery, *National Income and Employment Analysis,* 2nd ed., in this John Wiley series.

During the early 1960s, the Federal Area Redevelopment Administration subsidized plant construction and expansion in areas of high unemployment. Should more government money be used to move capital to labor?

First the Southern states and, more recently, Northern and Western states have created "socialized" state banks to make government subsidized loans to attract manufacturers from other states. Sometimes, the state-subsidized (or city-subsidized) plant locates in an area of high unemployment, sometimes not. "Conservative" state governors have played up these subsidizing programs and, in their campaign literature, have stressed the number of firms they have subsidized through state-owned banks.

Should governments, federal, state, or local, provide money to help selected communities expand old plants or obtain new plants? In nearly every case, the new production facility, obtained with government help, would have been built elsewhere in the absence of government intervention. If the new plant had been built elsewhere, the unemployed of the poor community *could* have moved to the other location—although they might have been reluctant to do so. Should the governor of a state or the director of a federal agency be allowed to use public money to divert production facilities to the places that he favors?

The Watts riots called nationwide attention to an urban area of many square miles that lacked any means of public transportation. The Watts situation appeared to typify a developing big-city pattern in which public transportation is arranged to connect the middle-class suburbs with the central-city mercantile and industrial centers, while it leaves the inner-city low-income areas without transportation with the exception of private automobiles or walking.

It is not enough for a man to be able to do a job, nor is it enough for him to know of a job that he can do—he must be able to get to the job. In many big cities, direct bus routes from the black ghettos to factories cannot cover costs. Should government subsidize these routes? Most of the middle class go to work by car (usually one person to a gasoline-burning car) on roads built with government money. Would the social benefits of subsidized public transportation between the poor and jobs exceed the social costs in a particular case?

B. *Permitting Mothers to Enter the Labor Force*

In the spring of 1970, the federal government was providing full or partial financing for day-care facilities for more than 600,000 children under various War on Poverty programs. These day-care facilities permit a woman to leave her preschool children in institutional care while she takes a job as a supplementary income earner or as the sole source of earned income for her family. In 1969, there were 4.2 million working mothers with preschool children; in 1960, there were 2.9 million. Head Start programs last all day and permit mothers of 3- to 5-year-olds to work if they want to do so. But even mothers of Head Start children are not free to work if they have children too young for Head Start and if no child-care agency is available for the younger children. Mothers may not choose to work if the only available child-care center is a private agency that charges so much that the woman's earned income net of travel, special clothing, and a child-care fee is less than AFDC. Quality full-time day care for preschoolers cost about $1600 a year in 1970.

Are day-care centers a desirable arrangement? Is it better (1) to have mothers home with their children although in poverty even with transfer income, (2) to have the mothers home with their children and receiving from the nonpoor the transfers that raise them out of poverty, or (3) to separate the mothers from their small children 2 or 4 or 8 hours a day while the mothers work and the children remain in institutional care? More narrowly, should government money be spent to operate day-care centers that give mothers a choice?

C. *Government as Employer of Last Resort*

During the Great Depression of the 1930s, the Public Works Administration (PWA), the Works Progress Agency (WPA), and the Civilian Conservation Corps (CCC) provided jobs for up to 3 million people a year. With one fifth to one seventh of the labor force unemployed, the federal government acted as employer of last resort for a fraction of the labor force that was unable to find other employment.

In 1966, the National Commission on Technology, Automation, and Economic Progress recommended that the federal government serve as employer of last resort and employ those who seek work but who are unable to obtain any other jobs.[7]

Garth Mangum has essayed a careful and lively analysis of the proposal and suggests that the potential clientele in 1966 would have been the following numbers:

Unemployed more than 26 weeks	840,000
Unemployed continuously, 15 to 26 weeks	295,000
Males 25 to 49 years of age, out of labor force but able to work	500,000
Involuntary part-time who usually work full-time (nonagriculture)	1,183,000
	2,818,000

Mangum estimates that $1.50 an hour for this number plus likely overhead cost would run to a total of $12 billion a year.[8]

Mangum suggests the following kinds of work that might be done in such a program:

> Conservation,
> Two mail deliveries a day,
> Cleaning and repairing public buildings, streets,
>   parks, and neighborhoods.

Some War on Poverty Programs have involved small employer-of-last-resort features. Should the federal government act as employer of last resort? If not for a wide clientele, should it act thus for a subgroup, for example, for heads of families in the categories listed by Mangum above?

An alternative but closely related arrangement would be for the federal government to subsidize private employment of the people Mangum listed. Should the federal government do this?

D. *More Human Capital for Children*

In the United States, most children of poor families attend schools that are inferior in teachers, buildings, equipment, and

---

[7] *Technology and the American Economy*, U.S. G.P.O., Washington, D.C., Feb. 1966, pp. 35-37 and 110.

[8] "Government as Employer of Last Resort," in *Towards Freedom from Want*, Levitan, Cohen, Lampman, eds., Industrial Relations Research Association, Madison, Wisconsin, 1968, pp. 135-161.

course variety in comparison to the schools attended by the children of nonpoor families. Public policy may react to this difference in one of three ways:

1. The difference can be maintained.
2. The schools can be "equalized" so the schools of the children of the poor add as much to the Intelligence C of their children as the schools of the children of the nonpoor add to the Intelligence C of their children.
3. The schools can equalize total education by compensating for educational defects of home and neighborhood so that the poor child and the nonpoor child of equal Intelligence B both rise to the same Intelligence C.

Exactly what Choice 2 would mean in actual programs is not certain. It might mean the same number of dollars spent on the education of every child. Its intent would be that the public school educational effect would be the same for every child; but home and neighborhood environments would contribute less to the Intelligence C of the poor than to the Intelligence C of the nonpoor. A nonpoor child would attain a higher Intelligence C than would a poor child of equal Intelligence B if Choice 2 were implemented.

Which of the three choices *should* be adopted by the United States? The 1965 Congress committed itself to helping children from poor families to "catch up" in Intelligence C with nonpoor children of equal Intelligence B. But congressional help in this direction has been modest; by and large, the same people continue to teach in schools attended by the poor.

Since America is a federation, Choice 2 or Choice 3 can be adopted for a part of the nation. Should Choice 2 or 3, if adopted, apply just within each school district? Or each metropolitan area? Or each state? Or the entire nation?

In generation after generation, children of the poor have grown up to become not poor by exercising their inherited high Intelligence A. Perhaps, we have now reached a stage where the poor are those who had "reasonable" opportunities but who remained poor because of limited Intelligence A, which limitations they tend to pass on to their children.

In this respect, there may be a great difference between blacks and whites and between majority-group whites and the members of other minorities. It may be that whites who are poor are poor because low Intelligence A led them to fail despite ample educational and employment opportunities. Blacks and other minorities are in a much different position. Relatively few have had an equal chance either in school or in the job market. Thus, poverty comes to some blacks because of low Intelligence A and to other blacks because of discrimination and in spite of high Intelligence A and high Intelligence B. If these generalizations are true, children of the white poor, on average, will have lower Intelligence A than the children of the black poor. And, if the differences in Intelligence B are not too unlike the differences in Intelligence A, a dollar spent educating poor black children will yield higher returns than a dollar spent educating poor white children. If these assumptions are correct, *should* more money per child be put into the schools of the black poor than into the schools of the white poor?

Kenneth Clark and others[9] have argued that schools for children from poor families, especially for children from poor minority-group families are inferior because of the following reasons:

1. Their majority-group white teachers do not expect the children to learn.

2. Their majority-group white school administrators do not expect the teachers to teach.

3. The teachers suffer no penalties when the children do not learn.

To counteract these conditions, the salary in teachers' renewal contracts could be determined by the *percentage* of increase in average scores on standardized tests taken by their students at the beginning, the middle, and the end of the school year. The percentage rule would mean that students rising 5 points from a score of 50 to a score of 55 would justify a salary increase equal to that justified by a rise of 10 points between scores of 100 and 110 points. Thus, the system might work with slow classes as well as with faster classes. Teachers convinced that they would

---

[9] *Dark Ghetto,* Harper & Row, N.Y., 1965, pp. 132-139.

not receive pay raises because their prospective students were "unteachable" would elect out of the schools and might be replaced by teachers who could and would teach. Should teachers be paid in proportion to their accomplishments? Should the system suggested here be used to elicit better teaching in the schools that are attended by the children of poor families? Should some other system be used that would be more effective in reaching that objective?

E. *More Human Capital for Adults*

Adult education was once an exclusively private affair. It no longer is. Many school districts offer adult-education courses. Some districts charge fees high enough to cover all operating expenses; some levy only nominal charges and pay other expenses from school tax receipts. States now provide funds for adult-training programs. In the Manpower Development and Training Act and in the Adult Education Act of 1966, the federal government undertook to finance adult education. How much adult education and training *should* government taxes provide? Which levels of government, if any, should participate?

Every school district offers twelve years of free schooling. How much more *should* government provide? Every state subsidizes four additional years of school for those who care to go to college. Furthermore, parents who send their children beyond college to professional school (for example, to a law school) can do so at public expense by sending their children to a state university. There is no "need" test; any family choosing this route is able to benefit by having the powerful state tax all citizens—poor as well as nonpoor—to obtain the funds used to subsidize their sons' or daughters' advanced specialized education.

Lee Hansen and Burton Weisbrod examined the value of the subsidies going to students in California public colleges and universities in 1964.[10] They reported a subsidy of $1700 a year to students in the University of California. That would be $6800 over four years. They did not calculate graduate education sub-

---

[10] "The Distribution of Costs and Direct Benefits of Public Higher Education: the Case of California," *The Journal of Human Resources*, Vol. IV, No. 2.

sidies; but if a guess of a $3000-a-year subsidy to law students is accurate, the son of a $35,000-a-year lawyer going through seven years of the University of California undergraduate and law-school program would receive a subsidy of more than $12,000 taxed from the poor and nonpoor of California.

Should a state do this? There is no issue; all states do, and there is no criticism. Having taxed the poor to help pay the educational costs of advanced degrees for the nonpoor, *should* a state, school district, city or federal government tax the nonpoor to provide testing, counseling, education, and training for adults who are poor but who are neither qualified for nor interested in a state-run college or professional school? An alternative having the same implications for equity would be to reduce state taxes and to end state tax support for colleges and professional schools. Should tax subsidies for the education of 19-, 20-, and 25-year-old offspring of the nonpoor be ended? Or reduced?

In March of 1970, President Nixon urged new research initiatives to identify the factors essential for good education. How much should be spent on efforts of this kind?

We do know that the character of the teacher makes a great difference in the learning of the student, adult, adolescent, or juvenile. What will happen to those most able as teachers in the generation that reads this book? Will they teach? Will they teach where their teaching can be most effective? Or will they take up other occupations and leave the teaching to persons less qualified than they would be?

V. ZERO POPULATION GROWTH?

In 1968, the SSA criteria counted 10.7 million children in poor families. Of the 10.7 million about 4.5 million lived in homes with 5 or more other children. Almost 40% of the 10.7 million lived in families in which the family head worked full time all year during 1968. These family heads combined low employment productivity with high reproductivity. Adults held jobs but, with low productivity, they produced and earned little. Given low productivity—or unemployment—families already poor can avoid more severe poverty by practicing birth control. The potentially poor can escape poverty altogether by restricting the growth of their families. In the summer of 1970, the Senate authorized a $1 billion program to acquaint the poor with birth control and to provide contraceptive devices to anyone who wants them.

The arithmetic and economics of birth control as a means of reducing poverty are straightforward. The moral issues remain. Should governments provide birth control information and devices to the poor who request them? Should governments provide this information and these devices to unmarried women? Should governments advertise to encourage the poor to practice birth control? The answers to these questions will affect a majority of the poor in the United States. If the answer in each instance is "no," what alternative policies are appropriate?

In all states except Hawaii and New York abortion is not a question left to women and doctors; instead, male legislators have used state power to impose restrictions on women. Thus far, women have allowed the laws to remain and have gone in large numbers to back-room abortionists. Oregon's Senator Robert Packwood has advocated repeal of all state laws restricting pregnant women's freedom-of-choice and has proposed legislation to legalize abortion in the District of Columbia. Should states restrict abortion?

Senator Packwood has also advocated a change in the customary so-much-per-each-child income tax exemption—now $600. He suggests a $1000 deduction for the first child, $750 for the second, $500 for the third, and $0 for any other children. This proposal, if adopted, would raise taxes for people with many children and might discourage new pregnancies among poor women. Should such a change be made?

VI. MINIMUM WAGE LAWS

Given a less than perfectly inelastic demand for labor and given a perfectly elastic (competitive) supply of labor, any minimum wage law that raises wages will reduce employment. (Haveman and Knopf explore the situation in which an employer is a monopsonist, that is, the supply of labor slopes up to the right, and a minimum wage law can induce an increase in employment.[11]) People drawing a minimum wage may be poor; people laid off because of a minimum wage may become poorer—or they may become better off if they become eligible for welfare assistance denied them—in any amount—while they worked.

The effects of minimum wages still are not clear. Attempts to observe them have been frustrated by the effects of other ongoing changes in the economy. Jacob Kaufman and Terry Foran recently reviewed the work of others and summarized it as follows:

The conclusions of this paper—which, it must be stressed, are not all conclusive—are:

1. Minimum wages raise the wages of workers.

2. Minimum wages create adverse employment effects, but there is no strong evidence that this unemployment is unequally distributed toward the "disadvantaged" groups in society.

3. Minimum wages may very well have the effect of redistributing income in favor of labor, thus creating a tendency toward less inequality in the personal distribution of income.[12]

Minimum wage legislation is a perennial congressional issue. Should the federal minimum wage be raised? Lowered? Eliminated?

Since 1962, teen-age unemployment has been five times the adult unemployment rate. Between 1948 and 1962, the ratio was three to one. In March 1970, a Labor Department study reported that a differential between youth and adults in federal minimum wage would reduce teen-age unemployment. During the 1960s, the teen-age population grew 40%; during the 1970s it will grow only 12%; hence, the five-to-one ratio may fall back toward three-to-one as the years pass. In the meantime, should the minimum for persons below 21 be cut below $1.60? Should their rate be left at $1.60 while the minimum for persons 21 and over is raised above $1.60?

---

[11] *The Market System,* John Wiley & Sons, N.Y., 1970.
[12] The authors explain the basis for these conclusions in "The Minimum Wage and Poverty," in *Towards Freedom from Want,* Levitan, Cohen, Lampman, eds., Industrial Relations Research Association, Madison, Wisconsin, 1968, pp. 189-218.

VII. TAX REVISIONS TO BENEFIT
THE WORKING POOR

The Packwood tax proposal might induce the working poor to limit family growth. Other tax proposals would raise the after-tax income of the working poor.

Chapter 7 noted that sales-excise and property taxes take a larger portion of the income of the poor than of the income of the nonpoor. Assuming a constant total tax collection, it follows that a decrease in the portion of the total collection coming from income taxes and an increase in the portion coming from other taxes means an increase in the share of taxes paid by the poor and a reduction in the share paid by the nonpoor. This issue is often faced in cities and in state legislatures when income taxes are proposed. What should be done? Should there be lower income taxes and higher other taxes to shift the tax burden somewhat from the nonpoor to the poor?

With the exceptions noted previously, the American public welfare payments rule has been that when a welfare beneficiary earns a dollar, he or she loses a dollar in welfare benefits. By taking a job, welfare recipients may receive zero extra income. Welfare beneficiaries who take full-time jobs generally lose all welfare assistance. Leonard Housman examined the earning potential of unemployed heads of families who received AFDC assistance in 1965 and concluded that 73% of the female-heads of AFDC assisted families and 41% of the male-heads of AFDC assisted families possessed such low Intelligence C that their income from full-time work would have been less than their AFDC income.[13] When those people take jobs, the "tax" on their earned income is over 100% when their earned income is less than their AFDC income would have been.

As pointed out in Chapter 7, for every dollar transfer in welfare assistance, 16 cents is spent on administration devoted not to helping raise the productivity of persons assisted nor even to

---

[13] Christopher Green, "Income Security through a Tax-Transfer System," *Towards Freedom from Want*, Levitan, Cohen, Lampman, eds., Industrial Relations Research Association, Madison, Wisconsin, 1968, p. 173.

alleviating their personal problems but, instead, is devoted to the determination of eligibility for the several categories of assistance. Other programs might cost less and help the poor more.

A negative income tax has been proposed as a low-cost means to provide assistance to all in need—not just to those in specified need categories (for example, blind, disabled, dependent children) —and to provide work incentives, or more precisely, to remove welfare-program work disincentives. Negative income tax proposals vary in detail as among proponents. The proposal of James Tobin is representative and is shown in Table 9-1. Tobin proposes that the federal government pay each family $400 for every person in the family and impose a 33 1/3% tax on all of the other money income of the family.

Table 9-1. Negative Income Tax of the James Tobin Type

Family Income Before Income Supplement (Dollars)	Size of Family				
	1	2	3	4	5
	Income Supplement Family Is Entitled to (Dollars);				
0	400	800	1200	1600	2000
600	200	600	1000	1400	1800
1200	0	400	800	1200	1600
1800		200	600	1000	1400
2400		0	400	800	1200
3000			200	600	1000

Source: Christopher Green, "Income Security through a Tax-Transfer System," *Towards Freedom from Want,* Levitan, Cohen, Lampman, eds., Industrial Relations Research Association, Madison, Wisconsin, 1968, p. 165.

Such a program would be much easier to administer than the existing welfare programs; only two questions must be answered (asking for the answers would take more than two questions):

1. How many people in your family?
2. How much money income does your family receive?

The work disincentives of the present welfare programs would be replaced by the work incentive that of every extra $3 earned, the earner would add $2 to his net income.

The tax rate can be higher or lower and the basic per-person income supplement can be higher or lower than in Table 9-1 without changing the basic scheme. The higher the per-person income supplement, the more people who would be included—and the more expensive the program; the higher the tax rate, the lower the program cost, but the smaller the work incentive.

The negative income tax proposal may appear less unorthodox if one thinks of the present federal income tax in the following ways:

1. It places a percentage tax on income without dependent exemptions.

2. It provides a federal payment of so much per dependent.

Viewed in this way, a five-person family with a marginal tax rate of 25% pays $2,500 to the government on its $10,000 net income *without* dependent exemptions while it receives $150 per dependent (25% of the $600 exemption), $750, from the government. In effect, this is what *is* done except that the tax payment and government $150-per-dependent payment are netted when the tax return is completed; and only the final net $1750 changes hands. The special feature of the existing system is that the $150 per dependent only goes to people with taxable income of $600 per dependent. A five-person family with a $50,000 or a $5000 taxable income benefits from each $600 dependent exemption. A five-person family with a $1000 income does not.

A negative income tax would expand the coverage of welfare benefits to all persons in "need" as defined by the tax law. Both the "needy" unemployed and the "needy" employed would benefit, and work incentives would be increased. Should a negative income tax be introduced to supplement the present welfare system? Should a negative income tax be introduced to replace the present welfare system?[14]

VIII. RACIAL DISCRIMINATON

Legislation restricting the practice of racial discrimination expands the range of action, the freedom, of some people while

---

[14] For more details about negative income tax proposals see either Green, *op. cit.,* pp. 162-188, or Martin David and Jane Leuthold, "Formulas for Income Maintenance: Their Distributional Impact," *National Tax Journal,* Vol. XXI, No. 1, March 1968.

it reduces the range of action, the freedom, of other people. Some white American managers dislike blacks and refuse to hire, train, or promote black Americans even when this refusal reduces the firm's profits. These discriminating whites lose some of their freedom of choice when legislation compels them to hire on the basis of present and prospective Intelligence C rather than on the basis of race.

There are white union members who dislike blacks and who wish to exclude blacks from their unions and from their line of work. These union members lose some of their freedom of choice when legislation forbids them from excluding blacks.

There are white school board members who dislike blacks and who allocate more money per white pupil than per black pupil. These whites lose some of their freedom of choice when legislation forbids them from discriminating in the appropriation of public funds.

There are white parents who dislike blacks and who prefer to have their children bussed longer distances rather than have their children attend school with blacks in schools nearer home. Southern "segregation academies" are now bussing more of their students, and are bussing them farther than are public schools in the South. Whites lose some of their freedom of choice when legislation (the Constitution) forbids bussing to achieve segregation.

Some white parents want local schools that segregate whites and blacks in conformance with housing segregation. These parents lose some of their freedom of choice when legislation compels them to accept schools that bus children—white and black—from other residential areas.

Some whites prefer to exclude blacks from their residential areas (when the California legislature passed an open housing law, realtors placed a repeal constitutional amendment on the ballot, and California voted two to one for discrimination although leaders in both parties and most church leaders vigorously opposed repeal of the open housing law). When legislation forbids housing discrimination, most whites lose some of their freedom of choice.

Blacks and members of other minority groups gain freedom of choice when legislation forbids discrimination by employers,

unions, school boards, and realtors. W
choice, blacks can acquire additional physica
and can make more productive use of their Intelligc.
Should the federal government forbid racial discriminati
the market? Should the federal government cancel contracts with
firms that discriminate? Should the federal government cancel
contracts with firms that do not take "affirmative action" to employ and train members of disadvantaged minority groups?
Should the federal government cancel contracts with firms that
fail to employ blacks at all levels in the proportion in which
blacks are represented in the local population?

Blacks pay 10 to 25% more than majority-group whites for
urban housing of any given quality. The difference is not a result
of conspiratorial landlord greed. Instead, it results from white
prejudice that limits the number of urban houses and apartments
available to blacks. Whites may buy or rent any house or apartment in town (if they can afford it). Blacks have access to only
a portion of the houses and apartments in each American city.
Consequently, they bid up prices and rents in their ghetto areas,
and black dollars become second-class money, which buys less
housing, dollar for dollar, than white dollars buy.

Effective "fair housing" legislation would expand the portion of
urban residential housing available to minority groups; it would
reduce minority-group housing costs, thereby reducing the second-class value of minority-group dollars. This legislation would
expand the freedom of minority groups; it would curb the freedom of the many majority-group whites who very much want to
discriminate against minority groups in housing. Is such legislation desirable?

Black Intelligence C lags behind white Intelligence C and
will continue to do so on average for a number of decades because so many adult blacks were limited to the $6.67 a year
educations that were the Southern Way of Life and because so
many blacks have been and are now in the nonteaching schools
in Boston (as described by Jonathan Kozol) and other cities. One
way to accelerate black catching-up is to mix black poor and
white nonpoor children from the first grade on. If the education
of white children is somewhat less in these circumstances than
it would otherwise be, should such mixing be the objective of

VIII. Racial Discrimination of
With this added freedom of ... and human capital
...tion in
223

...NG
WORK

... the policy issues raised have referred to
...diately or potentially work to reduce their
... share in the earned income of others. In this
... policy issues considered refer to persons who are
le.... ...o work or to share directly in the income of other
work ...eople.

Three categories of people have been considered in this book:

1. Those who can escape poverty through their work or the work of people who share with them.

2. Those who can escape poverty or who can have their poverty alleviated only by transfers from the nonpoor.

3. Those who can alleviate but not escape poverty through their own work or the work of others sharing with them.

This section deals principally with policy issues formulated in terms of people in the second group, but most of the transfer payments also can affect people in the third group.

The first question is: Should there be any government transfer payments at all? The availability of government transfers does lead some people to work less than they would otherwise; the higher general relief payments are (relative to the consumer price index) and the easier that it is to obtain general relief, the greater will be the number of people who choose relief over work.[15] The work disincentives of transfers can be reduced but never fully eliminated.

The poverty gap discussed earlier showed that if Americans poor in 1968 had received an additional $9.8 billion in income distributed in a way that would have lifted all of them to their pov-

---

[15] Carl T. Brehm and T. R. Saving, "The Demand for General Assistance Payments," *The American Economic Review,* December 1964, pp. 1002-1018.

erty thresholds, America would have had zero poverty in 1968. Since America's GNP was $866 billion in 1968, an additional transfer of $9.8 billion from nonpoor to poor might appear a not unreasonable price to pay to wipe out poverty.

But if every low-income person were assured a poverty threshold income whether he worked or not, how many of the working poor would stop working? If a working family earned an income $500 above the poverty-threshold transfer income of the unemployed but otherwise identical family next door, would the working family stop working, give up the $500 gross extra (working does require extra expenses; so the net difference would be less than $500), and settle for the poverty-threshold transfer income? How many similarly situated working families would stop working? The arithmetic can be only an educated estimate at best, but Robert Lampman has estimated that the poverty gap of 1966 could not be closed for less than $20 billion and might cost as much as $30 billion in transfers.[16] Less costly changes would reduce the gap; or one might prefer changes that would increase it.

A. *Tax Forgiveness for the Elderly*

Property taxes assume a positive correlation between property value and current-income ability to pay. Elderly people often own their homes but have small current incomes. Property taxes are, therefore, an exceptionally heavy burden on their current incomes. Since most states force their schools to depend in large part on property taxes, elderly people are taxed far more heavily for school support than they would be if the same school revenues were obtained from income taxes.

Several states (California, Minnesota, Oregon, and Wisconsin) have granted a degree of property tax exemption to the elderly. The exemptions are in each state greater the lower the household's current income. In effect, these states transfer a property tax refund to the aged poor. What has been the effect of these refund transfers?

Yung-Ping Chen has studied those effects and the general problem of the property tax burden on the aged more thoroughly than has anyone else. He concludes:

---

[16] Cited by Green, *op. cit.*, p. 170.

. . . the average amount of financial assistance (tax saving) to elderly householders is relatively minor even though it represents a sizeable portion of their average income. . . . I believe that increment of income instead of decrement in taxes should be a preferred approach. Although tax reductions result in income increment, the increase is usually rather small.[17]

Chen found the average property tax on the aged poor to be $200 to $225 and average relief to be $150 to $175. Should other states grant property tax relief to their elderly poor?

B. *Federalizing Welfare Programs*

The present welfare system is comprised of a separate program for each state and the District of Columbia. Each jurisdiction sets its own payment schedules (for example, Alabama's $62, New York's $260 a month AFDC for a family of four). Congress could change the state system into a federal system by establishing federal standards for the nation (cost-of-living differences could be allowed for in the benefit schedules). Should the benefits be the same (apart from cost-of-living differences) in every part of the country?

C. *The Family Assistance Program*

In August of 1969, President Nixon proposed that AFDC be replaced by a Family Assistance Program that would provide a $1600-a-year federal transfer to a four-person family with less than $720 a year in income from other sources. To provide recipients with a work incentive, President Nixon announced that the program was designed to reduce the federal transfer by only $1 for every $2 received in excess of $720 from other sources. During the summer of 1970, Congressional probing revealed flaws in the program that would reduce the federal transfer by $1.60 for every $2 received in excess of $720 from other sources. Put differently, this meant a very small work incentive in that a recipient's total income (after social security, income, and federal

---

[17] "Burden and Relief of Property Taxes on the Aged: Some Notes," *Economics of Aging: Toward a Full Share in Abundance, Hearings, Special Senate Committee on Aging*, part 4, *Homeownership Aspects*, July 31— August 1, 1969, 91st to 1st, G.P.O., Washington, D.C., 1970.

medical insurance taxes) would increase only 20 cents for every dollar earned. In August of 1970, one could not tell whether or not the bill would be passed by the Senate in 1970, with or without major revisions.

In the original proposal, the benefit rate would be $500 for each of the first two family members and $300 for each additional member. The Family Assistance Program would apply to families with children but would include many more people than AFDC now helps, because families with working men could be helped. In families that received benefits, all adults would be required to register with a public employment office except the mothers of preschool children and the mothers in households where fathers were registered. The Family Assistance Program would add about $4 billion to present welfare costs. Eligible households would benefit from the cash transfers and from an expanded food stamp program.

Beneficiaries would not receive the same transfers in every state. If adopted, the Family Assistance Program would bring eight Southern states up from below the proposed minima. The other 42 states above the minima would not be allowed to cut rates.

The Family Assistance Program would apply to families with children. Other portions of President Nixon's "welfare reform" proposals would reduce interstate differences in the size of benefit payments to the aged, blind, and disabled.

The program's proponents emphasized welfare reform. Technically, the program is a negative income tax, and it would help both those incapable of earning anything and those capable of earning themselves part of the way out of poverty. Should such legislation be passed?

X. SUMMARY

Many programs exist to heal or to alleviate poverty. These programs use tens of billions of dollars each year. Many new programs are being proposed. The old programs are not necessarily good just because they exist. The new proposals are not necessarily bad just because they have not been tried. The old programs can be abolished, expanded, or cut back. The proposals for new programs can be accepted in whole or in part, can be modified, or can be rejected. To maximize social welfare, old programs can be cut back and new programs can be expanded until marginal social cost just equals marginal social benefits.

This chapter has considered a series of political issues that will be resolved by votes based on individual value judgments. All of these issues involve choices that will give more to some at the expense of others. For example, with regard to price movements, creditors and the fixed income group can benefit from falling prices while debtors and the variable income group lose—or vice versa, but all cannot gain at the same time (except from the effects of overall expansion). As regards price movements *and* unemployment, creditors and the fixed income group can benefit from falling prices only when debtors and the variable income group lose.

Gain for some means losses for others following other policy choices. More freedom for blacks to be employed, trained, and promoted on the basis of ability means less freedom for whites to discriminate. Education that permits children in poor neighborhoods to catch up with children in nonpoor neighborhoods benefits the former by reducing the relative advantages of the latter. Increased transfers to the poor leave less for the nonpoor. Even birth control that prevents the birth of unwanted children reduces the freedom of those who would use government power to keep others from practicing birth control.

This chapter has surveyed areas of conflict. It has not suggested solutions. Honest, intelligent, informed individuals will disagree on each issue raised. Each individual must decide on the basis of his own set of values.

XI. CONCLUSION

Most of the people in the world are poor. Most Americans are not because technology and the quantities of natural resources and human and physical capital controlled by Americans have raised the average product of American labor to a height unprecedented anywhere in the world. Over past centuries, over recent decades, the changes that have raised the average product curve of American labor have reduced the incidence of poverty in America. Over forthcoming decades further changes in those same factors will raise the average product curve of American labor still higher and—if population growth is not too rapid—will further reduce the incidence of American poverty. Recessions of the kind used during 1969 to 1970 to reduce the rate of price increases interrupt but do not change the direction of the long-run trend.

The fundamental principle underlying the division of American output is: "To each in proportion to his contribution to production." America's poor are in large part those who contribute little to production either because they are incapable of contributing much or because insufficient aggregate demand, racial discrimination, or some other factor keeps them from making the productive contribution of which they are capable.

President Johnson's War on Poverty concentrated almost exclusively on programs that would raise the Intelligence C, the productive ability, of individuals. Few Americans born nonpoor become poor; the poverty question is: "How many born poor will acquire the Intelligence C required to work their way out of poverty?" The War on Poverty and a decade of falling unemployment rates have not eliminated poverty, even among those with the potentiality to work their way out of poverty, but the 1960s witnessed a sharp reduction in the incidence of poverty among those people. The 1960s also witnessed an increase in government-administered transfers from the nonpoor to the poor, and these increased transfers reduced the incidence of poverty among people unable to earn their way out of poverty.

A host of issues now require decisions that will affect the rate at which the incidence of poverty continues to fall in America (and in the world *if* population growth can be checked). Few of these issues are to be decided in terms of all or nothing. Maximum social benefits require conditions that equate marginal social costs (presumed to be rising) and marginal social benefits (presumed to be falling). Since the value of social costs and benefits are in large part in the eye of the beholder, preferences as to the degree to which any given proposal should be implemented—if at all—depend on the value system of each American.

Index

AALA, gap, 40-41
  world, 66, 68
Abel and Seth, anecdote of, 100-104
Abortion, 217
Achievement motivation, 90-92
Adult Education Act of 1966, 215
Afghanistan, 39, 45-46
AFL-CIO, 129, 191
Age, geographic movement and, 175
  poverty count and, 11-12, 19, 22, 27
Aged, asset data of, 9
  housing, 159
  medical care for, 147-148
  poverty among, 22, 25, 27-28, 98, 165
  tax forgiveness, 225-226
  transfer payments to, 139, 146-149,
    151, 153-154, 161, 164-165
Agee, James, and Evans, Walker, 85
Aggregate demand, 96-98, 101-102,
    104, 127-128, 171-173, 178, 187,
    205, 229
  as determinant of national income,
    50-53, 55
Agriculture, 28, 102-104, 142, 181, 184
  Senate Committee, 68, 156
  U.S. Department of, 19, 155, 156
    in South, 111-112
Agricultural extension agents, 111-112
Aid, to the Aged, 148-149, 151,
    153-154, 161
  to the Blind, 148, 153, 161
  to Dependent Children, 148-151,
    153, 161, 192-193, 211, 219,
    226-227
  to the Disabled, 148, 153, 161
American Federation of Labor discrim-

ination, 110
Appalachia, 57, 87, 89, 91, 176, 209
Appalachian Regional Development Act
    of 1965, 176
Apprenticeship, 187, 202
Aptitude tests, 174
Area Redevelopment Administration,
    175, 210
Assets, 8-10, 16, 205
Assistance, general, 160-161
Attitude toward work, 49-50
Average product of labor, 57-61,
    170-171, 178-195, 200, 228, 229

Bakunin, Mikhail A., 66-67
Beecher, Henry Ward, 108
Bigart Homer, 157-158
Birch, Herbert C., and Gussow, Joan
    Dye, 93-94
Birth control, 216-217
Black power, 130
Blacks, 57, 65, 106-133, 149, 151, 173,
    182, 187, 189, 200, 210, 213, 214,
    222-223
  farming, 24, 46
  poverty among, 23-24, 27-30, 107, 172
  see also Discrimination, Negroes,
    Nonwhites
Bornet, Vaughn Davis, 143-144
Borrowers, 204-205
Brehm, Carl, and Saving, T.R., 224n
Brenner, Joseph, 121-122
Brotherhood of Electrical Workers dis-
    crimination, 111
"Buddy system," 89-90, 191
Bussing, 222

Capital consumption, 34, 180
Census, Bureau of the, 4-5, 7, 9, 16-18, 51, 174, 206
Census information, 16-19
   questions, 17-18
Charitable agencies, 139-140
Charity, depersonalization of, 143-144
Chen, Yung Ping, 225-226
Child Nutrition Act of 1966, 158-159
Children, poverty among, 22-23, 27-28
Choate, Robert, 158n
Churches, 139-140, 142-143
Citizens' Board of Inquiry into Hunger and Malnutrition in the United States, 84, 122, 144
Civil Disorders, National Advisory Commission on, 116, 123
Civil Rights Commission, 111
Clark, Kenneth, 130, 214
Coles, Robert, 86-87, 125-126
Collery, Arnold, 52n, 209n
Commerce, U.S. Department of, 10, 36-37
Community Action Agencies, 193
Concentrated Employment Programs, 193
Conrod, Alfred H., and Meyer, John R., 109
Constitution of the United States, 16, 49, 222
Consumer price index, 202, 205
Contract Compliance, Defense Department Office of, 178
Council of Economic Advisers, 96-97, 207
Counseling, 216
Credit Accessibility, 10
Creditors, 204-205
Current Population Survey, 16-19, 21, 31

Day care, 177, 201, 211
Debtors, 204-205
Defense, U.S. Department of, 178, 187-188
Deflation, 203
Denison, Edward F., 50
Depressed area assistance, 176-177
Diminishing average returns, 58, 69, 194
Diminishing marginal returns, 69

Disabled persons, 98, 148, 153, 161
Discrimination, 28, 102, 106, 109-117, 129-132, 172, 177-178, 221-224
   statutory prohibition of, 178, 222-223, 229
Distribution, systems of, 65-72

Eastland, Senator James, 68-69
Economic Opportunity, Office of, 185
Economic Opportunity Act of 1964, 2, 177
Economic rent, 78-79
Economic Report of the President, 1965, 10n
Economies of scale, 48, 50
Economy food plan, 19-20
Education, adult, 176, 186-193, 201, 215-216
   discrimination in, 124, 132, 134
   effect on productivity, 28, 46, 56, 88-94, 201, 213-216
   inferior, 28, 57, 124, 181, 212
   in Mississippi, 124-125, 182
   vocational, 92, 183
   see also Human capital and Intelligence C
Eisenhower, President Dwight D., 196
Eisenhower Administration, 26, 35
Elementary and Secondary Education Act of 1965, 159, 183
Elderly persons, assets of, 9
   housing, 159
   medical care for, 147-148
   poverty among, 22, 25, 27-28, 98, 165
   tax forgiveness, 225-226
   transfers to, 139, 146-149, 151, 153-154, 161, 164-165
Employment agencies, 89
   private, 173-174
   state, 154, 173-174, 188, 192
Employment discrimination, 109-114, 128-133, 177-178, 222-223
Equal Employment Opportunity Commission, 178
Equal incomes, 41-42, 65-66
Evans, Walker, and Agee, James, 85
Extended School Lunch Program, 158

Fair housing, 223
Families, poverty among, 21-24, 28-30
transfers within, 137-139
Family, definition of, 7
obligations, 94-95
Family Assistance Program, 226-227
Farm residence, 11, 19-21, 24, 27-28,
102-104
Fecundia, Republic of, 44
Federal Reserve System, 52; *see also*
Monetary policy
Females, poverty among, 23, 25, 30, 98
Fiscal policy, 26, 28, 52-53, 172-173
Fixed income groups, 204-205
Food stamps, 155, 157-158
Foran, Terry, and Kaufman, Jacob, 218
Full employment, 28, 30, 96, 170
Full-time work, 30
Future Farmers of America, 92

General assistance, 160-161
Genetic potential, 72-76
Geographic movement, 91-92, 173,
175-177, 201, 209-210
Gillespie, W. Irwin, 166-167
GNP price index, 202, 206
Government share of output, 62-63
Gray, Thomas, 85
Great Depression, 202, 211
Gross national product, 34-41, 44-46,
51, 54, 63-64, 195, 225
Growth of output per person, 44
Guideposts, wage-price, 207-208
Gussow, Joan Dye, and Birch, Herbert
C., 93-94

Hagen, Everett, 134
Handlin, Oscar, 133, 199
Hansen, Lee, and Weisbrod, Burton,
215-216
Harrar, George, 86
Haveman, Robert, 52n
and Knopf, Kenyon, 106, 217
Head Start, 184-186, 211
Health, effect on poverty, 11-12, 74,
86-88, 98, 120, 129
Herrick, Robert, 199
Hollister, R.G., and Palmer, J.L., 205
Home Board, Federal, 111

Hong Kong, 38, 44-45
Household, definition of, 8
female heads, 22-23, 98, 123-126, 177
male heads, 23, 26
Housman, Leonard, 219
Human Capital, growth of, 55, 109, 127,
131, 139, 171, 181, 193-194, 198,
200-202, 213-216
per person, 75-76
quantity of, 47-48, 50, 83, 170, 228
see also Intelligence C
Hunger, Senate Subcommittee on, 86-87

Illiterates, functional, 93
Illness and poverty, 28, 74
Immigrants, 199-200
Immigration, House Committee on, 199
Incidence, of poverty, 2, 5, 22-24, 64, 201
decline of, 25-36, 97-98, 172-173,
198-201, 229
definition, 21
of taxation, 166-168
Income, cash, 10-12
in kind, 10-11, 16
money, 7-11, 16
Income groups, fixed and variable,
204-205
Income inequality, 41-42
Income Maintenance Programs, Presi-
dential Commission on, 151
Income tax, negative, 220-221, 226-227
Income transfers, 63, 137-141, 145-165,
200-201, 224-227, 229
India, 39, 41, 47, 56, 65
Indian Affairs, Bureau of, 135, 175, 193
Indians, 24, 106-107, 117, 119, 120,
128, 133-135, 185, 187
Inflation, 30, 201-209
Intelligence, productive, 73-76
"A," 73-76, 79, 83-84, 93-94, 106,
117-121, 131-132, 213-214
"B," 73-75, 83-89, 93, 118, 120-121,
123, 129, 132, 181, 183, 213-214
"C," 73-75, 79, 83, 85-94, 106-108,
117-119, 123, 125, 127, 129,
131-132, 150, 183, 185-186, 188,
213, 219, 222-223, 229
Interest, 76-78, 203
International output comparisons, 37-38

Investment, gross, 54, 202
net, 54-55, 64, 201-202

Japan, 38, 41, 45-48, 50, 54-55, 80
Job bank, 174
Job Corps, 184-186
Job opportunities, knowledge of,
89-90, 171, 173-175
Job Opportunities in the Business
Sector (JOBS), 190-192
Job vacancy statistics, 174
Johnson, President Lyndon B., 2, 115,
184, 186, 190

Kaufman, Jacob, and Foran, Terry, 218
Knoblock, Hilda, and Passamanick,
Benjamin, 75n, 121n
Knopf, Kenyon, and Haveman, Robert,
106, 217
Kozol, Jonathan, 125-126, 223
Kuwait, 38, 44

Labor force participation rate,
126-127, 177, 201, 211
Labor mobility, 91-92, 173, 175-177,
201, 209-210
Labor Statistics, Bureau of, 51, 206
Labor, U.S. Department of, 185, 191,
218
Lampman, Robert, 155, 225
Leased housing, federal, 159
Leftwich, Richard H., 106
Legislation to reduce discrimination,
222-223
Lenders, 204-205
Lincoln, Thomas, 91
Literacy, 47
Location, effect on living costs, 12
Long, Clarence D., 95
Luck and income, 79-80
Lynching, 109, 115

McClelland, David C., 91n
Maimonides, Moses, 136
Malcolm X, 110
Males, poverty among, 25, 28-30, 98
Mangum, Garth, 212
Manpower Development and Training
Administration, 188-191, 215

Manpower Report of the President,
1968, 174
March, Michael S., 145
Marginal benefit, 201, 209, 229
Marginal cost, 88, 201, 209, 229
Marginal product, 69, 76-77, 79, 131
Marginal Resource cost, 70-71
Marginal revenue, 88
Marx, Karl, 42, 66-67
Mayer, Jean, 74
Medic aid, 153, 161
Medicare, 147-148
Mexican-Americans, 175
Meyer, John R., and Conrad, Alfred H.,
109
Migration from farms, 28, 142
Milk program, 159
Miller, Norman C., 156
Minimum wage, 95-96, 217-218
Minkin, Jacob S., 136n
Minority groups, 106-136; *see also*
Blacks and Discrimination
Mississippi, 124-125, 182, 188
Monetary policy, 26, 28, 52-53, 172-173
Monopoly power, 207
Mortality rates, 121
Mothercare, 138
Mothers with dependent children, 98,
123-124, 218; *see also* Day care

National Alliance of Businessmen,
190-191
National Commission on Technology,
Automation, and Economic
Progress, 211-212
National income, 34-37, 47
National product, 204
Natural resources, 44-45
Near poor, the, 99
Negative income tax, 220-221, 226-227
Negroes, 107-109, 174; *see also* Blacks
and Nonwhites
Neighborhood Youth Corps, 184-186
Net national product, 34-37, 54, 104,
182
New Deal, 173, 211
Nixon, President Richard M., 191, 208,
216, 226-227
Nonfarm residence, 11, 19-21, 24, 28

Nonwhites, 93-94, 120-123, 126-127, 189, 196
   poverty among, 21, 25
Number of poor, 21-29
Nutrition, 84, 86, 128, 158
   malnutrition, 84, 86-87, 120-122, 129, 132

Okner, Benjamin A., 168
Old Age, Survivors, Disability, and Health Insurance, 146-149, 151, 161
Old Age Assistance, 148-149, 151, 153-154, 161
On-the-job-training, 175, 181, 186-189, 190, 202
Operation Mainstream, 193
Our Town, 142
Output-to-population ratio, 33-36, 41-43, 54-55, 57, 62, 66, 68, 201
Ozarks, 57, 176, 209

Packwood, Senator Robert, 217
Palmer, J.L., and Hollister, R.G., 205
Part-time work, 30, 96, 98, 102, 172, 212
Pasamanick, Benjamin, and Knobloch, Hilda, 75n, 121n
Patents, 179
Per capita income and product, 37, 38, 45, 49
Personal disposable income, 36-37
Physical capital, access to, 127
   growth in, 28, 54, 109, 111, 114, 171, 179-181, 194, 198, 200
   per person, 45-46, 75-76
   quantity of, 45-47, 50, 54, 76-77, 80, 83, 119, 129, 131, 170, 181, 193, 228
Poage, Congressman W.R., 155
Poor, decline in percent of, 25-30, 97-98, 172-173, 198-201, 229
   residential separation of, 141-143
Population, growth, 44, 54, 60-61, 66, 103, 194-195, 201, 216-217, 229
   size, 33, 41
Poverty, in foreign nations, 38-40
   of spirit, 13
Poverty criteria, 5-15
   Social Security Administration,

19-21, 25, 42, 94, 96, 149, 164-165, 216
Poverty cross section, change in, 27-28
"Poverty farms," 103-104
Poverty gap, 30, 224-225
Poverty incidence, decline of, 25-30, 172-173, 198-201, 229
   definition, 21
Poverty line, 19
Poverty reduction, 25-30, 96-98, 172-173, 198-201, 229
   by increased production contribution, 21, 25-30, 170-196, 198-201, 229
   by transfers, 21, 28, 43, 137-165, 168-169, 200-201, 224-227, 229
Poverty threshold, 20-21, 29-30, 225
Prejudice, 28; *see also* Discrimination
Price changes, 19-21, 25, 28, 35-36
Price index numbers, 36, 202, 205-206
Price stability, 26, 202-209
Productivity, 28, 30, 99-104, 113, 178-193
Profit, 78, 208, 213
Project transition, 188
Public Assistance Programs, 148-149, 153, 161-164, 183
Public housing program, 159-160
Public schools, 182-186, 212-216
   in Boston, 125-126
   in Mississippi, 182
Public Works and Economic Development Act of 1965, 176
Puerto Ricans, 24, 106

Racial discrimination, 28, 102, 106, 109-117, 129-132, 172, 177-178, 221-224
Rent, economic, 78-79
Rent supplements, federal, 159-160
Roosevelt, President Franklin D., 115

Saving, T.R., and Brehm, Carl, 224n
School lunch program, 158-159
Scripps Foundation, 196
Segregation academies, 222
Seth and Abel, anecdote of, 100-104
Sex and income need, 19
Sharecropping, 168
Silberman, Charles E., 130

Slavery, 68, 107-109
  breeding, 108
Social insurance, 161
Social minimum wage, 95-96
Social Security Act of 1935, 148-149,
  154, 160, 177
Social Security Administration, 5-7, 9,
  11, 13-15, 19-33, 98, 148
Social security benefits, 18, 147-148,
  163-164
Social service, 160
Social Welfare, California Assembly
  Committee on, 160
Solomon, Frederick, 84
Southern Regional Council, 113n
Spanish Americans, 24, 106, 117, 119,
  128, 133, 185, 187, 191
Special Impact Projects, 193
Statistics, reliability, 18-19, 27, 206
  source, 17-18
  see also Number of poor
Subsistence society, 66, 68
Supreme Court, 125, 150
Surplus Commodity Distribution Pro-
  gram, 157
Survey Research Center, University of
  Michigan, 195-196

Taeuber, Karl E., 117
Taxes, 147, 165-169, 172, 183, 201,
  205, 215-221, 225-227
Technological change, 55-56, 99,
  100-104, 111, 142, 171, 179-181,
  200-201
Technology, 48, 59, 76, 181, 198, 228
Temporary Disability Insurance,
  152-153, 161
Tobin, James, 220-221
Transfers, government, 63, 145-165,
  200-201, 224-227, 229
  private, 137-141
Transportation, 210
Trescott, Paul B., 208-209
Twain, Mark, 51

Unemployment, 26, 28, 50-51, 95-96,
  101-102, 127, 152, 171-173, 175,
  178, 186-187, 189-190, 201, 216
  rate, 190-191, 201-202, 209

Unemployment insurance, 154-155, 161,
  164, 173
Unemployment-price-change relation-
  ship, 51, 202-209
United funds, 143-145
United Mine Workers, 110
Unrelated individuals, definition of, 8
  poverty among, 21-23, 27
Unwillingness to move, 92
Upper Volta, 39, 44
Urban renewal, 160

Value of marginal product, 70-71, 79,
  131
Variable income group, 204-205
Veterans pensions, 151, 153, 161, 164
Vietnam War, 26, 172
Vocational education, 92, 183-184,
  188-189
Vocational Education Act of 1963, 184
Voting Rights Act of 1965, 115

Wage-price guideposts, 207-208
"War on Poverty," 2, 177, 184, 186,
  211-212, 229
Watson, Donald S., 106
Watts, 210
Weisbrod, Burton A., 96n
Weiss, Leonard, 58n
White power, 106, 114
Whites, poverty among, 21, 23-25,
  28-29, 68
Wilder, Thornton, 142
Wilson, President Woodrow, 114
Women, as family heads, 98, 123-124,
  126, 177
  poverty among, 22-23, 28-29
Work Experience Programs, 192-193
Work Incentive Program, 151, 192-193
Working poor, 28-29, 177
Workmen's Compensation, 151-152,
  161, 164
Work week, length of, 49, 101-102
World Bank, 39n
World poverty, 39-41

Zero Population Growth, 216-217

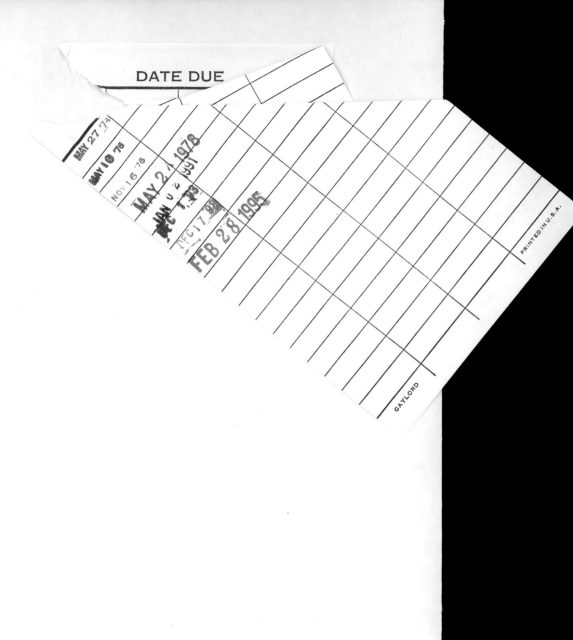

DATE DUE

MAY 27 '74
MAY 10 76
NOV 16 76
MAY 24 1978
MAY 22 1991
JAN 12 '93
DEC 17 '93
DEC 17 '93
FEB 28 1995

PRINTED IN U.S.A.

GAYLORD